The BR
LEATHER
SATCHEL

Published by Seacoast Press, an imprint of MindStir Media, LLC
1931 Woodbury Ave. #182 | Portsmouth, New Hampshire 03801 | USA
1.800.767.0531 | www.seacoastpress.com

Printed in the United States of America
ISBN-13: 978-0-9977466-7-9

The BLACK
LEATHER
SATCHEL

written by

PAULA CZECH

SEACOAST
PRESS

KIRKUS REVIEW

"A memoir about overcoming abuse to find happiness and fulfillment."
Kirkus Reviews

"Czech relates her struggle to make peace with her painful childhood and to learn to accept emotional intimacy in her life. Her story begins when her mother flees with her boyfriend and the author after losing a custody battle with Czech's father in Connecticut. The new family begins a new life on the Ben Davis Farm in Vermont, where the author says that she was later subjected to horrifying sexual abuse by her stepfather. Fortunately, she says several people helped her heal over the course of her life; she calls these people her "Angels." The first and perhaps most important of these was Philippa Bassinger, the landlord of the Ben Davis Farm, who became something of a surrogate parent when she convinced Czech's mother to allow the girl to leave home and attend first grade in Cooperstown, New York. Czech writes that other, later "Angels," including neighbors and college professors, gave her the confidence and compassion to overcome obstacles in life. Her decision to finally rebuff her stepfather at age 11 demonstrated remarkable strength. She ultimately severed all ties with him, but his influence lingered as she struggled with intimacy for years. _But the author's unflinching, vivid depictions of her worse memories are a testament to her strength as a writer, and her ability to share her darkest moments with such honesty is formidable."
Kirkus Reviews

"A moving story that will inspire fellow survivors everywhere."
Kirkus Reviews

REVIEW: THE BLACK LEATHER SATCHEL

Child abuse, and especially child sexual abuse takes a terrible toll on children and the adults they eventually become. Ms. Czech's book, *The Black Leather Satchel,* is a mesmerizing account of one of those victim's stories, her own. Ms. Czech persevered and succeeded, where many child victims never do, and she credits the people she dubs her "Angels." There is psychological research that studied resilient children, those who "made it" though growing up in chaotic poverty and neglect. The difference was that the resilient children were lucky enough to have found at least one adult who cared and believed in them. Ms. Czech was fortunate that she had more than one of these people at different times in her life.

Ms. Czech speaks about child sexual abuse as the kind of trauma that leads to PTSD. It is, but it is often more than that. There are usually repeated incidents. The abysmally low sense of worth or the need to block out the pain often leads adolescents and adults into poor situations and poor choices. There are predators out there who are particularly good at recognizing victims. So there are repeated traumatic events. Psychologists who treat survivors call this "complex trauma," or similar names, although there is no official diagnosis that encompasses this.

Consider a child. A young child's brain is developing, learning, rapidly—this is the time for learning trust, love, intimacy, curiosity. What the victimized child is learning is "love" entangled with pain, violation, distaste, confusion, shame, fear, hopelessness. So the victimized child's brain grows up differently, knows different things. The trauma suffered is at the hands, usually, of someone who is supposed to provide care, protection, nurturance, love. And it happens over and over and over again, maybe for years. The child victim has been set-up, for life.

In all my years of practice I have never lost the awe I feel for the courage of trauma survivors, but most especially, the survivors of child sexual abuse. Ms. Czech's story is worth reading.

-Loralie Lawson, PhD, (Retired) *Psychologist*

A NOTE FROM THE AUTHOR

I was motivated to write my memoir out of gratitude and a desire to educate others, fully aware that without my Angels' interventions, I may have become involved in prostitution and drug abuse, like many victims of child sexual abuse. My primary purpose is to enlighten the public through an honest and powerful narration, with the ultimate goal being to protect children and ensure their safety and nurturing. I believe more must be done to inform communities that abused children, like Veterans, also suffer from Post-Traumatic Stress Disorder. A similar awareness and intervention on behalf of the most vulnerable and fragile, our children, is necessary. They, too, have been traumatized by physical and emotional events.

It is my hope that every community will have an "Army of Angels" intervening in the lives of children, modeled after my angels. Sexual abuse continues to have a taboo stigma that hinders people from speaking up despite suspicions raised by their intuitions. Too many perpetrators abuse without consequences. Our children would be better protected if the public could readily recognize the signs of abuse and have the courage to report it. It is also my belief that the few predators who do appear before the judiciary are inadequately punished. The laws and sentences must be strengthened.

I have changed the geographic locations and the names of some people to protect their privacy, otherwise this is a factual accounting of my life.

PAULA CZECH

ACKNOWLEDGEMENTS

I wish to express my gratitude and acknowledge those special individuals (my angels) who recognized a troubled little girl and extended unsolicited and unconditional love through many acts of kindness. I remain indebted to: Philippa Bassinger, Louise Ball, Monetta Baldwin, Annette LaFrank, and also to those who recognized an angry young woman and provided help: Sharon Ball, Marie and Ray Nelson, Dottie DeCotis, and Denis Lesmerises.

To my wonderful, highly skilled and professional therapists: Jim Lianos, Ph.D., Bob Flynn, M.D., and Bernie Shaw, Ph.D., and the Women's Survivors Group. I dread to think where I would be without having received your help.

And special recognition goes to my Vermont angels: Jack Dodd, Avis Dodd, and Irene Strong.

To my two amazing brothers who have remained loyal and expressed their love and gratitude as the three of us navigated our way to adulthood: Butch and Sid.

I wish to thank all of my friends and relatives who patiently read passages of my manuscript and/or gave me encouragement to continue my mission: Sharon Marden, Dottie DeCotis, Sylvia Stewart, Jamie Lumbra, Carol VanGuilder, Durwood Sargent, Skip Hause, Eileen and Dennis Grabauskas, Ginny Rasch, Sally Ball, Mina Tajiani, Shelly Swain, Irene Strong, Edie Dimick, Shirley and Bruce Wilson, Gladys McDonald, Elaine Sylvester, David Hearne, Estelle Zatz, and Gillian Kendall.

To my mother, Zeta Eleanor McCarthy, who sacrificed her entire life for me.

I understand you did the very best you could considering all the complications in your life, and I know how much you loved me. A special thank you for believing me when I revealed my secret.

I also wish to extend thanks and gratitude to Seacoast Press, specifically JJ Hebert for supporting my desire to shine a spotlight on the long term detrimental effects of child sexual abuse. Special thanks to Kathy Lee for patiently working with me during the layout process and for bringing old photos to life. Thanks to Rob Rop, project manager for his prompt response to my inquiries.

Most importantly, I want to compliment JJ Hebert for providing the best possible match for my project, my editor and author, Joy Wooderson. Her editing suggestions enhanced my story and because of her empathy and understanding of the subject, I now consider her one of my "Angels."

And most of all to my son and his wife, who supported my project from the beginning by giving me subscriptions and other writing resources. They have remained steadfast despite the sadness they feel when reflecting on my life. Thank you so much for your love and loyalty.

Chapter 1
ROAD TRIP

The sun peeks over the church steeple at the center of Canterbury. I shuffle memories of Mom like a deck of cards, as I sip my morning coffee from the farmer's porch of my antique cape home in the historic district. The shared stone wall between my lawn and the village green is hundreds of years old, and I daydream about all the memories it keeps of the changing times.

Recently I have been in a reflective mood, typical of the elder years. My thoughts have scurried like a mouse, frantically searching for answers about my early childhood. Now that I am facing my mortality and taking inventory, I am driven to find the missing files.

As I walk over to my car near the two story barn, I obsess about morals and customs, recalling a time when women were required to wear hats to attend mass in the Catholic Church and everyone wore their best finery for weddings. Contrast this with contemporary practices, where brides walk down the aisle with swollen bellies and their young daughters accompany them as flower girls.

How different my Mom's life would have been if measured against today's values. The same morals and values once held to rigid standards in her era have now been thrown away as if they were yesterday's headlines. I grieve when I recall how often I witnessed silent tears rolling down Mom's cheeks while she stood at the stove and I helped her with supper by setting the table for our family of five.

My mind continues to wander... As a young girl it upset me to see Mom crying for what seemed no reason. During my teen years I found myself becoming irritated and then instantly feeling guilty for being insensitive. She would never divulge the cause of her sadness, but as I matured I began to put the pieces of the puzzle together.

Despite reflecting on my Mom's life, my mood remains upbeat, full of anticipation but somewhat anxious about today's potential revelations. In preparation for my long drive, I enter the address into the GPS, 1 Court Street, Middletown, CT. We will be on the road soon to discover why my mother absconded with me. I am determined to locate the final nugget of truth and find peace.

My best friend of sixty years, Sharon, will join me on my trip. I am so grateful and excited, it's as if we were still little school girls. For the past thirty-five years she has resided in Maine, several miles away from me, but we have remained connected weekly, a necessity to provide mutual nourishment to our souls. She instinctively knew I would welcome her presence for today's pilgrimage.

She knows my life story. We have been friends since the third grade where we first met on the playground, two little girls from dissimilar backgrounds. Sharon full of light and laughter, sandy colored hair and blue eyes, and me with a cloud of darkness floating above my brown hair and brown eyes. Sharon with a purity of innocence, me a little farm girl too mature for my age. Fate has brought us together in this moment, loyalty and bonds of friendship will help me through it.

Sharon bounces out of my house, overnight bag in hand, smiling broadly. My heart lifts. We can handle whatever today brings. At age sixty-nine Sharon is extremely active and continues to work as a night auditor in a hotel on the sea coast of Maine. Being a diabetic she is constantly worrying about not being able to lose the last five pounds, but I scoff at her concern over so few pounds because I am of a stockier build consistent with my Polish heritage.

Sharon has an upbeat, cheerful persona, not that she always feels carefree. She never allows herself to feel darkness or negativity. She is a Pollyanna, always a people pleaser. I boldly express my emotions and everyone always knows what I'm feeling and thinking. I often try to use some of Sharon's restraint but I fail, it is not my nature. It is unusual that we have remained soul mates when one of us is so full of lightness and the other is scarred by too much darkness.

Sharon intuitively understood the significance of this day, and during our phone call last week announced that she would like to accompany me. Our transitioning moments have often paralleled one another, as is true now. In a few weeks Sharon will be moving to Savannah, Georgia, having resided in Maine all her married years and more.

Today is a bitter sweet moment for us; there may be a long hiatus before we see each other again. We are facing our mortality and running out of time. This may be the last opportunity we have to share another adventure unique to our friendship.

We load our overnight bags into the back seat, uncertain if we will need them or not. We are truly on an adventure. And off we go... I turn my car onto interstate 93 south, the sun is bright, the fall air is crisp and cool, the leaves are turning color. Although we are driving toward a bygone era filled with turmoil, it will be lively and uplifting because we are together.

Thinking about our day I say, "Sharon, I will be devastated if the clerk doesn't find the papers. I wasn't able to give her the exact dates, I took a guess that the time frame was between 1944 and 1945. She told me those years were in the archive files in the basement."

Sharon replies, "She might need more time than the two days' notice you gave her, but we will have some other things to look into."

"Agreed," I respond.

About one hour into the trip we stop near I-90 for a bathroom break and so I can stretch out my back, as I have chronic back pain due to lifting patients over a fifty-year nursing career. On the road again, within a short distance I see the large overhead sign for SPRING-FIELD/ALBANY and a significant memory leaps to mind.

I turn to Sharon, "Did I ever tell you the experience I had in Springfield because of Joe, my stepfather?"

"No... I don't think so," she answers.

"I was sixteen and a new driver when Joe told me to drive the standard shift old white Ford Fairlane sedan and to stay on the bumper of his truck. And as you recall, when he issued orders, you had no choice but to comply. We were traveling on Route 5, a heavily traveled road, being the main route between Charlestown, NH, and Connecticut. It was about a 100 mile trip.

"The farthest I had driven was twelve miles to Claremont and I was yet to be a competent driver with a stick shift car, but I was managing until we arrived in Springfield, a big city. Route 5 was a long uphill road via the Main Street of the city and every light was red. I would push in the clutch, right foot on the brake, pull on the hand brake, my eyes on the rear view mirror noting how close the next vehicle was behind me.

"It was terrifying, sweat dripped down my face. Mom was next to me, with a tight grip on the arm rest, speaking words of encouragement to me.

"Oh God, then the light would turn green. I slowly released the hand brake, slowly let out the clutch, moved my foot off the brake and onto the gas pedal, praying the car would not stall and roll backwards into the car behind me. It was so frightening but I was determined not to stall the car and lose sight of Joe's pickup truck. I had several jerky starts and near stalls when my car would roll backwards, but I finally made it up the hill without crashing into those vehicles behind me."

I have never forgotten the panic and sheer terror of that car experience. Over the years I have often wondered if, in that moment, was it an innate courage that propelled me through it or did I adapt to the situation as a result of living with Joe and being at his mercy for so long? When I recall childhood events like this my anger stirs.

My Mom, Eleanor, was a petite soft-spoken woman, and courageous especially if it concerned me. She was the fourth and youngest child in her family and was pampered by everyone. She received dance and piano lessons at a young age, and by her early twenties was an accomplished dancer, to include teaching dance at her studio. But despite a comfortable childhood, later in life she lived under challenging circumstances and had no choice but to become resilient and stoic.

My father, a big man, broad-shouldered and six-foot four-inches tall, was often out to sea with the Merchant Marines during WWII, leaving Mom alone to cope with the hardships of wartime and the challenges of being a new mother. Unfortunately, the war years totally changed the trajectory of my mother's life.

We exit onto I-84 in Connecticut. We are within a few minutes of arriving at the Court House. My anxiety increases, and I think to myself, "Oh please, clerk lady, have the papers ready for me."

"Sharon," I exclaim, "I think that big building straight ahead of us is the Court House!" It is a large five-story gray concrete block structure with rows of windows appearing sterile and impenetrable. We turn right onto Court St., the Garmin woman announces arriving at destination: 1 Court Street.

We find the parking garage easily and the entrance to the building. There are several steps to climb and it is difficult to find the door because of the glass facade. I am surprised to learn we must go through a security process similar to those at airports, and as usual I mess it up and need to start over. The young gun-toting guard assures me it is okay, everyone gets it wrong the first time.

Too nerve wracking! I can't have anything prohibit me from completing my mission. We are directed to an elevator, the Civil Clerk's office is on the second floor. My heart is beating in my ears, hard to think. Getting extremely nervous, I begin talking to myself, "Calm down Paula, be calm."

A little confusion as we exit the elevator, but we are soon directed to the door of the Civil Clerks Office. We enter a narrow room, a few straight back chairs along the wall to our right. About six feet in front of us is the check-in area. One must speak through a small round metal louvered disk within the window pane.

The entire length of this side of the room is glass from waist high to the ceiling. There is a long wooden counter beneath the windows extending to the end of the room where it stops before a locked glass door. Looking through the wall of glass we see rows and rows of desks with all of the clerks facing forward. I feel uncomfortable peering through the glass wall watching the clerks at work. There are no cubby partitions, they are fully exposed.

I estimate there are fifty of them. Sharon and I are alone in this room. I approach the metal disk check-in area. There is a male clerk on the other side of the glass. "I'm here to view the Czech record, I was directed to ask for it here." I feel my voice tremble. It has been sixty-eight years since the Judge's decision.

The registration clerk thumbs through a stack of files to his left... not there... Oh no, I think, he couldn't find the record. He indicates he will be right back. With vigilance, I watch him question various clerks in the room. One after another, heads shake no until he is at the last desk in the back of the room farthest to my right. A brown haired woman pats a stack of folders at the top corner of her desk. He leaves. She stands up slowly, she is a tall woman.

Before leaving her desk she adjusts her clothing and seems to breathe in deeply while picking up the file. I sense a reluctance on her part to show me the record. As the clerk walks up the aisle of desks, toward the locked door, our eyes meet. I smile, but I feel my Mom's sadness filling my chest. When the clerk reaches the glass panel door and sees my eyes tearing, she also becomes emotional, and clears her throat a few times before speaking.

She unlocks the door, introductions are made. I can tell she is apprehensive.

I ask her, "Does it say why the divorce occurred?"

Eva answers, "Yes it does."

I respond, "Don't worry, I will be okay no matter what it reveals."

Her shoulders relax with relief. She stands aside as I thumb through the record. There it is in black and white dated April 17, 1945. It is mostly as Mom told me, so incredulous.

The court papers state: custody of the child Paula Czech is awarded to her father Joseph Francis Czech. Her mother Zeta Eleanor Czech is convicted of adultery, along with Joseph Thibault.

I find it difficult to comprehend that one's entire life could be devastated because of puritanical laws and harsh doctrines.

In an effort to understand my mother's dilemma, we must realize women were mostly housewives during the 1940s. Men were the bread winners. Few women had careers but due to WWII this dynamic was disrupted somewhat. With husbands away fighting the war, many women were enlisted into the workplace to support the soldiers by making airplane parts. These were the "Rosie, the Riveter" years.

Because my mother thrived on being in the limelight as a dancer, she craved the socialization of the work environment. However, challenged by balancing motherhood, work and running the house without my father, I have concluded she became lonely and vulnerable. Probably complicated by the fact that my stepfather and biological father were similar in appearance and had the same first name.

Eva directs me to the remaining court papers: there are the ORDERS OF NOTICE dated April 9, 1946 and June 19, 1946, whereby my father attempted to determine my mother's location. He was never successful. Additionally there is a JUDGEMENT OF DIVORCE dated January 31, 1947. Also a newspaper publication seeking my mother's location and two envelopes stamped returned never delivered.

I request copies of the entire record and pay thirteen dollars for it. I thank Eva for her help and she tells me she prides herself on being an expert at locating archived files and finds it satisfying to help those who are searching. With tears in our eyes we hug good bye.

Sharon has stood by quietly as a witness to my successful search. A final validation of why my mother maintained her fugitive status her entire life. I feel a responsibility and a deep sadness that my mother lived out her life without ever returning to her beloved little house on the hill located on Bell St., Middletown, Connecticut.

I have deduced that my mother and her boyfriend Joe fled with me, from Connecticut for Vermont within weeks of April 17, 1945. She could not risk losing me, so bravely and with a mother's deep love defied the Judge's orders.

Sharon and I leave the Superior Court with our emotions on high. With enthusiasm we talk over all the details of the morning events during lunch. Repeatedly I say how excited I am to have copies of the court records.

The reason why my Mom was always crying throughout my childhood and young adulthood is now clear. It is difficult to fathom the pain she suffered, so tragic, and I feel so guilty.

Following lunch I say to Sharon, "I want to see if we can locate my parents' home on Bell Street."

"Do you have the address?" she asks.

"No," I respond.

All I can think to do is put a phony number into the Garmin. Randomly, I punch in 300 Bell St., Middletown, Connecticut.

I do not know much about my mother's background except her birth was a surprise. She was the fourth child and fifteen years younger than the third child, a brother named David. She was treated as a princess being the youngest of the family and was adored by her much older siblings. I have learned her family history both directly from my mother and by reading letters and documents in the blue blanket chest.

Her mother was of German heritage and her Grandmother Rhode was a soprano soloist in St. Patrick's Cathedral in New York City. Her Grandfather assisted with drafting the plans for the George Washington Bridge.

Mom's father, George McCarthy, was very active in local politics. Her other brother George (Ned) followed in his father's footsteps and was running for Town Selectman when Mom fled Connecticut. He also played drums in the Tommy Dorsey Band.

Marie, Mom's sister was the oldest and was married with four children. Her eldest daughter Joan was my Godmother. Marie's brother-in-law was a priest, Fr. Gaffney.

I feel a deep responsibility to honor my mother's lifelong sacrifice by visiting all the places she spoke of with excitement and love. This is my mission for today. I am sad that I did not make this trip with her long ago while she was alive.

Within a few minutes the GPS directs us to the entrance of Bell St. Ahead on the corner I see a large red barn, my heart leaps for joy. I feel a connection with Bell Street, my early childhood was spent on a Vermont farm, The Ben Davis Farm.

We turn right and proceed slowly, taking in every nuance of the rural, beautiful lush green neighborhood. It feels like summer not fall in Connecticut, with the warmth of the sunshine and the light breeze coming through the car windows. A black paved road winds up and down slight hills and around curves. Tall trees line the road, nice homes sit on large lots.

Both Sharon and I scan the properties, determined to locate the little house up on the hill. We have driven the entire road a minimum of three times, speculating maybe it is that one or that one but none are as described by Mom. They are either too large, not on a corner or too new. On our last turn up the road I see a man on a lawn tractor.

I say, "Sharon should I interrupt that man and ask questions?"

"Yes, sure," she replies.

I stop the car on the wrong side of the road and park it barely off the road (typical of my defiance regarding obeying the rules of the road). I am emotional, my heart is pounding walking up to a stranger in hopes of learning the most compelling answer to a major piece of my life's story.

As I walk across the lawn, the man turns off the mower and removes his headgear. An instant attraction ignites... I think, this is a good-looking man, tall, gray haired, and as I am face to face, I see his beautiful blue eyes.

I extend my hand, "Hi, I'm Paula and I'm on a mission to find the house I lived in as a baby. Do you know if there was a McCarthy house near here?"

The blue eyes light up with recognition. "Sure," he says, and points across and down the road a short distance. I respond with both glee and doubt.

"How can you be sure," I ask?

"Well, because I have lived on this road all my life. This is my retirement house. I grew up on the farm at the corner... where the red barn is." I nod in acknowledgement.

He continues, "The McCarthy that lived there was also the Westfield Fire Chief for years." I react with surprise. We continue chatting for a while. I learn his name is Bob Massey and he is seventy-one years old, near my age. He gives me the name Corine Lewis and tells me she lives in the McCarthy house now. He encourages me to go visit her.

Bob says, "She will be happy to talk to you."

At the last moment I recall the house is supposed to be on a corner. I turn to Bob and say, "But the house is not on a corner."

He responds, "The road was changed to cut out the sharp corner."

"Okay," I answer.

We say goodbye and I thank him for all his help. As I walk away I wonder if he has a wife. I think he is a mighty fine man. I also fantasize about how much fun I probably missed by not growing up in this neighborhood.

Returning to the car, I am in awe and emotional because I have just spoken with a man who knew a blood relative of my mother's. All these years have passed with no contact with Mom's family. It feels a little like when I was reunited with my father. For the first time I feel connected to Mom's family. This is an exciting moment.

With surging adrenalin I spill out all I have learned to Sharon, who responds with excitement too. But suddenly I realize I made a mistake. I asked for the McCarthy house not the Czech house. For some reason I gave my mother's maiden name instead of her married name. How weird.

Then I think, once again it was divine intervention. If I had said Czech the time frame would have been too remote for Bob, because he was a baby when we Czechs lived there and most likely he would not have recognized the name. I surmise that one of Mom's brothers took ownership of the house once it was abandoned. Again it was synchronicity. I'm beginning to accept these moments as routine.

It is as though I have a guardian angel always present around me. I have always had a sense that I am living a predestined life and a belief that I have several guardian angels. But perhaps this is magical thinking. I've had extremely dark periods, but often I've been rescued by truly unusual, divine-like moments.

Sharon and I decide to check out Corine's house—aka my Mom's house. It is definitely up on a hill but it is a long tan ranch, not white or little, as described by Mom. It has random jut-outs indicating a few additions have been constructed over the years. So it is possible it was once a little house on a hill.

I knock on the door, no one responds although there are cars parked by the detached garage. We sit in the car for a while in Corine's driveway talking. I'm feeling sentimental thinking my parents once lived and walked on this land. I am overjoyed we found, "Mom's little house on the hill." I take a few photos and we leave.

What a day it has been, emotionally exhausting and we are both tired, after all we are seniors. It is late afternoon so we decide to find a motel room. We need to stay over to try again to meet Corine, and I want to locate the building where my Mom had her Dance School in Meriden.

The next morning we are eager to continue our detective work. Last night I found Corine's phone number in the motel room phone book and made a call. No answer, so I left a message with my cell number.

After breakfast we drive toward Meriden. I punch in 11 Colony Street, an address I've seen many times on the old supply receipts. My mother had been well known in the community for her dance performances in the local theater and because of her dance studio, The McCarthy School of Dance.

I have fond memories of hearing her stories about those days. She was once in a musical with Buddy Ebsen (Jed Clampet of the *Beverly Hillbillies*). As part of the musical, Mom and the other dancers were lying on the stage floor pretending to be asleep. But Buddy was whispering jokes to them, making it difficult for them to maintain their sleep postures. Mom said you could see their chests rise and fall with muffled giggles. As a child I used to have so much fun playing dress-up in her dance costumes, flapper style dresses, high heels and furs.

The GPS is confused in the city of Meriden and it delays us finding Colony Street initially, but in time we are parked on a side street perpendicular to it.

I look up and say, "Oh Sharon, there it is, see the sign!"

We jump out of the car, and walk a short distance to the intersection, a bland city street, except to our right is a free-standing tall black ornate iron clock. Historical street lamps complement the clock and there is a theater to our right. It appears we are in the entertainment section of town.

We cross the busy city street, dodging speeding cars and begin looking for number eleven. We soon locate it above a glass door covered with paper and a sign FOR RENT. The building is an old style masonry, mustard yellow, brownish structure with a flat roof. The second floor has a wall of unobstructed windows and in my mind's eye I can see students along the barre with all the light filling the dance studio.

We have found the location of Mom's dance school, but I am disappointed there is no one to talk to about the history of the building. Interestingly, there is a sign on a nearby building advertising dance lessons, so Mom's vocation remains in the neighborhood. I feel sentiment rising in my chest and I choke back tears.

I linger for a while feeling I am on sacred ground and that Mom is smiling down on me. Somehow I feel I am honoring my Mom's sacrifice with this trip. I regret I didn't mature early enough to bring her back with me.

Since my talk with Bob yesterday, I've been thinking about the McCarthy that was the Westfield (a section of Middletown) Fire Chief in the late 1940s. I'm wondering if it was Mom's brother George (Ned) who was running for Town Selectman when Mom left town, or was it David.

"Sharon, let's pay a visit to the Westfield Fire Department."

"Sure," she answers. "When you attended your uncle's funeral a couple of years ago you were impressed with the fire department ceremony."

"Yes that's right," I respond, "And I vaguely recall Uncle Al (on the Czech side) telling me many years before he died about a fire chief McCarthy, but I was too young to follow up on it. Maybe there will be some old firemen hanging around the fire department that might remember a McCarthy."

Back in the car I program the GPS for the Westfield Fire Department. We soon find the fire department and it looks familiar. I recall all the impressive ceremonial pageantry and seeing Uncle Al's casket on a fire truck in front of the fire house. I walk up to the building and try the door, all locked, no one around. I guess that makes sense, after all it is a volunteer fire department.

We decide to drive around the complex, it is quite large. No one at the rear of the building, but as we come around to the side I see a pickup truck parked, idling and an elderly man in the cab smoking.

I pull up close to the driver's side, put my window down and ask, "My uncle used to be the fire chief here, do you know where the cemetery is, seems to me it was close by?"

The man tersely responds, "What was his name?"

"Alfred Rasch."

He says, "Follow me, I will take you there."

I turn to Sharon as we are following the pickup truck guy and say, "This entire trip is so surreal, things seem to fall into place with little effort on our part. A higher power is certainly guiding our agenda."

She answers, "Yes, Paula, your angels are at work again.

I respond, "Probably because I am on a road trip, because we know I have a Car Angel."

We both laugh, so many car stories and potential speeding tickets in my life involving divine intervention.

Less than a mile from the fire station we turn into a rural iron-gated cemetery. The man parks his truck and walks over to Uncle Al's gravestone. He bends down and begins grooming the monument, leaves and some dirt have blown up on it. He stands up and is reverent and respectful.

Sharon and I join him and soon learn his name is Sid Hanson

and he had been a friend of Uncle Al's for years. He is quite talkative and reminisces about his times with my father's sister Julia's husband. When he pauses I question him about a fire chief named McCarthy. He recognizes the name but doesn't know much about him.

Then thinking of my babysitter whom my Mom spoke of often I ask, "Did you ever know a family named Aliff?"

He responds promptly, pointing across the street to a big white house, "Yes, they lived right there!"

I nearly pass out. Sharon and I exchange shocked looks. For a moment I am speechless. In hindsight I regret that I did not ask any questions about the Aliff's but I was so shocked at Sid's immediate acknowledgement, I was literally speechless.

Thinking about my babysitter Ruth Aliff, I recall a story my mom told me about the Aliff sons. They loved having me at their house and treated me like a toy. As teenage boys they enjoyed tossing me back and forth between their twin beds.

I say to Sharon, "Let's walk across the street and see if there is a mailbox with the name Aliff."

I am feeling a little like a voyeur, so we don't linger but I do see the house number is fifteen. No mailbox near the road, the house is on a corner, one side abuts a rural road, on the cemetery side and the other is in a development.

We return to the cemetery, I take a few photos including some of Sharon. I'm sensing our time is coming to a close and I want to hold onto her a little longer.

I announce, "Well it is late afternoon, we should get on the road for home."

Sharon nods in agreement. We are both amazed and delighted that we have experienced a triumphant trip. I am at peace. As we approach the Massachusetts Pike interstate 90, the blue tooth car phone rings. It is Corine Lewis, I tell her I will call her back when I arrive home.

Eleanor in Connecticut

My Father, Joseph Francis Czech

Mom's Little House on Bell Street

Paula in fur-trimmed snow suit.
Final photo of Paula
in Connecticut.

Aliff Sons with Paula

Sharon at Westfield Cemetery Gate

PAULA CZECH

Chapter 2

THE BEN DAVIS FARM

Mommy and Daddy have been fugitives for eighteen months, and we are on the move again, but with the addition of a new baby brother who arrived on Mother's Day, May 11, 1946. Butch was born at home at the Larrabe Farm.

Daddy continues to have a difficult time finding consistent work despite being back in Vermont and near his family. At the age of twenty-seven and as head of household he is stressed by the responsibility of supporting a family of four. However, on an early fall morning his luck changes. He decides to stop for a quick cup of coffee at Carrie's Restaurant in Elkins Falls, three miles from the Larrabe Farm.

Elkins is a small village and is the shopping area for three surrounding hamlets. Fifty miles to the south is Burlington, the major city in Vermont. Main Street consists of one restaurant, a gas station, and hardware, farm equipment, and feed stores. In the center is a park with a gazebo where Memorial Day ceremonies are held.

As Joe enters the restaurant he immediately notices Philippa, an attractive woman sitting on the end stool at the counter. It is unusual to see a woman alone in Carrie's at five a.m., normally it is only frequented by farmers and truckers at that hour before beginning their long work day. They gather for breakfast and to hear the latest news about increased prices for feed, fuel and to revel in the latest gossip.

The restaurant is small with a row of ten counter stools on the right and five booths on the left. There are menu specials tacked on the wall behind the counter with only one sassy waitress for the entire restaurant. Over time she has learned to manage the male patrons without risking good tips.

It is the fall of 1946 and Philippa is at Carrie's attempting to find someone to lease her beloved Ben Davis Farm where she has wonderful memories of summers filled with riding horses, working in the barn and helping her grandmother with the garden and canning. However, as a tomboy she much prefers to be in the barn near the horses, cows and the other farm animals.

Both Philippa and Joe are about the same age so when Joe, a tall dark-haired handsome guy with stunning blue eyes enters Carrie's, Philippa instantly notices him and likewise he is immediately drawn to the woman with strawberry blond hair worn in long braids and an ample bust, notable beneath a white turtle-neck shirt and a brown corduroy jumper. Her effervescent personality and childlike zest for life are obvious as she describes her farm in hopes of finding a farmer to lease it and return it to a vital working farm.

My stepfather is charming and often uses his good looks and persuasive personality to his advantage. I believe that is what occurs on this early morning in Carrie's when he convinces Philippa to bankroll his farm start-up rather than signing a lease and paying her a monthly rent.

Nestled in Sleepy Hollow, a small hamlet of Burton, is the Ben Davis Farm, one of four farms, two on each side of the gravel road all framed by rolling green meadows and distant mountains located seven miles from the Canadian/U.S.A border.

The Ben Davis barn was built in the late 1800s as a post and beam Dutch Gambrel. It was constructed using twelve-inch long wooden pegs and from huge timbers that were drawn to the site by a team of horses. Due to so much interest at the time, crowds gathered along the five mile route between West Burton and Burton to observe the procession of the logs. The barn remains a stately structure.

Alice was from a wealthy family in Cooperstown, NY, but lived a humble life with her husband Ben as everyday farmers. Typical of the time, they both worked long hours just to maintain sustenance. Alice as a housewife and mother of one daughter, Lillian, filled her day with gardening, canning, baking, quilting in addition to the usual cooking, laundry, ironing and mending of clothes. She was frugal, conscientious and diligently maintained a handwritten financial record of every monetary expenditure for items like flour, molasses, vinegar and the number of canned goods she produced from her garden.

Ben labored in the fields and dairy barn. So he mostly spent his day repairing machinery, milking cows, and caring for the young stock in an effort to build his herd. He also planted, harvested the crops, and went to the woods in early spring for sugaring.

But on Sundays he took his family to church in a horse drawn carriage with a fringe on top. He took pride in having the fastest horse and enjoyed sprinting ahead of the other buggies.

With Philippa's loan Daddy obtains his dairy herd, milking machines, and outfits the cow barn with updated equipment. Mommy is optimistic that Daddy has finally found a way to make a decent living.

On a September day, we arrive at the Ben Davis, with the fresh sweet smell of newly mowed hay in the air from the nearby farms. As Daddy turns the loaded truck into the driveway, we hear a crescendo of birds chirping and the loud flapping of wings as a flock of starlings swoop down in front of us and sail across the lawn. The gravel driveway on the east side of the large stately farmhouse is lined with a row of maple trees that stretch all the way to the barn. It is a beautiful, peaceful setting. I am three years old.

An enthusiastic Philippa walks down the steps of the screened porch. She is exuberant and her long braids tied at the ends with tiny colorful ribbons wave in the breeze. Her face crinkles with smiles and her deep, hearty, welcoming laugh puts us at ease.

She greets us warmly, throws her arms around me and scoops me up exclaiming, "You are the most beautiful little girl I have ever met! You are my little Rosebud."

After setting me back down on the ground, she turns her attention to my new baby brother Butch in the arms of my mother. She coos, "Mon Petit Chou" (my little cabbage) to him.

Mommy passes Butch to Philippa's waiting arms. With him in her arms she proceeds to give us a tour through this formerly chocolate brown farmhouse, now its rich facade faded and in need of paint.

I see a smile on Mommy's face and I can tell she is happy, as we enter the large L-shaped kitchen from the welcoming screened porch, accented by wicker rocking chairs and a hammock strung across the far end of the porch. The floor is covered with rag rugs.

Once in the kitchen we see gleaming maple hardwood floors, wide cherry wood baseboards, and woodwork. I immediately run into the sewing room to the right of the kitchen where I see a black treadle Singer sewing machine. I begin playing with the flywheel, but Mommy calls to me, explaining we must stay with Philippa.

Next Philippa escorts us past the large wall drying-rack into the spacious sunlit living room with two large picture windows on opposite walls. Flanking both sides of the west wall are an upright piano and a matching organ. I entertain myself by spinning on the piano stool.

The wall near the dining room is lined with four oak Barrister glass-door bookcases five sections high. They are stacked full of various books, to include Shakespeare, Aristotle and other classics, law journals, books on farming, and nutrition journals.

Philippa walks over to one of the book cases and takes down the framed photos of her grandparents, Ben and Alice, and reminisces about the many summers she spent with them as a child. She tells Mommy about her thoroughbred riding horse and how difficult it was to teach him to stand with all four feet balancing on a large round rock out in the meadow, but so satisfying when she accomplished the trick.

Through the cherry wood paneled double pocket doors, we proceed into the dining room located on the back side of the house. It is another bright room with three tall windows, a brick fireplace, and a built-in china hutch with two glass doors.

Peering into it I am fascinated with all the pretty floral china tea cups dangling from brass hooks. A beautiful room-size oriental carpet in burgundy and navy blue colors completes the dining room.

We have walked in a circle from the kitchen and have now returned to the opposite entrance of the kitchen.

Daddy carries Butch's crib into the kitchen, "Tell me which bedrooms will be ours." Mommy had requested it be the first item off the truck.

Philippa instructs him to put the crib in the second bedroom on the left.

Moving day has been busy, tiring and we are hungry so Philippa shows Mommy around the kitchen and tells her to use anything she needs. Philippa has a well-stocked kitchen and begins helping Mommy prepare supper. Like the Larrabe Farm all cooking is done on a wood-burning stove, which Mommy has now mastered.

Philippa and Mommy are bonding on several levels. They both share a strong intellect, a love of books and they both come from enriched backgrounds. Combined with Mommy's vital curiosity, political interest and Philippa's genuine love and generosity they are developing a strong connection.

As yet they are unaware, but on a deeper level they also have shared emotional pain. Both have endured monumental emotional loss. Philippa at the age of twenty-three lost her mother and two sisters in a car crash. Mommy at the age of twenty-seven lost everyone except me.

Over the next few months our little family settles into the rhythm of farm life and we all seem to be adjusting to living in Vermont.

Philippa lives in Cooperstown, but visits the farm about every three months and when she does I hear Mommy laughing and engaged in lively discussions with her. Philippa has been a great support for Mommy, helping her to adapt to farm life, a culture shock and hard work.

My mother is an avid reader, often reading in bed until the early morning hours. She has a plethora of books to choose from in the living room bookcases. During Philippa's visits I observe an animated Mommy discussing Pearl S. Buck's books on China. I am eavesdropping through the upstairs bedroom floor register in the kitchen ceiling. I spy on everyone. Mommy is worried that China will become a superpower and a threat to our country.

All this talk about war scares me. There is a Motorola radio in the kitchen and Mommy listens to the Arthur Godfrey show every morning. I hear the newsman reporting on the Korean War and about the bombing missions. In bed I have nightmares about the house being bombed, then I wake up crying.

Philippa has been a wonderful friend and a positive influence on our family. First by bankrolling Daddy for a start-up in farming, restoring some culture to Mommy's life and for playing with Butch and me.

Years later Philippa would tell me that Daddy never repaid her the three thousand dollar loan or paid any rent.

We thrive on Philippa's love and attention. She frequently scoops us up in her arms, cuddling and cooing, "My little Rosebud" and "Mon Petit Chou" (my little cabbage).

We especially love it when Philippa gets down on the floor and plays bucking bronco. While on her hands and knees she mimics the sounds of a horse nickering and whinnying. One at a time Butch and I climb onto her back, grab her pigtails for reins while she jumps around until we all end up on the floor laughing.

Philippa is a wonderful friend to our excitement, she bubbles with enthusiasm, laughter and entertains us with funny antics and stories. Her genuine love of children makes her a perfect playmate.

I don't ever remember having a Christmas tree or celebrating Christmas while living at the Ben Davis Farm but I do remember a soft rubber head, cloth body doll and a doll carriage given to me by Philippa. Shortly after receiving it our cat had a litter of kittens in my doll carriage and I considered it ruined because of the stains left by the kittens and never played with it again. Butch was given a red radio flyer wagon that we both enjoyed.

There have been several significant changes in our lives during the initial years in Vermont, but finally Daddy is farming successfully and able to support our family. Mommy has adapted to rural life with Philippa's friendship.

The landscape of Vermont inspires a feeling of tranquility with its expansive green meadows, gravel back roads threading their way through the canopy of trees, the brooks bubbling over the boulders leading to secret trout pools with frequent surprise sightings of wildlife along the way. Unfortunately, for Mom and me life in Vermont was never calm nor peaceful.

Ben Davis Farmhouse Late 1800's

The Everyday Buggy, Philippa and Grandfather, Ben Nearby

Ben Davis Farmhouse Early 1900's

Ben Davis Barn and Philippa

*First Photo of Paula
in Vermont, Age 3
with Butch and Mom*

Stepfather's Starter Herd of Holsteins/Back Meadow

Mom with Butch and Paula on Side Lawn

*Philippa teaching Horse
to Stand on Rock*

Chapter 3

THE FIELD IS ON FIRE

Daddy manages his dairy herd well during his first years of farming, as evidenced by a high milk production and the birth of several healthy calves and the acquisition of three pigs, a team of horses and a Morgan horse. But once haying season arrives in the summer of 1948 things begin to change.

His hired man, George, is unreliable and today he is provoking Daddy's anger. Daddy, dressed in his green Dickies and cap emblazoned with the Farmall tractor decal, storms around the manger of the cow barn cussing at George for putting too much bedding in the calf pen.

George is a twenty-year-old, tall, lanky guy who moves about the barn in a lackadaisical, sensual stroll. He does not give a damn about Daddy's troubles, so the vulgarities and threats from Daddy do little to motivate him. His mind is not on the chores but on sex. He often makes sexual jokes and brags about his latest conquest. Today he is being erotically descriptive about a girl he danced with at last Saturday night's barn dance.

Daddy turns his attention away from George for a moment but just in time to see his saddle horse, Brownie, from the barn window soar over the lane's three-strand barbed wire fence. Brownie is racing up and down the field of oats.

In a panic to save his oat crop, Daddy runs out of the barn toward him, yells and waves his arms at Brownie to direct him out of the oats. Of course this causes Brownie, a beautiful legendary Vermont bred Morgan horse, to run for his life, thus trampling the oat crop.

I am near the back of the barn beside Daddy's pickup truck when I see him running in my direction. I freeze in place thinking I'm in trouble for something. But he races past me and opens the truck door. He reaches beneath the driver's seat and retrieves his Colt 45 pistol and fires the gun at Brownie.

With the first gunshot my hands fly up to cover my ears as the loud bang vibrates my small torso. Each time Daddy shoots, Brownie's ears flicker as the bullets whiz between his ears, just missing his forehead.

He rears up on his hind legs and swerves in a different direction each time a bullet is fired. Brownie is in stampede mode and destroys the oat crop. Finally, out of bullets, Daddy stops the madness. I am grateful for the silence and especially that Brownie is still alive. I am convinced Daddy was going to kill him. The gun scares me.

Daddy's anger has turned to rage, not only has he lost his entire oat crop but the mowing machine requires repairs before he and George can start cutting the only remaining crop, the Timothy in the meadow along the maple tree lined driveway.

When in this state of mind, Daddy's desperation usually leads to self-destructive behavior. He has always been a risk taker and impulsive, so he begins plotting illegal schemes.

To add to his stress, Butch and I are also an annoyance for him. We are constantly under foot, full of energy with an abundance of curiosity, our liveliness only heightened by the hustle, bustle and chaos we observe. I vigilantly observe my stepfather. I never know when he will be mean, weird or playful and allow us to ride on the wagon with him.

Mostly he yells, "Get out of here... Get to the house!"

The following day Butch and I leave the house after lunch to find something fun to do and I suggest we play in the cow barn. There is an overcast sky and it feels like it is going to rain. We are not supposed to be in the barn without the adults due to safety issues, especially because of the gutter cleaner.

The gutter cleaner is a chain mechanism that runs in a channel behind the cows and moves the manure out of the barn. If we were to step into the gutter cleaner while it was accidentally turned on an amputation could occur.

We enter the barn through the milk house and stand just inside the cow barn door gazing down the manger, waiting for inspiration. I think the empty stanchions resemble the bars along a jail block, and I am about to suggest to Butch that we play jail when suddenly we see Daddy.

He is surprised by our presence and not happy we have interrupted him. We are not expecting him to be in the cow barn, as it is not chore time. Daddy is sitting on a milking stool in a corner of the barn. His back is to us and we cannot see him clearly because he is in the darker side of the barn where there are no windows. He stands up and magazines slip to the floor while he quickly rearranges his pants.

He soon becomes mean and begins swearing, "Jesus Christ, God Dammit!"

Suddenly, he charges toward us, grabs Butch and with one swift motion stuffs him into a cloth brown burlap grain bag, then he swoops me up and piles me on top of Butch, and loosely ties the top of the grain sack. He runs holding the bag with us screaming and thrashing over to the silo door. Opens the door, drops us down four feet to the silage at the bottom and bangs the metal door shut.

Coughing and wiping the grain dust out of my eyes, nose and mouth, I finally free us from the bag. We are standing in the wet, soft, slimy, smelly, silage up to our ankles. With survival determination, I begin to try to climb the fieldstone rock foundation of the round silo to reach the door four feet above our heads. But it is futile. Butch and I are terrified, crying and screaming. The rocks have sharp edges and I slip off the rock wall again and again scraping my knees because my shoes are slippery from the silage. Even though it is daytime, there are only a few cracks of light shining into the silo through the wooden slats due to the rainy, gloomy day.

In a total panic, we scream, repeatedly calling out, "Daddy let us out, please let us out!"

There is no response to our cries for help. After a while I stop crying for help and my fear rises, I think we are never going to be able to get out of here.

Time passes slowly, my anger at Daddy builds, I begin cussing him... thinking I am going to die in this silo.

I say to Butch, "Daddy is a Goddamn son of a bitch! He is going to let us die in here." I hear Daddy and the hired men swearing a blue streak all the time so the defamatory expletives roll off my tongue. It is a long, lonely, petrifying afternoon but by chore time he opens the door to retrieve us and he is still angry.

His only admonishment, "Get to the house!"

We never tell Mommy that we were physically abused by Daddy. We are ages two and four-and-a-half.

Haying season is almost over and Daddy doesn't have enough feed stored in the barn for the winter. We observe him throw tools against the barn wall in frustration and his anger escalates because he cannot find a way to raise money to purchase extra hay and grain for the winter.

Butch and I have learned to avoid Daddy when his mood is volatile. He can be extremely frightening so we try to stay close to Mommy in the house.

A month later, with fall approaching, it is time for Philippa's quarterly visit to the farm. Butch and I are delighted and as if on pogo sticks we bounce around the kitchen. After a while Mommy encourages us to go out on the porch and watch for Philippa's car to appear.

Out on the front porch a soft breeze from the huge maple trees gently moves the porch screens back and forth like sails billowing. Our dog Ring, who is a beautiful black border collie except for a white circle around his neck, is curled up on a rug at the far end. He has learned not to nap in the traffic path to avoid either Butch or me stepping on his tail. It is a beautiful October morning.

A car can be heard coming in the distance so we eagerly keep our eyes on the crest of the hill, and then we see Philippa's black Dodge sedan with the orange plates peek over the ridge of the gravel road, puffs of gravel dust roll out behind her car like tumbleweeds.

I call out to Mommy, "Philippa is coming! Philippa is coming!"

Mommy, Butch and I go out to the yard to welcome her. She turns into the driveway with the car loaded to the roof. Philippa's Elkhounds are stacked double decker style in the back seat. Two are on the seat and two more are on a plywood board above the seat, level with the rear window and the back of the front seat. Ingrid, Amos, Big Boy, and Little Girl tumble out to greet us with tails wagging, licking our faces, and running around joyfully.

Philippa turns to us exclaiming, "My beautiful Rosebud and Mon Petit Chou," drowning us in hugs and kisses. "You two are growing like weeds!"

She and Mommy hug hello and Mommy asks about her trip. Philippa says it was fine except for when she stopped by the side of the road to pee.

Her cheeks are flushed pink as she gushes about a tractor trailer driver who caught her in an embarrassing situation. She had both car doors open on the side away from the traffic so she could squat between the doors. Apparently the driver could see her from his high vantage point and blew his air horn at her.

Philippa is appalled by the incident but at the same time it is obvious she enjoyed the male attention. Daddy arrives just in time to hear the last part of her story and gives her snappy off-color retort, something like so you were flashing your flower, causing Philippa to turn beet red.

At times the behavior between them is quite flirtatious, but somehow Philippa always appears too naive to actually be accused of flirting with another woman's husband. All three of them enjoy a salacious laugh over it.

Philippa is soon in the kitchen helping Mommy with lunch. She has brought some home canned ripe cucumber pickles, known as tongue pickles by the farmers, and some relish.

The spacious kitchen soon shrinks with all the extra adults milling around waiting for lunch to be served. With Philippa and the extra hired man it makes seven of us gathered at the large round oak table.

There is high energy in the room due to Philippa's visit as we sit down for lunch. Everyone is talking over each other and there is lots of laughter. As the meal is winding down, the high energy conversation continues while Mommy gets up to clear dishes before serving coffee and dessert.

Surreptitiously, Daddy rises from the table but locks eyes with me, he winks and motions with his head for me to go with him. He has a stern authoritarian presence, so I obediently get up from the table and follow him out the back door that leads to the woodshed.

He takes me by the hand and leads me to the secluded walled-in corridor that runs along the outside wall of the woodshed. It is about twenty feet in length and the only light comes from a small window at the end where there is an old two-hole outhouse, with removable wooden covers.

On a previous day I had removed the covers and peered down the holes, and was scared to see that it was a long way down to the bottom. I would not want to be thrown down the outhouse. A fecal odor remains detectable despite the outhouse being abandoned for years. I am puzzled why there are two holes when people go to the bathroom alone. I think how awful it would be to have to sit next to someone. I hate being in here.

Daddy is eager for me to be with him, I sense his excitement, his breathing doesn't sound normal and he has a weird expression on his face. He sits down facing me and begins his usual talk.

"Now Cooky, you know you are Daddy's special little girl, you are my favorite. We are going to have fun playing the tickle game again."

I think to myself, it wasn't fun the last time or the times before that.

"Do you remember it is our secret?" I nod yes because I'm too nervous to speak.

"You can't tell anyone about this, especially don't tell Mommy."

Next he takes his white handkerchief from his pants pocket, folds it in a triangle, spins me around so my back is to him and proceeds to blindfold me. He ties it tightly, and tucks the edges in ensuring I can't see.

He turns me back so I am standing between his legs. I cannot see anything but I can hear. His breathing gets louder and then I hear his zipper. I'm getting very nervous because I'm not sure what he is going to do this time, it varies.

He says, "Cooky, now Daddy is going to tickle you."

Daddy pulls my pants and my panties down around my ankles. It is cold in here and I shiver.

Soon I feel some wetness on my pee pee, then after a long time I feel pressure on my pee pee that intensifies and it hurts a little. I feel like I'm standing in front of him for a long time and I become impatient. I attempt to squirm away but his strong left hand on my shoulder holds me in place. He does not talk to me the entire time.

I think, what is he doing? This does not feel like tickling and I don't like it. I do not like that this game takes forever, I find it tiring standing in one place for so long.

Eventually there is even more pressure on the outside of my private parts and lots more wetness. I hear his zipper and I'm relieved because I know he is done.

His breathing is slower, and his demeanor is calmer. He pulls up my panties and pants, then removes the blindfold. He stuffs the handkerchief back in his pocket. He looks me in the eye and reminds me once again not to tell, this is our secret. He puts his fingers up to his lips and says shhh.... I am four-and-a-half years old.

We return to the kitchen just as Mommy is serving pumpkin pie for dessert. The high energy conversation is the same as when we left. It doesn't appear as if anyone knew we were gone.

Of course at four-and-a-half I do not understand what just happened to me but I do know how it makes me feel. I feel dirty, scared, and so sad, about to burst into tears, but somehow I realize I must not cry, and I don't.

I want to go to the bathroom and clean myself but I have to sit through dessert first. Even though I am very young I know I've been treated like an object, like a nothing... It was like he didn't know I was there. There was no interaction with me. I am a scared little girl who resented standing in place for twenty minutes. He didn't hug me or speak to me, I was used.

My emotional distress makes me think about Philippa's dog, Ingrid. When Philippa scolds her, I see Ingrid squirm around, twisting her body as if to turn inside out.

Because of the frequency of these events, I am already dreading the next time and I stay alert around Daddy, but at the same time I am usually within his proximity because I love the daily hum of life on the farm. There is so much to see, milking of the cows, graining the animals, mucking out the horse stalls, harnessing the horses to the wagon, and standing by hoping Daddy will allow us to have a ride on the wagon.

At chore time Daddy orders me, "Go to the house and bring back the kitchen scraps for the pigs".

I throw the kitchen scraps into the pig trough and watch the mommy pig scoff up the scraps, fascinated as I observe the twelve piglets pull on the teats and bump their heads against the mother's belly as they nurse. I love to hold the baby pigs, and stroke their soft, silky hair. It is so different from their mother's stiff bristle brush hair. The baby pigs are so cute and I love them.

A few days later I am in the carriage house, it is attached to the wood-shed off to the right. It is a two story oversized barn used to store large pieces of farm machinery and I'm feeling bored and restless when my attention turns to the new tractor.

The tractor is the only piece of equipment in the carriage house. Because it is new I am attracted to the shiny exposed motor parts. I explore every nook and cranny of the motor with my tiny fingers touching the spark plugs, wires and other motor parts.

Aha, a great idea pops into my mind, I'm going to give the tractor a grease job like I've seen Daddy do many times. There is a fifty-gallon drum filled with maple syrup in the nearby workshop. It is laying on its side in a wooden crisscross frame made to accommodate the barrel. A spigot at the end of the barrel can be turned open to allow a stream of syrup to flow. I rummage through Daddy's work bench until I find an old coffee can, fill it with maple syrup and grab a paint brush.

For a brief moment, I think... I should not do this but I quickly shrug that thought away and proceed to have fun.

With meticulous care I paint every working part of the tractor to include the steering wheel, shifting levers, spark plugs and the dials with thick maple syrup. I step back and admire my work and then with excitement run to find Butch to show him my grease job.

Daddy doesn't discover my grease job until a few days later. By now numerous insects, flies and bees have become stuck in the syrup, giving the tractor parts an appearance of a one-day-old beard.

Daddy is enraged when he comes to get me, he grabs me by the arm and marches me into the kitchen. He initially scolds me for damaging the tractor and then demands I pull down my pants and lay over his lap. I receive a bare bottom belt spanking and I scream out loudly because it stings.

Since the silo incident Butch and I are playing in the house near Mommy. We like to help her with her work so when she unpacks groceries she hands me the clear plastic bag the size of a confectionary sugar bag. It is filled with Crisco and is used as margarine.

My job is to squish the red dot in the center of the bag until the entire bag turns a buttery yellow. It feels really good to squish the bag and I enjoy squeezing it firmly for several minutes.

I pay close attention to where Mommy puts all the groceries, mostly in the pantry that has the window over the sink. The last items to be put away are cartons of cigarettes. There are three cartons, Camels for Daddy, Chesterfields for George and Lucky Strikes for Philippa. Mommy goes to great lengths to climb up on the counter and using all of her five feet two inches height stretches to reach the top of the cupboard. This whole process intrigues my mischievous mind.

Thinking back on these days my memories of my mother include seeing her either standing in front of the black wood-burning cook stove stirring a pot, in the pantry rolling out pie crust or peeling potatoes with a butcher knife, her favorite kitchen tool. She has little time to interact with Butch and me but does her best to entertain us in the house.

I am amazed at my mother's resilience and strength because there were none of the modern day conveniences that we take for granted. Mom's daily routine consisted of cooking all foods from scratch on a wood-burning cook stove summer and winter. There were no prepared box items or frozen foods. She baked daily to include biscuits, cakes, pies, rag muffins, and cookies. I can still visualize fresh baked pies cooling on the pantry window ledge.

Then in between there was mounds of laundry using a wringer-type washing machine. It was impossible to get all the water out of the clothes making them heavy to hang on the wall drying rack during the winter or carrying them to the backyard to hang on the clothes line if summer. My mother only weighed 105 pounds.

I have been in the house for days and I am bored when I remember the cigarettes. Without Mommy nearby I climb up on the pantry counter but I'm too short to reach the top of the cabinet. Seeing the metal bread box I pull it over into position, then climb on top of it and succeed in reaching the cigarettes. I know the brand of cigarettes smoked by Philippa, Daddy and George and decide to take the hired man's carton.

Later in the day I take matches from the stove and go behind the house out of sight and sit near an open cellar window. Oh what fun it is to light the cigarettes and take a couple puffs. Initially I do not inhale. After the cigarette burns down half way, I toss the lighted cigarette through the cellar window and light another cigarette.

It is not long before there is a big mound of cigarette butts on the dirt cellar floor. Over the ensuing weeks I closely observe Philippa, George, and Daddy and learn the technique of inhaling. Eventually I share with Butch the cigarette escapade and then we both have fun smoking cigarettes.

Each week I steal a different brand of cigarettes. The three adults begin complaining and accusing each other of taking their cigarettes.

After a while I begin to have stomach pains, both Mommy and Philippa are concerned and hover over me, constantly checking my temperature and placing cold cloths on my forehead thinking I may have appendicitis. This routine continues over a few days until my savvy stepfather, the master manipulator, begins to get suspicious as my sickness continues without a fever.

"Cooky, come over here," he orders. It is after supper and the entire household members are present.

I walk over to Daddy who is sitting at the end of the kitchen table. Mommy and Philippa are washing dishes in the pantry but they stop to see what is happening.

Daddy instructs me to open my mouth to check my throat but immediately recoils saying "Whew!" Apparently my breath reeks of cigarettes.

Daddy has an idea, "Cooky, let's have a cigarette together."

"Okay," I respond.

He pulls up a high stool and places it in the middle of the kitchen, picks me up and places me on the stool. All the adults have gathered to watch what Daddy has planned.

He lights two cigarettes and hands one to me. I smoke my cigarette like a pro, much to everyone's shock... I nail cigarette smoking! Both Philippa and Mommy are flabbergasted.

But Daddy is annoyed that I'm not failing his smoking test so he rummages through a desk until he finds an old stale cigar, then proceeds to break it down into shredded tobacco. He packs his pipe with the stale cigar tobacco, lights the pipe and hands it to me. I take a big draw on the pipe and immediately begin coughing and gagging. I become dizzy and nauseated.

The pipe ends my smoking adventure. I turn five-years-old on November 1, and this time I don't get a spanking.

But my mischievous behavior continues... as I react and cope with the abuse from my stepfather.

One afternoon near the end of fall when the garden season is almost ended, I notice that the neighbor's garden located on the border of our lawn is full of big fat yellow cucumbers. Mrs. Edward is deliberately allowing them to become overripe so she can make tongue pickles. But I have a better idea for them.

I go to the kitchen and take two sharp knives from the pantry. Then Butch and I crawl through the barbed wire fence, and into the garden and gather armfuls of yellow cucumbers. We return to our lawn and pile them up beneath the maple trees along the gravel road.

Next, on a beautiful fall afternoon, we proceed to cut up the cucumbers into big chunks then throw them into the road, and with glee we watch the cucumbers smash all over the road. By late afternoon we have accumulated a large area of slippery cucumbers in the road causing cars to slide around.

But when Daddy's truck comes along and hits the smashed cucumbers I'm in big trouble again. By this time Mrs. Edward has called to complain and is demanding restitution. Daddy gives her some money and then of course yet again I receive a severe bare bottom spanking with Daddy's belt. This time it leaves red welts. But it does not deter my behavior, instead it increases the frequency of my mischievous acts. I am in a battle of wits with my stepfather.

The following Spring during the evening after supper, when darkness has fallen, Daddy rushes into the kitchen. He yells for Mommy, "Come to the barn with me, I need your help!" They both rush out of the house but not before Mommy tells me to stay in the house. Well that may as well be an invitation for me to leave the house. This is not the usual routine so my interest is piqued and I feel rebellious and want to know what is happening in the barn, so once they are out of sight I sneak up to the horse barn.

Hiding in the horse barn I peer through a knot hole where I can see into the cow barn. My initial impression is... Oh no! ... it only has one leg, not realizing the calf is only partially born. Both Mommy and Daddy are wearing long rubber gloves. This is a breech birth and both the cow and calf are in danger. With Mommy holding one leg off to the side, Daddy reaches in up to his shoulder and struggles to unfold the other leg. Finally he is able to position the leg straight and between the two of them they pull the calf out. Once I see the long strings of gelatinous membranes dangling out of the cow, I am repulsed and scared away. I run back to the house. They never know what I have witnessed, at the age of five-and-a-half.

The next day Butch and I long to venture away from the house. I want to see the new baby calf and we both miss wandering all over the ninety acres to include the meadows, pasture, woods or even down to the forbidden reservoir.

Immediately after breakfast we go to the barn. The calf is in a small pen and is being bottle fed by George. It is a male so Daddy will take him to auction because he will not grow up to be a milking cow. The calf has only beef or veal value and Daddy is distressed because he is trying to increase his herd. But Butch and I think he is cute and we have fun petting him and watching him suck on the big baby bottle.

After playing with the calf we decide to go up in the hay barn. To make extra money Daddy has started holding barn dances on Friday nights. He has made a snack bar in one of the small rooms adjoining the hayloft. Daddy sells soda, chips, and candy bars during the square dances. Lots of people bring their own beer and whiskey and go out to their cars to drink. We are surprised to find a big watermelon sitting on the counter with a sharp knife.

I decide we are going to have some of it, so I give Butch the knife to carry and I pick up the watermelon. It is extremely heavy, I can barely hold it in my arms. Butch and I go behind the chicken house and down the meadow a short distance. We cut off chunks of the melon and have fun spitting seeds at each other. Within one hour we have eaten the entire watermelon and we both have stomach aches. There is no time to go to Mommy for help. We vomit the watermelon in the meadow. Butch and I are so sick, and to this day I can still smell it and have never been able to eat watermelon since.

Daddy doesn't discover the missing watermelon until one hour before the dance starts and by that time we are in bed, so I avoid the usual spanking.

The next day we go down to the reservoir where there is a waterfall at one end. There is a two-foot wide cement walkway high above a waterfall that connects our property with the neighbor's. By walking along it we can cross to the other side of the reservoir. I like to cross over to see what the neighbors are doing but I need to hold Butch's hand so he doesn't fall down over the waterfall.

We also like to play in the hay mow, the second story of the barn. The hay is loosely piled high to the top rafters where there is a big hay fork. It is controlled by ropes and is used to move hay down to the manger through a hole in the barn floor.

It is difficult to climb on the hay to the peak of the barn because the loose hay acts as a spring bouncing us about like a trampoline, causing us to fall down giggling. Once we are at the top we move to the edge of the hay pile overlooking the wood plank floor twenty feet below. Then as if we are at the top of a playground slide, we slide to the floor bringing lots of hay down with us, making a huge mess.

To hide our antics, we sweep the loose hay down the scuttle hole. This is an open hole in the barn floor with a sliding wooden cover that allows hay to be pushed down eight feet to the manger to the cows.

Butch and I also enjoy jumping through the hole, landing on the hay pile, but one time there was not enough hay on the cement floor below to soften my fall so I hurt my back. I did not go to the house for help because I feared the wrath of Daddy. My back and legs were painful for about a week.

The tickle game with Daddy resumes. On a warm sunny day he has taken me to the back meadow behind the barn, out of sight of the house. We continue a long walk until we get near the reservoir. The reservoir is surrounded by a high hill covered with dense low-hanging evergreen trees with only one easy way to access the water area. The entry point is at the bottom of the meadow where a shallow stream runs into the reservoir. Just before entering the woods and near the stream are the Jack in the Pulpit flowers. I love to play with them by lifting the flap and peering in at the brown Jack.

However, before we reach the entry point we hear men's voices on the opposite side, on a neighbor's land. Daddy panics and rushes us to the hillside with the low-hanging tree boughs and forces me to crawl on my belly to hide within the trees and then squeezes in behind me. The small branches are scraping my face and arms and as I lie face down, the dry rust-colored pine needles stab me. We lie there a long time until we no longer hear the voices.

We come out of the woods and proceed to the stream and into an opening where the reservoir pond is fully visible. It is a peaceful area, the trees that surround the reservoir are reflected in the smooth glass-like surface. Birds are tweeting and at the far end there is a blue heron standing on one of his tall skinny legs bobbing his head in the water. The dam is at the opposite end and we can hear the water spilling over it, the same place where Butch and I walked over to the other side.

Within the reservoir basin the hillside tree boughs are higher on the trees, making it easier to sit upright gazing down at the water but still be hidden in the woods. Daddy has me sit between his legs with both of us facing the water. He unbuttons my pants and slides his hand down the front of them. I can feel a bump in my back while he strokes my private parts. Again I feel like I am a nothing, an object, he does not talk to me and my thoughts drift away from the present moment. After a while he tells me to stay where I am and he moves away out of my sight for a few minutes.

Later on, during our return walk back to the house, he reminds me this is our secret. But I'm more focused on my painful scratched arms and I really don't like the sticky pine sap on my hands. I am five-and-a-half years old.

The Sunday following the reservoir incident and after the noontime meal, the adults are taking naps. Butch and I have too much energy to take naps so we go out to play.

We are behind the woodshed near the meadow between the Edward's white farmhouse and the Ben Davis house. There is a three strand barbed wire fence separating the two properties. I have an idea, we are going to pretend we are camping.

I tell Butch to go find a board in the woodshed and when he returns with a four inch wide by two feet long plank, I lay it across the shallow ditch that runs between the two properties. Now we can build our camp fire and cook our pretend beans. We pull up tufts of dry brown grass, piling it high beneath the plank.

When we left the house I had taken a few matches from the box of wooden matches on the black stove. I take out a match and light it by scratching it against an old nail in the board. As soon as I get near the grass... whoosh it flames up instantly in the noon sun.

Quickly the fire begins to race along the sides of the ditch toward the neighbor's house. At first I try to stomp it out with my feet but it spreads too fast. I become scared and run to the house and into the kitchen.

Daddy is asleep, mouth open and snoring on the roll top headrest of the antique chaise.

Standing next to him I yell, "Daddy, Daddy fire!" He comes flying off the chaise, dazed, so I yell again, "The field is on fire!"

Now he can see the flames from the kitchen window, he grabs a broom and races out the back door. By this time most of the field is ablaze and the edges are racing toward the Edward's house. Within minutes all three families from the neighboring farms, about ten people have arrived to help fight the fire by circling it and tamping it down with brooms. The fire is within inches of the fence when it is finally completely out.

Into the house the three of us go, Daddy is swearing and yelling at me. He immediately has me pull down my pants and lie across his lap, bare bottom exposed. I receive a spanking with his belt, but I barely whimper, I've become used to these spankings and stubborn enough to try to not make a sound. Butch is considered too young to be spanked, besides I'm always the instigator.

After receiving the spanking we are ordered up to our room. While up there I discover an orange rubber hot water bottle full of water. I look around the bedroom until I find a diaper safety pin and proceed to poke holes in the hot water bottle. My will, will not be broken.

Butch and I amuse ourselves by squirting water at each other for the remainder of the day. Late afternoon Mommy comes upstairs to retrieve us for supper. She sees the destroyed hot water bottle, the wet bedspread, our wet clothes, but says nothing. She gives us hugs and helps us to change into dry clothes.

The tickle game continues in the woodshed but when the weather becomes too cold it moves to Daddy's bed. I'm not sure why but my mother and I sleep in a double bed with Butch in a crib in the same room. Daddy's bedroom is down the hall one door away.

I suspect that when Butch was a small baby it was for convenience so Daddy could get ample sleep and/or when he rose at four a.m. he did not disturb baby Butch.

To this day I do not know how I would end up in Daddy's single-size bed. But I was there on several occasions. I recall one incident clearly.

I'm placed in his bed half asleep but something is different, this time there is a blanket that has been rolled like a log down the middle of the bed. I'm groggy, not fully awake, but I recall wanting to cuddle up against Daddy's back but the blanket roll is in the way. This frustrates me as I struggle to get it out of the way to no avail.

The next memory I have is of Daddy reaching back to me, and grabbing my hand and placing it on his penis while teaching me to stroke his erect penis. I am so sleepy that my hand repeatedly falls off.... but he puts my hand back on it. I soon fall fast asleep and I do not know what happens after that or when I am returned to Mommy's bed.

So the obvious question is how did he remove me from my mother's bed without her knowledge? Is it possible she was so exhausted that she slept soundly through the night? She certainly worked extremely hard as a housewife. I always woke up back in bed with Mommy.

It is normal for children aged five to six to go through social and emotional stages of development that include awareness of gender and sexuality. Both Freud and Erikson have theories describing how sexuality develops and usually this stage proceeds smoothly, setting the child up for a healthy adulthood. But in my case because of the outrageous sexual acts perpetrated against me by my stepfather, my emotional development is disrupted and my learning is opposite of normal. I learn that sex comes before affection and love, causing me to have a confusing and anxiety provoking adolescence and young adulthood. I am being taught that affection and love are only given once my body is used for sex.

Daddy continues to scheme to get extra money to cover the grain and hay he will need for the winter so he makes a visit to his Uncle Chet who lives in Richford, on the Canadian/United States border. He soon tells Mommy that he has a second job requiring trips to Canada two to three times a week.

He leaves the farm after dark in his three-quarter ton truck with the wood sides, stops by Uncle Chet's and together they drive toward the border. Uncle Chet guides him over abandoned logging roads near the border. Once they sneak into Canada by avoiding the Customs Station they load the truck with contraband loot.

When they return in the wee hours of the morning, they hide the truck contents in the hay mow in the barn, usually it is pin ball machines and refrigerators. Then the next day buyers driving tractor trailer trucks arrive under the cover of the night sky to haul away the smuggled goods to be sold in the southern states. At last Daddy has made enough money with his Canada job and the barn dances to feed the cows through the winter.

Early photo Davis Road/Ben Davis Farmhouse

Farmhouse as it Appeared when we Moved into It

Silo with Field Stone Foundation   *Brownie, The Morgan Horse*

Paula age five and Butch on his
third birthday.

Butch and Paula near
Chicken House

Reservoir/Dam at End

Reservoir/Opposite End

Chapter 4

HOPE

In the spring and summer of 1949 the abuse continues. I am five-and-a-half years old and I no longer have any childhood innocence. Due to living on a farm I have witnessed sex between several animals, the bull and the cows, between horses and of course the dogs. But I do not make the connection that I am being sexually abused; however, I do realize the tickle game makes me feel badly about myself.

What is happening to me feels more emotional than physical. It damages my self-esteem and causes me to be nervous and vigilant. Daddy makes me feel dirty and used and I believe I am a bad little girl because I receive lots of spankings. I feel guilty, it must be my fault because of all the spankings. I am confused, scared all the time, and have no confidence. I'm always on guard... always watching others, especially my stepfather.

When out of sight of the adults I am motivated to eavesdrop on most of their conversations, as I try to understand my reality. Sometimes I pretend I'm playing but I'm listening nearby. Other times I peer down the bedroom floor register and watch and listen to everyone in the kitchen. I am sneaky.

I am also becoming savvy regarding Daddy. One day Butch and I are playing trucks and cars in a sand pile near the bottom of the porch steps. It is unusual that we have toys, Philippa must have purchased them. The porch door opens and I hear it squeak and then recognize Daddy's footsteps. I'm immediately on guard and nervous.

As he walks down the steps toward us, he calls out, "Cooky."

I respond but do not raise my head to avoid eye contact with him. He stands near me and waits for me to lift my head, the silence is roaring, my heart is racing and I am terrified, but I'm having too much fun playing with Butch and do not want to go to the woodshed. I persevere and do not raise my head and avoid making eye contact with him. I do not want to see his signal to go with him. Reluctantly he gives up and walks away. A slow, triumphant smile spreads across my face.

I'm not sure if Daddy knew I had purposely avoided eye contact with him, but the next day he tells me we are going to do something special. We are going to have a picnic up by the old apple tree at the top of the meadow. I think that sounds like fun so I'm eager to walk up the meadow.

It is the same meadow that is on the other side of the driveway but it extends a half-mile up the road and ends just before the woods. When we get to the top of the meadow there is an apple tree on the edge of the woods that attracts several deer in the early morning and at dusk. It is located downhill from the road, so we can hear the traffic but barely see the rooftops of the pickup trucks.

Daddy spreads a brown blanket under the apple tree, it is a beautiful sunny warm day. We lie down on our backs and gaze up at the blue sky and clouds as he cuddles me close.

I have a worn out dress on, faded pink with some of the lace dangling from the bodice. Daddy says, "You are a pretty little girl Cooky, you know you are Daddy's special little girl don't you?"

I am instantly nervous but nod yes... So this is not a picnic after all.

He removes my panties and plays with my private parts, no blindfold this time. Then he has me lay on top of him and I feel him pushing his bump up against me. Once again, no conversation. After a while we leave with Daddy carrying the blanket. I am feeling tricked and I am angry.

As we walk back down the meadow he says, "Cooky, because you were such a good little girl Daddy is going to buy you two new, pretty dresses."

This sounds wonderful and I'm feeling hopeful and happy; my anger has dissipated by the time we return to the house.

A few days go by... no new pretty dresses and I realize he is not going to buy them. I am deeply disappointed and think Daddy is mean and now I'm extremely angry with him. No one is aware of my distress.

A week has passed since the meadow picnic, Mommy is up in her bedroom relaxing on her bed reading an Erle Stanley Gardner murder mystery. I join her and snuggle under her arm. She puts her book down.

"Paula are you feeling sick?" she asks.

"No Mommy I'm not sick." And then I just blurt it out...

"Daddy touches my pee pee."

My mother bursts into tears, grabs me and holds me close, rocking back and forth with me in her arms. She strokes my hair and repeatedly kisses my head, saying over and over, "Mommy loves you so much."

Then she announces, "Paula, you have a much nicer Daddy that loves you too, but he lives in Connecticut far away from here."

She gets off the bed and goes over to the blue blanket chest and pulls out a black leather satchel. I love the sweet smell and the softness of it, I have fun threading the strap through the closure loop. It is overstuffed with documents about my father, mother, her family and everything that connects me to my roots. Mommy takes out a letter that she tells me is from my real father. She reads a portion of it that says he can't wait to come home from the war and meet me and that he loves me. She tells me someday I will get to meet him.

Over the years, I view the black leather satchel as a family member. Whenever I am sad, lonely or feeling adrift, I seek out the black leather satchel. I hold the photos of my maternal grandparents and my father in my hands, scanning the faces for a resemblance. I never meet any of Mom's relatives. When I see my father's name in print on ration booklets and my parents' marriage certificate, he becomes more real. The black leather satchel also holds memories of a happier time in Mom's life.

Later that evening when Butch and I have been put to bed, I am awakened by a loud argument. I get out of bed and go over to the floor register and peer down to the kitchen. At first I can't see Mommy and Daddy but I can hear my mother screaming at Daddy. But after a while they move into my view. Mommy is waving her butcher knife in Daddy's face.

Soon after the revelation about a nicer Daddy from my mother, I begin calling my stepfather, "Daddy Joe" but it only lasts for a couple weeks because he becomes irritable when I address him as such, so I eventually stop.

I believe Mommy soon begins making a plan to protect me from Daddy. Initially she insists Butch and I stay in the house all day with her or play on the porch.

Her options are limited because she is a fugitive and if located by the Connecticut authorities could be arrested and sent to jail for six months due to the adultery conviction. An even bigger concern for her is the risk of having to turn me over to my biological father.

My mother is isolated in upstate Vermont, in a rural area with no driver's license, no money and ostracized by her family. Who is she going to turn to for help? She is in a no-win situation. Additionally, there are no laws or prison sentences for pedophiles in the 1950s. The only emotional support she has comes from Philippa, and she is too fearful to share her fugitive status with her.

Butch and I amuse ourselves in the house with Mommy over the following week. Mostly by helping Mommy. She allows us to play in the sink by helping her wash the dishes and we repeatedly stack cans of food in the second pantry.

We listen to the Motorola radio and "The Sparky Show." He talks about God, teaches us to wash our hands, brush our teeth and pick up our toys when we finish playing. Butch and I don't have to concern ourselves with that rule. We also listen to Mommy's favorite, "The Arthur Godfrey Show" with Julius LaRosa singing.

Lots of times I notice Mommy has silent tears running down her cheeks. By the end of the week I try to console her by putting my arms around her waist, looking up at her and asking, "Mommy, why are you crying?"

She gives me a brave smile and reassures me that she is okay. I think she decides it's time to do something fun with us outside the house.

When Butch and I come downstairs the next morning, Mommy looks up, with her dark brown eyes smiling. She is standing in the pantry adjoining the kitchen, to her back is the cast iron sink. The window above the sink is open, and the white muslin cafe curtains are fluttering in the breeze. The perfume from the lilac bush floats into the pantry, as a precursor to the day.

Mommy is excited about a surprise for us, and eagerly tells us we are going on a picnic. All morning she has been baking pies and cookies, preparing food in advance so she can take some time away from the kitchen to go play with us in the fields. She speaks softly, "Put on your boots, we are going down to the brook."

The three of us step off the farmhouse porch and walk up the maple tree lined gravel driveway in the direction of the meadows. Mommy is carrying a basket containing our peanut butter and jelly sandwiches, oatmeal raisin cookies and a quart of orange soda.

I whisper to Butch, "Quick, let's go hide from Mommy!"

We run ahead into the two feet tall hay that beckons us to come in and play. From behind we hear Mommy joyfully chuckling. Once in the tent of Timothy, I lie down while waiting to be discovered by her. I become entranced by the green grasshoppers crawling up and down the sheaths of grass, and with intense concentration I attempt to capture one but its long legs spring away time and time again.

Mommy has caught up with us and she is repeatedly calling out "Butch, Paula, where are you?"

We stay quiet and motionless so as not to sway the grass. Suddenly she is standing over us and she happily shouts out, "I found you!" We jump up with squeals of delight.

As we approach the brook, yellow buttercup wild flowers surround us. Mommy picks one of them and instructs us to lift our chins. As we do, she passes the flower beneath our chins. In the sunlight our chins light up yellow, and Mommy exclaims, "Oh see the yellow, this means you like butter!" We are intrigued and amazed at this new discovery.

At the brook we run ahead to splash around in the water, float sticks, old tin cans, and look for polliwogs. Around noon Mommy spreads a blanket and we gather for our picnic. During lunch Mommy tells us stories and educates us about the nearby flowers and birds. I love the trilliums with their blood red, three pointy petals on top of the three pointy green leaves. I have fun pulling the milkweed pods apart and watching the white fluff float away. But then I need to rinse my fingers in the brook because of the stickiness from the pod.

After lunch I lie down gazing up at the white puffy pillows in the blue sky, wondering if I can see God up there. Sparky on the radio is always talking about how God has love for everyone. I think God is not always there for everyone and I'm not sure he knows where I live. Butch and I say our prayers every night, but I don't trust that God will always protect me. I think I always need to be ready to take care of Butch and me.

My stepfather and his three siblings worked on the family farm in Highgate, a small rural town a few miles away, but they all experienced a childhood full of pain. When Daddy was nine years old his mother died of cancer. He was devastated. Being the oldest, he was extremely close to his mother and the most aware of her illness. Life was difficult for his father Ovila trying to run a farm plus raise four young children.

Joe is not successful at farming, not for lack of capability but because of a drive for get-rich-now dreams and schemes. It is unfortunate and sad be-

cause he is a hard worker.

He grew up in a crisis centered environment and it seems to be his lifetime model. As an adult he is constantly in the throes of chaos, usually self-imposed due to failed schemes.

I like to think about meeting my real Daddy someday. Mommy has told me he is a really big jovial man, and I like to believe he is stronger than my stepfather. Thinking about my real Daddy makes me feel happy.

A Very Sad Paula with Eleanor

Joe Raking Oats with Brownie (1949)

Ring, Mom, Butch, and Paula/Open Cellar Window

Butch Hoping to Ride on the Wagon/Ring

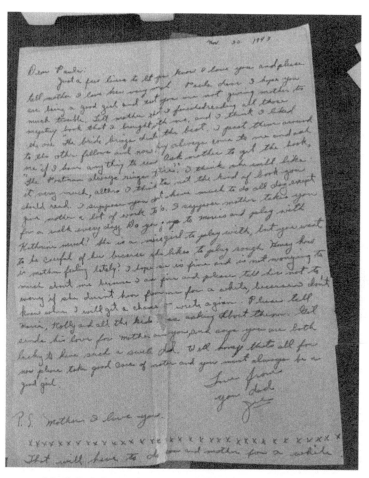

My father's letter to me as a one month old baby. He did not meet me until I was six months old.

The Envelope

The Black Leather Satchel

The Drying Rack

Chapter 5
FIRST GRADE

It is the summer of 1950. Daddy and Mommy have been fugitives in Vermont for four years, and my mother remains fearful of being found by the Connecticut authorities and losing me to my biological father.

Despite Mommy trying to protect me from Daddy, he still manages to find ways to be alone with me. It is the first week of July, Mommy and Philippa are sitting at the claw-foot oak round table in the nook drinking coffee. I am six-and-a-half years old. The afternoon sunlight from the porch window leaves a dappled pattern on the vinyl tablecloth near Mommy and Philippa's coffee mugs.

The second window looks out onto the maple tree lined driveway. To the left of the drying rack is a doorway leading to the living room. Where Mommy and Philippa sit, they can see across the kitchen into the sunlit, bright living room with the two picture windows.

I am listening to them discuss my school situation. Mommy didn't send me to school last year for fear my biological father would find me through school records, but of course she doesn't share this information with Philippa, but instead provides an alternate reason.

Mommy says, "Philippa, I am worried that she won't get a good start up at the Center in the two-room country schoolhouse."

Philippa replies, "I am not sure either. I could always take her back to Cooperstown with me and enroll her in the Cooperstown Central School. They have an excellent school system with access to testing and evaluations through the Clark Foundation." Cooperstown is an affluent town, and the Clark's are the owners of the Singer Sewing Machine Company.

But Mommy is hesitant about letting me out of her sight. "I don't think I could give her up for that long," she replies.

Philippa is reassuring, "I could bring her home for visits during school vacations, and besides the school year is only nine months long. We would leave in September and return for our first visit at Thanksgiving."

Mommy remains reticent, but because I have revealed what Daddy is doing to me she is giving Philippa's suggestion serious consideration. I see the frown lines on her forehead as she ponders her decision. Mommy is a pretty woman with shoulder length, soft wavy brown hair. She is dressed in a white tee shirt and loose fitting jeans. She wears thick glasses that turn dark in the sunlight.

I am listening to their conversation but pretending to be busy at my school table. It is a fold-up sewing table with a yard stick imprinted on the front edge of the top of the table. Mommy and Philippa do not sew, but Philippa's grandmother Alice used my school table to make most everything they needed from clothes to curtains. The sewing table is one of many antiques in the house that previously belonged to Ben and Alice Davis.

Butch and I are on the front porch near the screen door. I am writing my ABC's and numbers and Butch is playing with Ring, our border collie. Mommy started my schooling last year by teaching me to print my name. Except, I practiced writing my name on the wallpaper near the upstairs landing. Philippa was not happy with me.

I'm thinking I would like to go to school in Cooperstown and live with Philippa for a while, not forever because I would miss Mommy and Butch. I've been on a visit to Philippa's house in Cooperstown, when Philippa's father was still alive. I would sit on Harold's lap and he would play magic tricks with me. He once made a quarter disappear and then pulled it out from behind my ear.

Five weeks have passed since Mommy and Philippa's conversation, Mommy has decided to allow me to go to first grade in Cooperstown. I am excited, but when I think of leaving Mommy and Butch I feel sad and scared. When I'm gone Butch's only playmate will be Ring.

Mommy packs my clothes, they are mostly ragged knee jeans, shorts and tee shirts but I do have a nice black and white diagonal pattern skirt that Philippa gave me last year. She told Mommy she plans to buy me some new dresses and shiny shoes for school. I love shiny shoes.

With the new skirt, Philippa gave me black patent leather strap shoes and I am so thrilled with them, I take them to bed every night and keep them beneath the covers for weeks. I love running my hand over the smoothness of the patent leather as I drift off to sleep.

But one time the shiny shoes caused me to slip on the stairs. I was trying to carry Butch like a baby and I slipped and we both fell down the stairs, bouncing up against the door with the door opening, causing us to land against the kitchen wall. Luckily no broken bones but a few bruises.

After we are done packing, Mommy and I sit on her bed as she looks for my birth certificate in the black leather satchel kept hidden in the blue blanket chest. I enjoy the times Mommy goes through the satchel because she seems happier. Today she shows me a photo of herself in a dance costume.

We can feel the cool fall air nudging summer away, even though it is only August. It is time for Philippa and me to leave for Cooperstown. I will turn seven years old in three months. Her new black Dodge sedan is overloaded with our suitcases, a Victorian marble top table, and Ingrid and Amos, two of Philippa's six Elkhounds. Mommy has packed a lunch of roast beef sandwiches, potato salad, chocolate milk for me and a thermos of hot coffee for Philippa. And for dessert we have Mommy's oatmeal raisin cookies.

I hug and kiss Mommy and Butch good bye. Both Mommy and I cry when we hug. I'm feeling sad but looking forward to seeing my new school. Daddy is off working somewhere on the farm. Philippa is cheerful and reassuring, saying that we will be back soon for Thanksgiving.

As we drive away from Mommy, Philippa distracts me by telling me about all the fun things we will do in Cooperstown. She is going to take me to swimming lessons at the Colonel's gym, and give me art lessons at the Art Association. I think, I'm going to have fun at Philippa's and Phyllis's house at 44 Chestnut Street.

Late that afternoon we arrive in Cooperstown, it has been a long drive because Philippa only drives thirty-five to forty miles per hour. Ever since her mother's fatal car accident she is a nervous and slow driver. A trip that would normally be three hours has taken six hours.

As we pull into the driveway, I am intrigued by a cement creek that runs near the left edge of the driveway. It is about four feet wide and five feet deep. I have never seen a brook running through a cement trench. It continues beneath the street to the other side. The water is only about a foot deep but is running swiftly and making beige frothy ripples. I'm eager to throw sticks and old tin cans in it and watch them float, like Butch and I do at the brook on the farm.

Since the death of Harold, Philippa and Phyllis have been living together at the Chestnut Street house because he left them equal shares of it. Not the ideal situation. It is a comfortable home on one of the major streets of Cooperstown and it connects to North Main Street. At the end of the gravel driveway is a two-car garage and to the right is a big fenced-in yard for the Elkhounds.

Also Madge Bennett lives in an apartment on the other side of the house. When Philippa and her sisters were young she was their nanny and also the Bassinger housekeeper for several years, now retired. I am fascinated by her Scottish accent, but I have a hard time understanding what she is saying.

Phyllis is ten years older than Philippa and the recent widow of Philippa's father, Harold Bassinger, a renowned lawyer. The youthful age of Phyllis has always rankled Philippa. I think it was hypocritical of her father to marry a much younger woman, almost Philippa's age, but forbid Philippa to marry her true love, a New York City policeman. She remained heartbroken her entire life.

Her parents were prominent residents of Cooperstown, New York. Her father was a well-known lawyer who saved the homes of many townspeople during the depression years by bankrolling second mortgages, many of which were still on the books when he died, and her mother was a well-respected piano teacher.

In some ways Philippa is the original hippie and feminist. I hear her railing against preservatives in food, dyes in clothes, and advocating for vitamins and organic foods.

We make weekly trips out into the countryside to buy farm fresh eggs and place orders for grass fed beef and free range chickens, but only from farmers Philippa has thoroughly vetted and she is formidable during her questioning.

She wears only white cotton, and when she is out and about in Cooperstown she wears slacks, causing the ladies to whisper about how shocking it is that she is not in a dress. But Philippa ignores the whispers and innuendos. Instead, proudly and with conviction she wears her white cotton clinical type jackets with matching white cotton slacks, while taking every opportunity to preach about the atrocities of dyes in clothing. She is certainly eccentric.

I am thrilled to have my own room upstairs with a yellow and white bedspread on a twin size bed. Philippa has given me a wicker desk with two drawers downstairs in the foyer, where I can do my school work and color. Nearby, the grandfather clock chimes every fifteen minutes and I count the hour each time it gongs.

Philippa keeps a black velvet bag of her mother's favorite jewelry in the bottom of the clock. There are oriental rugs throughout the house and many crystal and bone china dishes in the glass door cabinet. I am particularly intrigued by the sterling silver lazy Susan that holds vinegar, oil, and other seasoning bottles. I love spinning it around.

On the first day of school, I wear a pretty red polka-dot new dress, my favorite color and new shiny brown shoes. I am so proud of my new clothes and I have four other new outfits. The school is on the same street where we live. It is a two story brick building trimmed in white wood. Philippa drives me on the first day but it will usually be a ten minute walk. Miss Champlain is my teacher and there are about twenty-five kids in the class.

In the first few weeks, I have fun playing with all my new friends. Miss Champlain is constantly telling me to wait until recess to talk with them, but I often forget to wait.

One day something happens that I never recover from emotionally. I am so embarrassed and ashamed. The music teacher comes to the class and calls each student individually up to the piano. I am scared because I have not listened to much music or tried to sing.

I have only heard Julius LaRosa on the "Arthur Godfrey Show" on the radio. When it is my turn, the music teacher plays and sings the scale. She instructs me to sing and when I do, she is quickly annoyed and with irritation says, "No, like this," and then she sings *doh re mi fa soh lah ti*. I try again but with the wave of her hand she dismisses me. I return to my desk and I never again try to sing. Music remains an enigma for my entire life.

I do not tell Philippa the music teacher shamed me. I have been trained not to tell.

Another bad thing has been happening to me on my walk to school, it started about two weeks ago. Except for this situation and music, I enjoy school. I especially like walking on the smooth sidewalks with my pretty shoes instead of over the bumpy pasture back home. My shoes click on the sidewalk like the horses feet do on the barn floor.

At the farthest section of my walk, I pass by these two huge cement lions gracing tall wide pillars in front of a mansion. After passing the lions I am surprised to feel a hard painful punch to my back between my shoulder blades. I nearly fall. Stunned, in pain and hunched over, I see a boy running away.

For two days, I am hit from behind, but on the third day I hear his footsteps and anticipate his assault. Before he can hit me, I whirl around face to face with him. My dark brown eyes full of rage, a litany of swear words spews forth.

"You Goddam Son of a Bitch, you better stop hitting me!" And I give him a shove. He takes off running and he never hits me again nor do I ever see him again.

I have heard plenty of swear words from Daddy and the hired men so I know them well, but swearing is not part of my everyday language. Mommy would never allow it.

I do not tell Philippa or anyone about the bully.

A long time ago on the farm, when I was walking in the meadow, with the blue sky above and the white puffy clouds, I remember thinking I have to take care of myself, no one else is able to.

Most days after school, I go to Mrs. Bennett's until Philippa comes home from the office. I have lots of fun with her. She always has yummy snacks and I enjoy listening to her accent. Today she serves me tea from a pretty tea pot and shortbread. I love the cookies.

I tell her, "You are a great cook like my Mommy." Then I add with disgust in my voice and nodding to the other side of the house, "They don't know anything about potatoes," referring to Philippa and Phyllis. Mrs. Bennett responds with hearty laugh. I am missing my Mommy's farm cooking.

Mommy is a stickler for manners, especially table manners. She has taught me how to hold my fork correctly and to place the napkin in my lap and how to discreetly dispose of a piece of tough meat. Mommy will not tolerate anyone holding their fork in the meat like a dagger. She gets very irritated when she sees someone doing it. "And no using a knife like a saw," she says.

I am having fun in Cooperstown with Philippa and Phyllis. They have nicknamed us "The three peas in the pod," Philippa, Phyllis, and Paula.

Phyllis grew up in New York City, where she was a secretary in a law office. One day her boss introduced her to Harold when he was in the city to visit his brother Percy. Phyllis speaks with an Upper East Side New York City accent and is polite and well mannered. She is sophisticated. Phyllis has straight black, chin length hair with bangs. There are a lot of laughs between the three of us and we are always dashing here and there.

Many evenings we drive out to Fairy Spring, on Otsego Lake for dessert. We go to a small restaurant with a screened porch overlooking the water called Millers. When we sit out on the porch at small round tables with wobbly legs it reminds me of the Ben Davis porch and my school table. Philippa loves their homemade pies. All three of us order different kinds and then share some of each. I love the warm apple pie heaped with vanilla ice cream. Philippa likes her pie with a large piece of cheese.

Other times we go out to local Churches for baked bean suppers. They are usually held in church basements and we all sit together at long tables with white paper tablecloths. The room is noisy, with many people talking simultaneously, a friendly atmosphere interspersed with laughter. Philippa is so proud that I am living with her, she is constantly presenting me to members of the community.

With much ado Philippa will say, "Oh you must meet Paula, a darling little girl who is living with me for the school year. Isn't she pretty and she is doing so well in school." I feel special when all these people tell me how pretty, smart, and polite I am. I feel like a princess with all this attention. It boosts my low self-esteem and builds my confidence.

At home Philippa cooks unusual foods, she calls them healthy foods, like beef heart and tongue. She is a dietician. Philippa was educated at Wellesley College, an all-girls school in Massachusetts, then Columbia University in New York City. Her minor was in religion. She did her clinical studies at Presbyterian Hospital.

While at Presbyterian she learned of the fatal car accident that claimed the lives of her mother and sisters. She was so distraught that she never returned to take her Boards. And has never worked as a dietician because of not being registered.

Philippa is always preaching the importance of taking vitamins, especially A, and all of the B's, C, D, and vitamin E. The pantry at Ben Davis smells like vitamins, because there are so many jars of them in the cupboard. She also uses cod liver oil, lecithin and Brewer's yeast. Ingrid and the other Elkhounds are fed raw eggs and wheat germ oil daily.

I have noticed that Philippa is treated like a princess too, like when we go to Danny's Market on Main Street for the organ meats. There is usually a line at the counter. But when the butcher looks up and sees Philippa he will immediately call to her and say, "Why, Miss Bassinger, how are you today and what would you like?" He makes a big fuss over her and then he turns his attention to me. Philippa likes to make a meat loaf with part ground beef heart and ground sirloin, so he grinds the beef heart for her.

The Bank President also treats Philippa as special. She has trouble almost every month balancing her checkbook. I am fascinated with it, a ledger size black leather, soft cover book with four checks on each page. I like to watch Philippa hold the checkbook on her lap in the car, write out a check, with flourishing penmanship. Then she carefully rips out a check and pays the garage attendant for the tank of gas.

We often go to the bank where Philippa meets with the white-haired President in his large upstairs carpeted office. We are welcomed by his outstretched handshake, then seated in front of his executive style desk. He always speaks to me and gives me something off his desk to play with, we are there for a long time. He has a snow globe that I have fun tipping upside down and sometimes I play with a music box that is in the shape of a bank.

Philippa has a trust fund created by her father and she can only have so much money per month, but she frequently needs to ask the bank President for an advance or help with balancing her checkbook. Sometimes he can give her an advance and sometimes he cannot. I like the days when she gets the advance because it is less boring and quicker.

Across Main Street from the bank where the pretty flowering baskets hang from the light posts, and at the corner of Lake Street is Harold's former law office. Currently, Philippa is attempting to start an insurance business in her father's former office. But Phyllis complains that Philippa is not working hard enough to learn the insurance business. Phyllis goes to the office daily to close out Harold's law firm affairs.

I hear her tell Philippa you need to spend longer hours in the office. Phyllis is annoyed that Philippa delays arriving at the office until almost noon. But of course Philippa has never held a job and is not used to waking early. She is more like Mommy, a night owl. She likes to read late into the night. Except Mommy has to get up early, farm life gives her no choice.

One day I was supposed to go directly from school to Philippa's office instead of going to Mrs. Bennett's. But when I got near the office I noticed the lake was down the street a few feet. I was so surprised to see the lake, I forgot to check in with Philippa. It did not seem unusual to proceed directly down the street to explore the lake area. After all at the farm Butch and I roamed all over the ninety acres almost every day.

For about one hour I amuse myself by checking out all the boats at the dock and then I try to get close to the ducks on the grassy bank of the lake. But they are not friendly, they run away quacking and flapping their wings. Eventually, I return to Philippa's office, where she has been trying to find me by calling the various store owners on Main Street. She is so angry with me when I arrive at her office. She scolds me severely.

At night she hears me whimpering in my bed, I am missing Mommy and Butch. I cannot understand what I have done wrong. Philippa takes me in her arms and explains it was dangerous near the water alone, I could have drowned. She has me go lie on her bed, where she cuddles me in her arms, saying "Oh my sweet little Rosebud, you know I love you so much and I can't have anything bad happen to you." But I am still homesick for a few days. My feelings have been hurt. Mommy never scolds me like that, she always explains things in a calm manner.

The following Saturday Philippa decides it is time for me to take swimming lessons. We go to the gym at the corner of Main and Fair

Streets where there is a two story stone building. It resembles a castle with a turret and curved stone, steps to climb to the main entrance. As we approach the steps, Philippa sees the Colonel and they begin a warm friendly exchange.

I am so fascinated by him especially with his pipe, I can't take my eyes off him. He is short and has a slight figure with a gray beard and a fancy curly mustache. He is dressed in a military jacket with beautiful red and gold epaulettes, but most interesting is his large pipe.

It is made of intricate patterns of carved pear wood and the stem is curled and there is a short chain attached to the bowl, with a flat round metal cover that has a design with cut-outs. As he puffs on the pipe, multiple circles and various smoke patterns float out and around the pipe.

I hear his foreign accent and I think he must be a very important person. But he is an old man so he can't still be in the army. He notices how intrigued I am with him and I can see he is pleased, as he occasionally glances down at me with smiling eyes. Later Philippa tells me he is Russian and he owns the building.

Philippa registers me for swimming lessons and helps me into my bathing suit in the locker room. There are about ten other girls, some older than me. We follow the instructor to the pool. It is huge. The room is steamy warm and it has a chemical smell like the milk house at the farm but stronger. At the deep end, above the pool on the second floor, there is an open balcony for the parents. Philippa is seated up there and waves to me.

I have fun hanging onto the side of the pool and kicking my feet. One by one the instructor teaches us to hold our breath and put our face in the water. By the third week I am feeling comfortable in the water. Near the end of the lesson the instructor allows us to play or practice what we have learned.

During our individual play time, the colorful balls with the rope strung through them and stretched across the pool catch my attention. So, I begin walking toward the rope, but soon my feet step off into air and my head sinks below the surface of the water. I am in a panic.

I repeatedly jump up to get my head above water and cry for help but the pool is too noisy and no one can hear me, so many kids are squealing as they toss a ball. I am in a total panic. After several bobs and mouthfuls of water, an instructor rushes to my side and pulls me to the shallow end. She gets me to the edge of the pool.

With a vice-like grip I hang onto the side. She tries to coax me back out into the middle of the pool but I refuse, then she tries to forcefully loosen my hands but I will not let go. I am not going back out into the middle of the pool. I scream, "No, no, I want Philippa." But Philippa has gone to run an errand and is not up in the balcony as usual. She returns at the end of the lesson to find me terrified. This is the last swimming lesson I take.

Next Philippa signs me up for art lessons at the Cooperstown Art Association. It is diagonally across the street from the Colonel's gym. We walk up a long sidewalk to a building with huge, white round pillars. Once inside we are in a large room with a tall ceiling. The floor is marble and there is sort of an echo in the room and it feels drafty. Near the end a long distance away, there are about five kids my age standing in front of easels with paint brushes. But they appear tiny in this giant room.

I am intimidated by the environment. It is not a kid friendly place. There are marble statues on tall pedestals along the walls and enormous size artwork on the walls. I do not enjoy painting because I am so distracted by the gigantic room. I tell Philippa that I don't want to go back to the large, cold marble room.

I am not fond of Philippa's cooking, I especially do not like poached eggs in vinegar or her chocolate milk. One morning before school I wasn't drinking my chocolate milk because it tasted sour to me.

"Paula, you must finish your chocolate milk before you leave for school," says Philippa.

I respond, "But I don't like it, it doesn't taste good." This battle continues for several minutes.

I dawdle until I'm late for school, Philippa finally allows me to leave.

Of course coming from the farm I am used to drinking raw milk, directly from the cows. Perhaps it is the store bought milk taste that I find repulsive. It has a different taste from what I am accustomed to.

When I arrive at my classroom, Miss Champlain tells me I must go the Principal's office. I am scared, not sure what he is going to do to me. It is a long, anxious walk down the darkened corridor to his office. Once I arrive, he seems friendly, but wants to know why I am late.

I promptly reply, "Philippa made me drink a full glass of sour chocolate milk."

"Oh I see," he says. Then he asks, "Does that happen often?"

"No, but I don't like a lot of her cooking," I reply.

Then he gives me a speech about not being late for school and sends me back to Miss Champlain's room. When I return home after school, Philippa tells me the principal called her about my sour chocolate milk. I can see Phyllis is trying to stifle a laugh and Philippa is trying to hide a smile. Luckily, I never had to drink sour chocolate milk again.

One noon time Philippa is eager to have Phyllis and me try her new recipe, a warm cucumber soup. It is terrible. Phyllis doesn't like it either but to be polite she is trying to eat it. The telephone rings in the living room, Philippa leaves the table to answer it and she becomes involved in a lengthy conversation. Phyllis admits to me she doesn't like the cucumber soup either so she begins clearing our dishes.

"What am I going to do with this soup... maybe I should dump it in the creek?" as she gives me a mischievous grin.

I am thrilled and giggle, "Yes, yes do it!

This totally delights me... mischief should be my middle name.

Playfully and with a big grin Phyllis says, "Yes, that's exactly what I will do."

Phyllis grabs the pot and runs out of the house, across the driveway over to the creek and dumps the soup into the water. She comes back in with a smile. I'm giggling and surprised she actually threw it in the creek.

Phyllis says this is going to be our secret. I promise I won't tell. When Philippa returns to the kitchen Phyllis is washing the dishes and putting the kitchen in order. There is no further talk about cucumber soup. Phyllis has been subjected to several of Philippa's new recipe experiments and many times dislikes her concoctions.

In the spring I develop a toothache so Philippa takes me to her dentist in Oneonta. He is an elderly white-haired man with no patience. Philippa has gone to sit in the waiting room. I have never been to a dentist so all of this is new to me. He draws up the Novocain and tells me to open my mouth. I'm trying to be brave and cooperative. I do as he asks but the needle prick startles me and I jump and pull away from him. He slaps my shoulder and sternly yells at me, "I told you to sit still."

I never tell Philippa that the dentist hit me.

After the dentist visit Philippa takes me to the Bresee Department Store nearby and tells me she has a surprise for me. When we walk into this large store, just inside the entrance there is a live Holstein cow on display munching on hay. I'm so excited and happy to see something familiar but think it is weird to have a cow in a store. Philippa talks with the person in charge and I get to pet the cow. It helps to take the sting off the dentist visit.

I think Philippa can tell I am getting homesick for Mommy, Butch and farm life so she and Phyllis decide to take me to the Farmer's Museum. It is a few miles outside the village of Cooperstown. There are many animals and old farm tractors and plows. We watch a man driving a team of oxen by tapping them with a stick, no reins. I particularly enjoy the blacksmith shop where I watch the blacksmith make a horseshoe nail ring, and then Philippa buys it for me.

But then I stumble onto the Cardiff Giant display. The Cardiff Giant is the result of a hoax from the late 1800s. The story is that a farmer had a discussion with a religious man who stated emphatically everything in the Bible was true, to include that giants once walked the earth.

The farmer does not believe it so he decides to play a prank by hiring a stone cutter to carve a huge ten foot tall man. He buries the stone man and invites a scientist to come examine what he has just unearthed. Initially, many people believe it is a giant, but in later years it is proven to be a hoax. Somehow it has ended up on display at the Farmer's Museum.

We join the long line of people waiting to view the giant. Up a steep hill there is a fence around a deep hole in the ground. The crowd of people move slowly up the hill and then along the rim of the hole to view it. Peering a long way down into the hole, I see the huge stone man.

He is lying on his back with one arm across his stomach and he is not wearing underwear. He is naked. I can't stop staring at his penis and thinking so that is what it looks like. I have never seen Daddy's penis, only had it pressed against me and touched it. Philippa is attempting to distract me and move onto something else but I am totally mesmerized and I resist moving along the line. Philippa moves ahead of me hoping that it will encourage me to follow her.

Finally I make a connection and I yell over to her and say, "Philippa, his pee pee is as big as Brownie's." (The horse at the Ben Davis.) People in the crowd are chuckling, but Philippa's face is on fire.

A few months later on Phyllis's birthday we all go to dinner at an upscale restaurant at an Inn downtown, all dressed in pretty dresses. It is nighttime and there is a lantern glowing beside the door as we enter the restaurant. Each room contains a few tables with white tablecloths, crystal goblets, lit candles and sparkling chandeliers overhead. A gentleman dressed in a tuxedo welcomes us and seats us at a table in the middle of the room. I am excited to have dinner here and look forward to the meal. I enjoy food and do miss Mommy's cooking.

We have a tomato salad, roast leg of lamb with mint jelly, baked potato (finally) and a special flaming cake that Philippa had ordered ahead of time. After dessert the maitre d' presents a finger bowl to all of us. Philippa tells me to dip my fingers into the glass bowl of water with the sliced lemons and then the maitre d' presents the white linen towel that is draped over his arm for me to dry my hands.

"You are a well-mannered young lady," he says.

"Thank you," I reply.

I had so much fun with the finger bowl. Another princess moment and I can't wait to tell Mommy.

The end of the school year is a three months away and Philippa has decided to take me to New York City where she went to college. Once in the city, our initial visit is at Uncle Percy's, Harold's brother who lives in a Manhattan basement apartment.

We take the third avenue elevated train to get there. I will not sit down in a seat because it feels like the train is going to tip over and fall off the tracks. It leans to the side way too far for my comfort. There are loud creaking sounds and it is bouncing and shaking along the tracks. Philippa is in a seat, but I refuse to sit beside her. I stand up in the aisle the entire trip, holding onto the backs of the seats across the aisle. People in the seats watch and smile at me. It is terrifying and I don't want to go on this train again.

When we get to Uncle Percy's apartment there is a wrought iron railing around a hole in the sidewalk. The entrance to his apartment is down cement steps. He reminds me of Harold. They both have round faces with round wire rim glasses and they are both plump and jovial. Philippa tells him we are going to the Bronx Zoo and then to Coney Island. Our visit is brief at Uncle Percy's, just time for tea and biscuits and to give Uncle Percy an opportunity to meet me.

At the Bronx Zoo we see a snake the size of an alligator in diameter, called an anaconda. I am both fascinated and fearful of it. I return to the cage several times, pressing my face against the glass to study it and watch it slither around and curl up on itself. I have only seen the garter snakes in the grass at the Ben Davis.

Next we go to Coney Island and Philippa says, "You need to be able to say you were in the Atlantic Ocean." It is a windy April day.

We both remove our shoes and walk across the sand to put our feet in the waves. We are the only people near the water. I am delighted as the waves chase me back up the sand. The ocean is freezing cold but lots of fun.

Next Philippa decides we are going to record a voice message. We stand together in a booth and speak into a microphone saying hello to Mommy, Daddy and Butch. Philippa says, "Hi Eleanor and Joe, we are at Coney Island in New York City."

I tell them I'm at Coney Island and I will be home soon and I love them. After making the recording Philippa retrieves a small four-inch round black record in a tan envelope that can be mailed but we don't mail it. Philippa says we will bring it to Mommy when we go for Easter.

It is critical that I have this year away from the Ben Davis Farm. In some perverse way, I am prepared to cope with the insensitive music teacher, the mean dentist, the boy bully, and the near drowning. I am the total focus of Philippa and Phyllis and I am showered with love and attention. All the new experiences stimulate my intellect, and give many joy-filled days. I am free from any interruptions from my stepfather.

My first year of school in Cooperstown is an exciting adventure and memorable. I learn much more than the usual first grader. The social events I attend, the travel, the arts and the fine dining are life-altering. To occur between the ages of six to seven, important formative years, makes all the difference and I am sure help me to cope with the trauma perpetrated by my stepfather. I believe Philippa is one of my "angels." The ones that always appear at serendipitous moments, when I need them the most.

School is out, I am ready for summer vacation and to go home to Mommy and Butch. Vermont here I come!

Philippa, Butch and Paula

Paula Wearing the Dress

Paula's Name Scribbled on Wallpaper

Wicker Desk and Grandfather Clock

PAULA CZECH

Voice Letter Made at Coney Island

Philippa with her Elkhounds

Playful Phyllis on Dog Sled

Philippa Dressed in White

*Paula Feeling Good about Going
to Cooperstown*

Chapter 6

DAMAGED GOODS

Philippa and I left Cooperstown early on Saturday for the Ben Davis. I will miss Phyllis, my food ally, and especially her sense of humor. As we hug goodbye I feel sad.

After a long six hour ride, we arrive in Elkins Falls, only three miles more before I am home! As we leave the village, I shout, "There is the water tower." It is located immediately past the McMillan Trucking Company whose tankers transport milk all over New England.

The water tower is a landmark, as well as the water source for Elkins. Resembling a barn silo in height but much larger in diameter, it is silver, situated high on a hill with Elkins Falls in tall letters along the rim of the tower. I am so excited to see it because it signals we are near the turn to go to Burton. We travel two miles up a long hill to the corner of Davis Road. At the top is a beautiful three-hundred-degree view of the mountains, to include Jay Peak, a popular Vermont ski area. There is a picturesque farm with a pond on the corner and a hobby farm diagonally to it. This area of Burton typifies the slogan, "Vermont, the Green Mountain State."

Philippa's black Dodge car with the bright orange New York State license plates always provokes curiosity, and I imagine the neighbors are on the phone to each other announcing the eccentric New York woman with all the Elkhounds is visiting.

I see my baby brother Butch waiting patiently on the front lawn. As soon as he recognizes Philippa's car he runs to the house to alert Mommy. We enter the driveway with Mommy already coming down the steps smiling and waving. I jump out of the car and run into her arms. Butch is looking up at me with his shy, sweet dimpled grin. We hug hello.

Daddy also welcomes me home with a big hug and says, "Hi Cooky, we have missed you around here." He is the only one to call me by my nickname even though Mommy gave it to me, when I was six months old because my big brown eyes and round face reminded her of a chocolate chip cookie.

After welcoming me home, Daddy returns to the barn. It is a busy time on the farm, nearly July fourth and time for the first cut. The meadow that borders the line of maple trees is high with the sweet Timothy grass, its feathery heads wave in the breeze announcing it is time for mowing.

I am eager to escape to the serenity of nature and Butch wants me to go play with him. While I've been gone he has been walking up the road to Jack Dodd's farm, our neighbor. Jack is a special man. When he was twenty-seven years old he sustained a terrible farm accident resulting in an amputation of his right arm and fingers from his left hand in a corn husking machine. We always know when it is time for him to come home from his second job at the feed store. So we wait on the edge of the lawn because he always waves to us from his black coupe.

Despite his handicap, he has been a successful farmer and admired by the entire community. He has a natural mechanical acumen so farmers frequently seek his help with repairs to their farm machinery, especially tractors.

Jack has a calm, kind demeanor, and he and his wife, Velma, take in high school boys who are not succeeding in school. It is a mutually satisfying arrangement because Jack always needs extra farm help and the boys need a break from their unhappy lives.

While I've been gone Jack has allowed Butch to hang out in his barn and ride on the tractor with him, recognizing Butch is lonely without me. Jack is a compassionate and understanding man.

Unlike Daddy, who has no patience with Butch and me when we ask for a ride on the horse drawn wagon. Daddy much prefers the company of adults who are captivated by his outrageous stories and dream ventures. He is a risk taker, impulsive and he is often on the wrong side of the law. He is currently maintaining his smuggling trips to and from Canada.

The following week Daddy receives a call from his sister Camile, who lives in Rockville, Connecticut, begging him to allow her twelve-year-old son to come spend the remainder of the summer with us on the farm. During the recent school year, he had been expelled and had spent a month in reform school.

Within a few days, Aunt Camile arrives with Calvin. He is five years older than me, but acts like a grown up. As soon as he arrives he begins giving me orders. "Show me this, get me this, do this." "I want to go get the cows."

He is taller than me with black hair and has a stocky build. I have an instant dislike for my city cousin. He is a bully.

The next morning I am eager to leave the house without Calvin. Quietly, I slip down the stairs, not to disturb anyone, especially him. I reach the bottom tread and with quiet concentration I turn the doorknob, slowly opening the door without making any squeaks.

Ring, his head resting on the hardwood kitchen floor sleepily opens his eyes. His tail thumps a friendly, sweeping greeting. Together we go out the back door, through the woodshed to trek down the lane behind the barn. We share the responsibility of bringing the black and white patched Holstein cows to the barn for morning milking.

The sun begins to light our way at the end of the lane as we climb the hill to the pasture, winding through the bumps and turns in the paths carved out by the cows' repeated trips to the barn. Cupping my hands to my mouth, I call out "Co, Boss, Co, Boss." I repeat the refrain over and over again. The cows hear me and begin to gather.

Ring excitedly circles back and forth behind them, nipping at their heels. Without hesitation, they fall into a single line, a regiment of soldiers marching up the lane toward the barn.

When I was much younger Butch and I had gone to the pasture to get the cows. Ring was still a puppy and not well trained. He spooked the cows with his racing around behind them and barking. They broke into a run and were racing right at us, but I couldn't get out of the cow path quickly enough. Number Eleven, a white cow and the only one with horns put her head down when she got close to me, her horn caught my sneaker, ripped it open and I got tossed in the air. My breath was knocked out of me when I landed. I lay rolling around on the ground, and in my fear I told Butch to run... go get Mommy... I am dead.

Butch runs into the kitchen yelling, "Paw wow wa is dead, Paw wow wa is dead!"

My poor mother realizes something is drastically wrong and immediately leaves the house. When she finally finds me, I'm sitting on a milking stool in the barn behind Number Eleven cussing at her. My foot is red, swollen and has an abrasion over the top of it and I am giving the cow hell because she destroyed my sneaker.

I enjoy this time alone before the others are awake because I feel free and less anxious. I am able to identify all twelve cows and know which stanchions they belong in once we reach the barn. After my year in Cooperstown I feel older than seven and more confident as I go about my job.

In the barn I snap all of the cows individually into their stanchions. George is already in the barn preparing the milking machines and has turned on the compressor. I notice him looking at me, similar to the way Daddy does, so I hurry to the house for breakfast. Mommy allows me to make my own toast by laying it directly on top of the black cook stove, then turning it over before it gets too dark. I can also make scrambled eggs.

Later in the day, I open the door to the woodshed to return to the barn and I am startled when I come face to face with George. He immediately picks me up and begins pushing me against the bump in his pants. I instantly recognize what the bump means and I am scared. I begin kicking him and hitting him in the chest with my fists and screaming, "Put me down, put me down!" He drops me down to the floor and quickly turns around and returns to the barn. He never touches me again.

I do not tell Mommy about the hired man.

A few days later I see Calvin running out of the carriage house yelling at me, "Where have you been?" Fear rises in my chest, he meets me midway between the cow barn and the house.

Calvin begins swearing and threatening me, saying "You knew I wanted go with you!" Earlier I had sneaked away from him because I didn't want to play with him.

He is much bigger than me, so he scares me. I do not verbally respond to his threats, I am too busy concentrating on how to get around him and to the safety of Mommy. I try to move past him but he suddenly pulls out a switchblade and holds it within inches of my nose. I am terrified.

Lucky for me, Daddy comes out of the house and sees what is happening. He runs toward us, grabs Calvin by the nape of his shirt and pulls the knife from him. I run to the house to tell Mommy what just happened.

Daddy drags Calvin into the kitchen, yelling at him, "What the hell is wrong with you?

I'm calling your mother right now. You can't stay here."

He makes him sit in a chair near the pantry, then he calls Aunt Camile to tell her to come for her son today. Calvin didn't even last a week on the farm.

Butch and I are relieved when Calvin leaves, he was dangerous. Too bad he isn't a good kid because we don't have many playmates out here in the countryside.

The only playmates we have are the Edward kids next door, Laverne, Luke and Danny. Danny is the youngest, closer to Butch's age so they are often together. The twins Laverne and Luke are my age, Laverne prefers to stay in the house with her mother most of the time so Luke and I spend a lot of time together.

It is a week before school starts, Luke and I are playing in the hay mow. We have been playing for a long time sliding to the barn floor, falling in a heap together, giggling and laughing. Luke suggests that we slide down a small area between the studs on the back side of the barn. The large barn door to our left is open allowing the daylight to light up this section of the barn. When we land we are face to face in a small, close hiding space.

Luke says to me, "Let me see your pee pee, then I will show you mine."

I giggle. "No I don't want to," I answer.

So, he pulls his pants down and pulls his pee pee out in his hand so I can see it.

For some reason this prompts me to pull down my pants, I grab his pee pee and try to rub it against mine. He is giggling and having fun but I am confused because his pee pee is too soft and limp. I find this frustrating and soon become disinterested in Luke's game. We pull up our pants and continue sliding down the hay.

Daddy is having financial problems again. Now he must buy more grain and hay to get the cows through the winter. The few heifers he has have yet to freshen and a couple calves have died so his herd is not expanding on schedule.

Mommy and Philippa are in the kitchen discussing Joe's troubles when suddenly, Philippa has a childhood memory.

Philippa says, "When I was a little girl, my mother and grandmother were talking about this very mean Thibault woman who lived in Highgate."

This woman was the stereotypical mean, abusive stepmother. She seemed to take out all her wrath first on the oldest boy then his remaining three siblings. She physically beat all of them with belts for the most minor infractions but mostly for not doing household chores.

They were saying she had some cruel punishments that included tying a string around a young boy's penis and then walking him down Main Street by the string.

"Eleanor, they were talking about Joe and his stepmother."

"Oh no, I hope not! What a horrible thing to do to a child!" Mommy continues, "Joe doesn't say much about his childhood but he does speak fondly about his real mother saying that he was close to her. He used to help her with the cooking and baking. He knows how to bake a great loaf of bread and he can also operate the sewing machine."

Daddy seems to crave thrills and engages in risky behaviors. To generate more income he also continues his smuggling trips in and out of Canada.

When Butch and I do stay in the house, mostly on rainy days, Mommy keeps us in the kitchen with her. As usual she listens to "The Arthur Godfrey Show" on the radio. With her dance and musical background she especially enjoys the music acts that perform on the show. On Saturday mornings Butch and I continue to enjoy the "Sparky Show."

I am happy to be back home from Cooperstown because I missed Mommy and Butch. I didn't miss Daddy because when he is around I become nervous and watchful. Now that Philippa has returned to Cooperstown, I miss her too.

Unfortunately it didn't take long before Daddy resumed abusing me. So there are more trips to the woodshed, but one afternoon I have a terrible… terrible experience at the hands of Daddy. It is the worst thing he has ever done to me! I am seven years old.

Earlier in the day I notice a stray dog in the yard, it appears to be a ragged, grayish terrier. His behavior is unusual because he is running along the perimeter of the carriage house frantically, sniffing the ground and the hair beneath his belly has a few strings of fluid dripping near his hindquarters. His belly and his legs are muddy. He is a filthy appearing dog.

Late afternoon near chore time I pass through the carriage house on my way to the barn. Suddenly Daddy appears out of nowhere at the end of the carriage house with the stray dog. He startles me.

Without speaking to me he takes me by the hand and leads me outside beneath the maple trees that line the driveway. We are in view of the road and Jack's home a few feet up the meadow and across the gravel road. If Velma were standing in her living room window she would be able to look down on us and see what is happening to me.

Daddy tells me to get down on my hands and knees in the low scruffy brown grass. Next he pulls down my pants so that my bare bottom is visible. I don't like this at all and I try to move away but he firmly tells me to hold still. I am feeling vulnerable and worried someone will see me with my pants down as I am out in the open yard.

The next thing I feel is the dog's toenails digging into my shoulders because Daddy is trying to make the dog have sex with me. He pushes the dog's snout into my butt, I don't like his wet cold nose. He then places the dog on my back.

I feel an emotional surge of sheer shock stab my chest and belly. I cannot believe Daddy is doing this to me and I think, "Oh no, he thinks I am a dog!!!"

The dog is not interested in me and does not cooperate. Daddy is angry with the dog and reluctantly gives up after trying several times to make the dog perform. In frustration he walks away leaving me to pull up my pants. Not once did he speak to me or acknowledge my presence.

I am devastated, totally degraded.... I feel like I am a pile of shit... I feel so tainted and I am so shocked. I go into the carriage house and collapse on an old truck seat and sob and sob. All I keep thinking is, "Daddy thinks I am a dog!"

I never tell Mommy about the worst thing Daddy ever did to me.

A week later it is time for second grade. School begins tomorrow and I will be going up to the Burton Center School, the two-room school house. There are four grades in each room. At the back of the room after the last desk, is a huge bulging potbelly black wood stove where we all gather in a circle for lunch.

In the morning Mommy packs my lunch box with a small bowl, spoon, a piece of buttered bread folded in half and some dessert. At noon the lunch lady arrives with a huge steaming hot covered pot. The menu varies each day from American chop suey, beef stew, corn chowder, beans and hot dogs, mac and cheese or chicken soup. Then the teacher gives each of us a carton of milk. We line up with our bowls while the lunch lady ladles out the meal and then we all squeeze next to each other on the floor around the stove.

When the meal is over we go out to play in the nearby pasture. We have fun playing king of the mountain by jumping off a tall, monstrous flat rock, or Cowboys and Indians. I learn to ride a bicycle on someone's bike on the dirt path that circles the school house. I balance myself with one hand by reaching out and touching the side of the building until I don't need to anymore. During the school day I feel happy and relaxed.

I enjoy going to this school. The teacher gives an assignment to the third and fourth graders, then she teaches us our lesson. Today it is penmanship and I have fun practicing my letters in cursive style. There are two rows of first graders, second graders and third graders and only one row of fourth graders because some of them were moved to the fifth grade in the next room. I can practice my cursive assignment and still enjoy listening to the big kids reading stories out loud. My spying abilities are always ready.

At the end of the day a station wagon car with brown wooden panels takes us home. We are all milling around in the front yard waiting for the school bus to arrive when I notice Luke is talking to a group of boys, who are whispering and occasionally glancing my way. They giggle and then turn away from me.

Oh no, something is wrong and it concerns me. Then I realize he must be telling them about us touching our pee pees together. I am very embarrassed and ashamed because I feel shunned by the boys. After a while my shame evolves into intense anger at Luke. I vow to never play with him again and I don't. In general I am becoming angrier and angrier.

I never tell Mommy about this shameful and ostracizing moment.

I am only seven years old but my self-image is tainted, any self-esteem has been totally stripped away, I am anxious most of the time and I have little confidence. The only thing I know for sure is I must stay away from Daddy.

Butch's Dimples

Cows Marching up Lane/Jay Peak Visible on Horizon

Cows Snapped Into Stanchions

The Number 11 Cow

Butch, Paula with Orange Soda Bottle

Brown Scruffy Grass Outside Carriage House

PAULA CZECH

Chapter 7

COPS AND ROBBERS

It is early winter of 1951, with drifts of deep snow on the ground. I recently turned eight years old and I am a second grader. A group of us kids are hanging out in the school yard waiting for the school bus. I look out toward home and I am surprised that I can see the top third of the brown Ben Davis farm silo. With all the leaves gone it is clearly visible way off in the distance.

Traveling by road it is three miles to home but I decide I will cut the distance in half by taking a shortcut across the fields and through the woods. The school bus is late and I have become impatient waiting for it. I become anxious and restless when forced to stand around or be in a waiting mode. The anxiety is so strong that it drives me to move and take some kind of action. I become impulsive.

Without much more consideration, I start walking home in the snow, dressed appropriately in my brown hooded snow suit, hat, mittens and boots. I crawl beneath the barbed wire pasture fence beside the school, walk past the big rock we all play on at recess, go down across the pasture and cross over the Watertower Road. I periodically look up to check the silo location. But eventually the terrain is so low that I can no longer see the brown silo, only the open meadows and the woods off in the distance. I remind myself to stay in line with the silo location by mentally keeping it in sight. I am on an adventure and I am having fun.

I climb over or under fences, whichever is the easiest, and walk through the back meadows of a few homes and three farms. Eventually, I am on the Pierre farm, it borders the Ben Davis but it is much larger.

Now that I'm down off the hills it is becoming more difficult to walk in the deep snow. I stop frequently to rest, the snow is up to my thighs. I have a moment of fear, when I have difficulty moving my legs, I'm almost stuck. Momentarily, I think I might get trapped in this deep snow but with a surge of adrenalin I am able to push forward.

With relief, I reach the stone wall and barbed wire fence of the Ben Davis property. A little more difficult to clamber over both fences, the stone wall is slippery and covered in snow but I make it over. I know every inch of this land so my steps become more confident as I proceed along the stone wall to the corner where the Pierre property ends. I turn left and make my way through the woods of tall white pine trees. It is a little easier walking without so much snow beneath the trees.

Darkness is beginning to fall, I come out on the ridge overlooking the back hilly meadows of the farm and can clearly see the silo within a short walk. I keep walking to my left until I'm in the pasture and then make my way down the cow paths to the entrance of the lane. I walk up the lane, and through the barnyard. The lights are on in the barn so Daddy and George are milking.

I feel tired and cold so I go directly to the house across the yard through the carriage house, left through the woodshed, through the back room, and finally, I open the door to the big kitchen and to Mommy. She throws her arms around me hugging me close.

Mommy is so worried because the school bus went by two hours ago. She has been making calls to all the neighbors to find me. She just got off the phone with the bus driver who tells her I never got on the bus with him.

"Paula, where have you been?" she calmly asks.

With excitement I answer, "I walked home from school Mommy. It was lots of fun."

Perhaps some of Daddy's risky, impulsive behaviors are influencing me. I'm not sure but I do get anxious with standing around and seek action.

It is now February and Daddy continues to have difficulty meeting his bills, so he decides he is going into the logging business. He finances a one-ton long wheelbase brand new Dodge cabin chassis truck. It is a beautiful truck, several people come to view it. Not many Burton residents can buy a brand new logging truck. Philippa takes several photos of Daddy in the cab and with him driving it down the road. He is so proud of his new truck and is soon involved in his next venture, logging.

About four months later, Daddy comes home in the early morning hours with his Uncle Chet. They are both exhausted and look like they were in a fight with a bear. Their coat sleeves are shredded and they have cuts on their faces. Everyone is speaking in hushed tones so I don't really know what has happened.

A few days later we are in Richford at Daddy's Uncle Chet and Aunt Connie's small house on the river. The U.S./Canada customs stations are nearby.

Whenever we go visit their home, Daddy insists Butch and I sit in the kitchen in straight back chairs with the adults while they visit. We must remain quiet and not interrupt the adults.

But Aunt Connie feels badly for us having to sit in chairs for so long. She showers us with attention by teasing us and telling jokes. She always has wonderful desserts to share and my favorite is her blueberry pie.

Throughout the visit she badgers Daddy, "Let these children off the chairs. They should be outside playing."

Daddy never changes his mind, we know he won't.

Butch and I are becoming bored and restless, but then I notice a different energy in the adult conversations. I can tell they are discussing something important, so I begin listening attentively. Uncle Chet and Daddy are telling their wives about their recent trip to Canada.

Apparently, smuggling grain is much more lucrative than refrigerators and pin ball machines. Over the last few weeks they have smuggled two huge loads of grain out of Canada on the bed of Daddy's new truck. His new truck is much larger than the wooden-sided truck, plus the bags of grain are easier to load and there are more nearby customers.

I continue listening to Daddy telling about when they had the truck backed up to the platform at the Canadian grain warehouse in the middle of the night. The truck was half loaded when the night sky suddenly lit up with bright spotlights shining on them. Uncle Chet and Daddy are on the truck bed stacking the bags of grain. With the glare of the lights in their eyes they can't see who is out in the blackness of the night.

Over a bullhorn they hear, "This is the Mounties, stay where you are."

Daddy and Uncle Chet realize they are in big trouble, they make a run to the back of the truck and jump off into the darkness of the warehouse as bullets begin to fly. Boom, boom, gunfire from all directions.

Again, over the bull horn, "We have you surrounded."

The Mounties continue shooting. Daddy returns fire with his Colt 45 pistol hoping he can make it to the cab of his truck. But the Mounties are getting closer to the platform with guns blasting. Daddy and Uncle Chet are outnumbered.

Uncle Chet says, "Jesus Christ, Joe, we have got to get outta here. Come on let's run for it."

Daddy is still hoping he can make it to the cab of his truck but at the last minute he orders, "Run!"

Behind the warehouse is farmland and it is five hundred yards to the United States border through the woods and a pasture. They split up to make the run for the border. In their panic and in the darkness they are tripping over stumps, falling and getting back up, running again until they crash straight into a barbed wire fence.

Freedom is within inches, but their coats are caught on the barbs.

With gunfire behind them and surging adrenalin they rip through the fence and run a little further before collapsing on the ground. They both have blood dripping from facial lacerations but they are safely across the border on U.S.A ground. They are free from the Mounties.

Back in the kitchen Daddy and Uncle Chet are laughing and boasting while they relive their shootout with the Mounties, but Aunt Connie and Mommy are totally disgusted with them.

Especially Aunt Connie, "You both are dumb bastards, you could have been killed!"

In early March, I'm in the kitchen watching Mommy whip up a cake for supper, when we hear heavy boots on the screen porch. Bang, bang, someone is pounding on the door. Mommy and I go to the door.

Mommy opens the door to see two Royal Mounted Police officers from Canada at the door and she is instantly very frightened. I am standing at her side and admire their beautiful red jackets, my favorite color.

One of the Mounties speaks to Mommy very sternly, "We are here to see Joseph Thibault about his truck. Is he here?"

Very quickly Mommy assumes a different persona. She is not sounding like herself. She seems to be speaking a foreign language, shrugging her shoulders, repeatedly saying, "Nein....Nein.....keinerlei!"

The Mounties become frustrated with her and eventually leave, but first they warn her they must speak to Daddy soon. They give Mommy a telephone number for him to call. Of course Daddy never makes the call, he accepts the loss of his brand new expensive truck. The Mounties impound his truck and never release it. An illegal, impulsive and expensive escapade that causes him to file bankruptcy later in the year.

My poor mother feels defeated, Daddy is always in trouble and she cannot relax or trust that he will conduct himself in a lawful manner. Her resources to improve her situation are nil. Silent tears roll down her face almost daily. My anxiety increases when I see Mommy so sad and I try to cheer her up by hugging her often.

When I hug her she puts on a happy face for a few days and appears brave. She goes about her household duties with grace and agility like the dancer she is, ready to fend off the next potential authority to knock on the door. My petite mother has a backbone of steel. She has a quiet strength.

School will be out for the summer in a few more weeks and I am eager for summer vacation although I have enjoyed the Burton Center School and made a lot of new friends. And I think Doug Wilson is a cute boy, much nicer than Luke.

The next day I am upstairs in the bedroom when I hear Daddy come in the back door from the woodshed.

He calls out, "Eleanor where are you?"

"I'm in the living room, dusting," she responds.

"Come here, I have something important to discuss," Daddy orders.

I lie on my stomach and peer down the floor register, they are out of my sight but I can hear them. Daddy says he was at Carrie's Restaurant and a bunch of guys were talking about the great jobs down in Springfield, it is about two-hundred miles south of Elkins Falls. Daddy is saying he thinks it is time to close down the farm and move on to something better, because he has worn out his welcome around here.

Of course closing down a farm can't be done that quickly, he will need to find a job, then have an auction to sell off the animals and equipment and finally tell Philippa their plans. It is going to be a busy summer. I am worried about moving away from the farm. It will mean going to yet another school and meeting new kids, sometimes that means bullies.

The next day Butch and I are playing behind the barn where the outside pig pen is located, when my mischief button is triggered. Daddy is away looking for a job in Springfield. I've been observing the six pigs pushing their snouts against the boards of the pen. I think they want to get out of there. So I go over and open the gate. The pigs begin running from the pen and down the driveway near the house.

I run into the house and yell to Mommy, "The pigs are out! The pigs are out!"

This is the last thing Mommy needs, to stop in the middle of doing laundry to chase pigs around the yard. After a while she grabs a pail of kitchen scraps and tricks the pigs back into the pen with Butch and me chasing them from behind. All of this nonsense has taken one hour and Mommy is exhausted and frustrated.

She asks, "Paula, why did you let the pigs out of the pen?"

I feel rebellious so I lie, "I didn't let them out."

Mommy is angry and begins lecturing me about not telling lies. I become increasingly adamant and sassy. It is not my usual behavior to be confrontational with my mother, but I feel saddened and threatened by the planned move. Additionally my anger has been building during the recent weeks.

Mommy rarely raises her voice but I have sparked her Irish temper and she gives me a proper tongue lashing saying, "I am your mother, you only get to have one mother, and you must never disrespect me by sassing me. And you must always follow the Ten Commandments: 'Honor thy mother and thy father.'" She escalates her harangue until Ring begins barking and jumps between us in an attempt to shield Butch and me from Mommy. He is our constant companion and protector.

This is the last straw for Mommy, she stops her lecture and returns to the house and to the laundry defeated and saddened. To see my quiet, kind mother in such a state, was startling to me and I feel really bad that I upset her. Mommy's message makes a significant impact on me and I never disrespect her again.

Although I hear a lot about God from Sparky on the radio, I have never heard about the Ten Commandments until Mommy mentions them. I already believe I am not worthy of God's protection so I worry about how the Commandments are going to impact me.

About a week later on the last day of school, June 19, 1952, I'm anxious about where we are going to be living. Philippa has not visited since April and I miss her, so I decide to write her a letter.

Dear Phil,
Summer vacation started today. I got good marks on my report card. I'm a third grader now. The pig

we have chases me and then bikes me a little. Daisy has 7 pups 5 males and 2 females. They are pretty. One is marked like Ring and Teddy is the father.

Robert says, that's mine!!

I hope we get a house to live in and plenty of land to play on. We like to walk around the fields.

Mommy says to tell you that Leonard Martin has passed away. You know him. You were at a party at his house.

Love Paula and Butch

Philippa receives my letter and calls to tell me she will come for a visit soon. Within one week she arrives and I am excited to see her. Everyone seems so much happier when Philippa is around. She brings lots of joy and energy to our household. She and Mommy stay up late at night talking and Philippa promises to visit us in our new house.

Fall has arrived and we have yet to move; however, Daddy is making frequent trips down to Springfield trying to get a job at the Foundry or Gear Shaper. Springfield has several factories with machinist-type jobs.

It is time for school to start and Daddy still does not have a new job which means Butch and I will attend the Burton Center school. Butch will be a first grader and he is excited to get on the school bus with me.

But within two weeks, Daddy is hired at Gear Shaper so we soon change schools before poor Butch has an opportunity to even get to know his classmates.

Daddy has sent all the animals to auction and Mommy is busy packing the household items. He spends the week in Springfield working and then comes home on the weekend to complete the bankruptcy process.

During the transition Mommy, Butch and I move in with the Anderson's. They are friends who live in a modest house on the grounds of the Elkins Falls Sawmill. This allows Daddy to save a few paychecks for an apartment. The bankruptcy took most of the auction money.

Bob and Charity are nice people, although we don't see much of Bob because he is gone all week working. Butch and I are fascinated by Charity because she has one leg that is shorter than the other. She wears a big black elevated shoe on her right foot. Her gait has a swing to it and the heavy shoe makes a clunking sound as she walks. She is warm and friendly and strives to make us all comfortable.

Because we now live with the Anderson's in town we must leave the country two-room schoolhouse in Burton. It is a long walk to the Elkins Falls Elementary School from the sawmill area. It is a white two story square building with lots of tall windows. There are several steps to climb to enter the building and it is a much larger school than the Burton Center School. Both Butch and I are scared to attend our new school. We don't know any of the teachers or kids.

It is especially scary for Butch, school is an entirely new experience for him. He is scared and sad and spends most of the day looking out the classroom window. The teacher repeatedly tries to draw his attention to the lesson but he is too sad to participate. He is a first grader and has experienced too many changes within a few weeks. We no longer have Ring and we don't know where he went. Butch misses Ring, his constant companion.

We are both affected by this transition period. I worry about Butch and remain the protective older sister. I am used to taking care of him on the farm, making sure he doesn't get hurt during our adventures throughout the day, especially making sure he doesn't fall off the reservoir dam. In an attempt to cheer him up, I take him to the Ben Franklin 5 and 10 Store every day after school. I hold his hand as we walk along Main Street.

It is a fun store. Down the last aisle on the left side there are trays and trays of small toys. Small farm animals, cows, chickens, pigs, little cars, trucks, tractors, tiny dolls, and several sizes of balls including paddle ball.

Sometimes we just walk up and down the store aisles admiring the toys, but other days I steal a toy for Butch or myself. Today I take a red tractor for Butch. It looks like the Farmall tractor we had on the Ben Davis Farm. The store clerk never notices when I take a toy because

I make sure she is not looking our way when I quickly shove it in my pants pocket or up my shirt. I am involved in my own form of cops and robbers and remain a very troubled little girl.

Living near the sawmill is both creepy and fascinating. I like to hear the hum of the saw and watch the logs move through the carriage and come out as boards. And I like the fresh clean smell of the sawdust as it falls from the logs.

The creepiness involves an old bum with baggy clothes who smells of urine and booze who lives in the sawmill. He has long, tangled hair and a wiry beard, and he sleeps in the sawdust bin which is always full of beer bottles. He also has a nasty dog that curls his lips and shows his teeth if we get too close. Luckily he is tied to a long rattling chain.

At the other end of the sawmill there are several cages of rabbits. I am fascinated by them, they come in all colors and sizes. I study their sweet little faces, big red eyes, cute twitchy noses and whiskers. I enjoy them because we didn't have rabbits on the farm.

Daddy comes home late Friday night in an enthusiastic mood because he has found an apartment. He and Mommy get up early Saturday to travel back down to Charlestown, New Hampshire so she can see if we will be able to adapt to a smaller space. Springfield is only six miles across the toll bridge from Charlestown. An easy commute for Daddy. This means we will be moving and soon changing schools for the third time this year. Poor Butch, not the ideal way to start the first grade.

I am nervous and feel insecure about leaving the Ben Davis. The sights, smells and sounds of the farm feel like a friend to me and more like an extension of myself. How will I soothe my pain without the refuge of nature? I am an emotionally damaged little girl full of fear and anger.

Boundary Line (behind row of trees) Between the Pierre and Ben Davis Farms

Ridge Overlooking the Ben Davis Farm

Daddy's New Logging Truck

Daddy Driving Down the Road

Daddy Logging

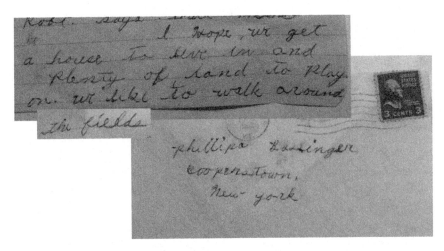

Paula's Letter to Philippa written on Last Day Second Grade

The Road to Canada

Chapter 8

THE FAIRY DELL

Saturday, October 24, 1952, moving day. Mommy and Charity are packing up the remainder of our belongings as Daddy and Bob return from the Ben Davis with the furniture loaded on his wooden-sided truck. Mostly the items Mommy brought from Connecticut, especially the blue blanket chest. Philippa said good-bye to us last week because she said, "I can't bear to watch you leave the driveway."

But Mommy insists this is not a final goodbye and invites her to spend Thanksgiving with us in our new apartment. Philippa agrees to come depending on the weather, she will not drive in the snow.

The four of us crowd into the truck, me in the middle and Butch on Mommy's lap.

Butch says, "I wish Ring was here."

No comment from Daddy or Mommy, so we don't know if Ring is alive or dead. It is a long drive to Charlestown, NH and Daddy doesn't like to stop for pee breaks. His response is always, "Just hold it a little longer, we are almost there."

Late afternoon we arrive in Charlestown, it has a lengthy, pretty

Main Street lined with tall elm trees. Route 12 is a major truck route but this portion is also Main Street. Most of the businesses are on the left side of the street. There is a multi-story inn, a diner, and an electrical parts store. A little farther down the street is a five and dime store, drug store and a bank.

On the opposite side of the street there are rolling front lawns with large colonial style homes. Most of the trees have shed their fall foliage. In the center of town is a large fountain near the post office and the Silsby Library.

We turn right after the library onto Railroad Street. The load shifts in the back of the truck, as we jostle over the railroad tracks and proceed down to Dell Street. We stop at the last house on the right, on a dead end.

Butch and I are excited to see there are woods beyond the end of the street.

I say, "Butch, let's go explore the woods after supper," and he smiles in agreement.

Daddy parks in front of an attractive two story white house with red shutters. Mommy and us kids clamber up the stairs to the apartment to use the bathroom. It is the biggest bathroom I have ever seen, it is the size of a bedroom with a slant ceiling on one side. There is a claw foot tub like at the Ben Davis beneath the slant ceiling. The toilet looks small and silly, sitting alone on one long wall. The opposite wall has the sink and a window. In a back nook is the area for the washing machine.

We continue checking out the four rooms, Butch and I will share a bedroom as usual. The living room is at the front of the house facing the street with two windows that look out across to the Tin Shop. I can hear a man welding in a garage-style doorway wearing a visor hood and see sparks flying all around him.

In the living room is a beige kerosene stove about five feet in height. It has a glass jar that occasionally gurgles as the kerosene feeds the stove. I am disappointed that we are in a much smaller place than the Ben Davis and it doesn't feel like home.

From the living room window and to my left I can see a large white house on the corner of Dell and Garden streets bordered by a white picket fence. I see kids swinging on a burlap bag swing hung high in an elm tree. I think, maybe I will get to play with them.

As soon as we finish supper Butch and I hurry downstairs to play in the woods. Mommy reminds us to come back in the house before dark. The woods are different than the Ben Davis, the trees are tall and do not have low branches. We can see all the way through the woods, no pricker bushes or pines with low branches to struggle through.

As soon as we enter the woods the terrain is downhill. We can see a clearing across the way at the top of a steep hill. As we get near the bottom of the hill the ground becomes moist and our shoes are sinking into the moss. Nearby we see a narrow stream, but because the ground is so wet and we do not have our boots, we decide not to cross the stream to climb the next hill.

With sheer joy we rush back to the house to tell Mommy what we found. She is smiling and telling us we can show it to her tomorrow but now we need to bathe and get into our pj's. We are all tired from moving day.

The next afternoon Daddy has his tools spread across the kitchen floor and he is busy building a wooden box. The kitchen is only slightly larger than the bathroom with only one window.

Always curious about adult activities I ask, "Daddy what are you doing?"

He replies, "I'm building a refrigerator."

I am puzzled so I continue watching him. Once he has a twenty by twenty-four inch box built, he goes over to the kitchen window facing the backyard and installs the box on the window ledge. He has the open end of the box facing the kitchen. By raising and lowering the window we can reach in for any cold stuff like milk, cheese, eggs and butter.

In the morning Daddy finds the milk frozen. The cream pushed the lid up from the bottle, Daddy scoops it off and eats the frozen heavy cream. Butch is standing by and wishes Daddy would share it with him.

Mommy is tired from the trip yesterday and is sleeping later than usual. Daddy takes me into the large bathroom and has me sit on his bump while we are both sitting on the toilet. I immediately feel irritable.... and then intensely angry.

On Monday, Mommy gets us ready for school and the long walk. The three of us leave the apartment, when we get to the railroad tracks Butch and I are excited to see a huge black locomotive with smoke billowing above idling at the train station. It is noisy. We are thrilled to see a train up close. I am fascinated with the huge iron wheels with the puffs of white steam escaping between them. We proceed up the street, passing the Elms Hotel, and as we near the library we hear the train whistle as it departs the station.

Mommy has us hold hands to cross Main Street. We walk by a factory that makes locks and keys. Our walk has been a constant slow incline and Butch is getting tired so we stop to rest. From the factory we look down the street where we see a Rexall Drug Store. There are some high school kids smoking in front of it.

We have only completed half the walk to school, so Mommy says we need to move along. We still need to walk uphill before we reach the schools. Butch and I will be in different buildings across the street from each other.

First Mommy takes me into the Holden School, a large two story white clapboard building. In front of us just inside the door is a wide stairway leading to the second floor. Kids are everywhere. Mommy presents my report card and meets my new third grade teacher.

Mommy and Butch give me hugs and tell me to have a good day, then Mommy takes Butch across the street to the Stucco School to register him for first grade. It is a much smaller one story gray masonry square building than the Holden School. This is the third school in less than sixty days for him. Butch has a difficult time adjusting to school and like me we are missing our former life at the farm. These are confusing, and scary days for us both.

I am shown to Mrs. Brown's classroom, to the left of the stairs, and down the hall to the last room on the left. She is very pleasant and has a big warm smile. Mrs. Brown shows me to my desk and tells the class my name. She is short, sort of dumpy and wears her light brown hair in a bun at the back of her head.

The first lesson in Mrs. Brown's room is arithmetic. She is at the blackboard writing numbers, teaching long division, and I have no idea what she is talking about. I am too intimidated to raise my hand and ask questions. In Elkins we were doing the multiplication tables and I know all of them up to the table of twelve. But I watch Mrs. Brown closely as she writes various examples on the board and after a week I begin to grasp long division. Although I eventually catch up with the class regarding arithmetic, I never feel confident about it like I do all my other subjects.

Recess is so different than the Burton school. There are brand new shiny swings, slides and monkey bars. We play marbles by digging a cup size hole with the heel of our shoe in the dirt. Next we take turns pushing our marbles with the side of our index finger into the hole. The winner gets to keep all the marbles in the hole. Of course during the first week I do not have any marbles, until I meet Sharon.

I recognize Sharon as being in my class. She has light brown, chin length hair and is wearing a pretty skirt and white blouse. I remember her because she often raises her hand to ask the teacher questions. I can't do that. But if the teacher calls on me to answer a question I'm okay. As I stand nearby watching her and the kids play marbles, she notices me on the edge of the group and invites me to play. But I do not have any marbles.

I ask, "Where do you get the marbles?"

Sharon responds, "Oh I have some extras, here take these."

She hands me ten brightly colored marbles with yellow cat eyes and swirl designs. I love the way they feel in my hand.

"Thank you," and I kneel down to learn how to play marbles.

Mommy seems so much happier living in town, she is always smiling and recently I have not seen her silent tears streaming down her face. Within the month Mommy is hired at Keil Lock, the factory we pass on our way to school. It is obvious she is overjoyed to be at work and on a job that is familiar.

Finally she has some independence, and her own paycheck. The work is similar to the airplane factory, working on an assembly line. With her dexterous fingers and quick mind, she produces more pieces than her quota and often has extra pay. When Mommy comes home at night, she is happy and talks about all the friends she is meeting at work.

On Friday nights we drive to Claremont, a much larger town than Charlestown, to do grocery shopping, and many times Daddy waits in the truck so Mommy can buy clothes for Butch and me at Montgomery Ward's.

After shopping we eat supper at a food truck parked in a plaza near the grocery store. It advertises foot long hot dogs across the side of the truck. Butch and I enjoy the steamed hot dogs piled high with chopped onions, mustard, relish and a sprinkle of celery salt. These are happy times for our family.

Mommy also buys bags of candy, mostly caramels. Both she and Butch love sweets, especially candy. In the evening Butch will sit in her lap while they munch on candy. I take a few pieces but I am not a candy fan like them. I prefer my meat and potatoes.

Daddy seems to be having a hard time at work. Every night at the supper table he is grumbling about his boss.

"He is a son of a bitch," says Daddy. "Always complaining that I talk more then I work. I tell him I can do two things at once, unlike him."

We are all looking forward to seeing Philippa on Thanksgiving. She sends a letter telling Mommy she canned some special pickles and will make a cranberry relish. However, the day before Thanksgiving the weatherman predicts we will have the biggest snow storm in recent years. On Thanksgiving Day, we learn that some places in New York State received more than ten inches of snow. So disappointed, we know immediately Philippa won't be coming.

One day walking home from school I notice a girl in my neighborhood playing with a cute small light brown dog. They are on the lawn of a two story gray house on the corner of Dell and Southwest Street. She is a pretty, petite girl with brown hair and I recognize her from school, so I walk over to see her dog.

"Hi Pudgie, I didn't know you lived this close to me. I love your dog, she is really cute. My brother and I miss our dog, Ring. He was a black border collie."

Pudgie asks, "Where did he go?

I respond, "We had to leave him in Vermont when we moved."

Pudgie says, "Oh that would make me cry, I don't ever want to be without Cindy. Where do you live?"

I tell her I live down the street in the last house on the right, and Pudgie invites me to come up after supper to play.

"Okay, I will."

The next day Pudgie and I walk home from school together and decide to play before supper. There is a two car garage to the left of her house where we go to find something to do. Thereafter, we spend lots of time together and I am happy to have a new friend that lives near me.

When we don't play in the garage, we play paper dolls in her bedroom with Cindy napping on the bed next to us.

"What kind of dog is Cindy?" I ask.

Pudgie tells me Cindy is a golden cocker spaniel. I really like playing with Cindy and Pudgie. Playing paper dolls is new to me. There is a cardboard girl figure that we clip into a plastic base so it will stand upright. Then we can cut out all different clothes for the doll and dress her the way we like.

I tell Pudgie I really like playing in the woods at the end of the street because they remind me of where we lived in Vermont. She tells me the woods are called The Fairy Dell. We become great friends and hang out a lot.

When the warm weather returns, Pudgie and I have fun playing dress-up in Mommy's old clothes and dance costumes. We pull out dresses with fringe skirts, feather boas, fur stoles, and high heels from the blue blanket chest. I like the fur piece that has tiny brown animal heads with beads for eyes dangling from it.

After we get all dressed up we struggle to keep the high heels on our feet as we wobble up the paved street to Pudgie's house to play in her garage.

One day I bring one of Mommy's china tea cups to the garage with me. Near the time to go home for supper I go to collect the tea cup but find it in smithereens.

"Pudgie," I yell, "You broke my mother's cup! Why did you do that?" Pudgie does not answer me. She is frozen in place, she has never seen me angry.

I gather up my things and yell at her again, "I'm not going to play with you ever again! I am really mad at you." And I never do. My anger has been intensifying since our move and it seems to erupt if someone betrays me.

I find other kids to play with in the neighborhood. They have a clubhouse in their backyard at the end of Garden Street. It is the last house on the left past the white house with the picket fence.

One Saturday four of us girls are in the clubhouse when one of the girls asks if anyone of us has seen a boy's pee pee. I am eager to fit in so I speak up and say I know what a Daddy's pee pee looks like. It has hair above it. The girls shriek in shock and run home.

Later that evening a man knocks on our apartment door. I am in my bedroom so I can't hear everything he is saying. But as soon as I hear a man's voice and something about his daughters, I am scared.

I am not sure what was wrong with describing a Daddy's penis, but when the girls ran away from me I realized I had said something bad. He is talking with both Mommy and Daddy. His voice gets loud at times but lastly I hear him say make sure your daughter doesn't talk about such things with my kids again.

After he leaves, I ask Mommy what the man was saying but she brushes it aside, "Oh it wasn't anything important." But then she sits on the couch with me cuddling me close and stroking my hair. But I am feeling guilty, ashamed and so confused.

Later that night I hear Mommy raising her voice at Daddy in their bedroom. They seem to be having an argument about me and the neighbor who came to the door. The next morning Mommy insists Butch and I be ready for school when she leaves for work at seven fifteen.

She says, "I want you kids to come to work with me and stay up-stairs in the break room until it is time for school to start."

I am bored sitting around for a half hour in the break room. It has a coffee machine but no snacks and I read the few magazines within minutes. But Mommy insists we go to work every morning with her thereafter. It is her way of trying to protect me again.

Within two months Daddy has another job, one day he yells at his boss and quits on the spot. As usual he finds another job quickly, also a machine shop job up in Claremont. Now he leaves for work before Mommy so Butch and I no longer need to go to the factory break room.

The girls who ran away from me shun me and never play with me again. I am confused and ashamed about this situation, it makes me feel very bad about myself. I have no confidence.

I go to the woods a lot when I'm upset. The heaviness slips away and I feel carefree when I am surrounded by the serenity of the woods. The tall trees, the whistling wind, then the quietness and the occasional dashing small creature give me comfort. I miss the Ben Davis Farm.

I do not tell Mommy I have been shamed and ostracized, because this time she is aware.

During the summer we all go to the Culvert to swim. It is a unique place, located in North Charlestown in the country. After walking along a meadow we come to a large swimming hole beneath the train trestle. The trestle is very high above our heads and below is a deep swimming hole. Mommy sits on the bank reading while Daddy, Butch and I go swimming. Because of almost drowning in Cooperstown I am not confident in the swimming hole. Butch stays near the bank in the shallow water near Mommy.

Daddy takes me out into the deep end by holding me by the hand. Near the trestle side there is a cement ledge with a small waterfall flowing over the ledge. He leans against the ledge with the water flowing over his shoulders. I am facing him and hanging onto him because with the force of the waterfall I feel safer.

With his hands beneath the water he tries to put his fingers in my bathing suit between my legs. He is trying to move the crotch portion over to the side to get to my genital area. My bathing suit is hurting my leg because it won't stretch far enough to allow access. Next he pushes his bathing suit down and tries to get his penis between my legs.

I repeatedly look over my shoulder to get Mommy's attention but she is reading her book. I am becoming more and more uncomfortable because there are nearby swimmers and I am embarrassed and nervous they will see what Daddy is doing. Finally he gives up because he can't get his penis inside my bathing suit.

When summer arrives Philippa comes to pick up Butch. Now it is his turn to spend time in Cooperstown with her. Because Butch has had such a confusing and traumatic first grade experience, Philippa suggests he attend some reading classes over the summer at the Mohegan Reading School. So he receives the royal treatment from Philippa and like me he thrives. He has a great summer in Cooperstown and enjoys his classes and does well.

By the time Philippa returns with Butch, Mommy and Daddy are talking about moving again. They say we need a bigger place and Mommy says the Keil Lock factory has apartments for rent.

Paula in Third Grade/Charlestown

Pudgie and "Cindy"

Pudgie's House and Garage

Our Gang in third grade.

Paula in Center Fourth Row Back

Chapter 9
THE HOYT MANSION

Mommy arrives home with news about a possible new apartment located across the street from Keil Lock. She says it is in the former home of a famous playwright from the late 1800s named Charles Hoyt. He was the first one to write a musical comedy. Mommy is enthusiastic about potentially living in the Hoyt Mansion as it appeals to her intellectual curiosity and artistic nature.

The following morning Butch and I race each other to the truck, eager to see where we might be moving. Daddy and Mommy are talking about the new furniture they will need to buy when we move to the apartment, a bed for Butch and a new refrigerator. The second-hand refrigerator they bought for the apartment is not large enough for our family.

As we approach Main Street we see a huge three story white house on a knoll across from the Unitarian Church, in need of a paint job, yet it remains impressive taking up a third of the block. There is a veranda that encircles three sides of the house, with a turret on the right side and a portico on the left.

The building manager describes the layout of the house. There are four apartments, one in the back where the former servant quarters were located, the other three are in the main house. Two apartments each consist of half the house with bedrooms upstairs. The expansive long beautiful stairwell is shared by the main house tenants. The fourth apartment is not rented at the moment but is located on the third floor in the turret.

Mommy and Daddy are interested in the apartment on the portico side of the house. Butch and I are pleased to see a large side lawn with a mulberry tree. There is a row of evergreen trees for privacy along the edge of the lawn on the Keil lock side.

We enter the apartment from the portico side porch into a small hallway with two doors. The one on the left leads upstairs to a bedroom over the kitchen. We enter the door on the right into a large dining room with a black marble fireplace. A small pantry and kitchen are to the left with a back porch overlooking flower beds.

In the dining room and living rooms are beautiful hardwood floors with ten-inch wide mahogany diagonal patterned borders. The rooms have fifteen-foot ceilings. We enter the massive living room through floor to ceiling mahogany folding French doors that span twelve feet in width. The living room has six floor-to-ceiling windows.

The skills taught to Daddy by his biological mother serve our family well because he is able to make curtains from inexpensive muslin cloth for the many over-size windows and they look great.

An elderly retired school teacher lives across the foyer from our apartment.

The grand stairwell with a curved bannister leads to the bedrooms. Upstairs on the left are two bedrooms the same size as the dining and living rooms but with white marble fireplaces.

We all love the apartment and Daddy pays the security deposit and first month's rent. I have the front bedroom overlooking Main Street and for the first time Butch has his own bedroom situated over the kitchen. Mommy and Daddy's room is through a small dressing room behind my bedroom.

The location of our new apartment is ideal for everyone, Butch especially is relieved he has a shorter walk to school, Mommy only needs to walk across the street for work and I am closer to Sharon. Finally we are in a spacious house even larger than the Ben Davis.

Sharon lives down the street about four blocks, also in a big apartment house on the second floor. I am intrigued that she can enter her bedroom directly from the main stairwell without entering the main door for the apartment, it appeals to my sneaky side. It is a short walk for us to go play with each other and we are always together.

We often get up early before school starts to see who can gather the most horse chestnuts from a tree halfway between our houses. I love the smoothness of them, of course only after they have shed their green prickly shells. I like to rub them between my fingers, I experience the same pleasurable sensation as I did with the marbles.

Many times Sharon and I play canasta on her bed. She sits at the head of the bed and I lean against the foot board of the bed. We have the cards spread out on top of the bedspread.

She teaches me to play and I love the game, but I become fiercely competitive. My anger soon surfaces each time she wins because she has a habit of holding two canastas in her hand then surprising me by laying down all her cards at once and going out. Sharon can be as sneaky as me. Without the usual indications that she is about to win the game it feels like a betrayal and my temper explodes.

It becomes more and more difficult to beat one another because we are so well matched. So then we make up additional rules to make the card game more challenging. Instead of needing two canastas to go out we change it to two red canastas. Eventually my tendency to become extremely angry spoils our fun and we stop playing.

Toward the end of the school year Daddy gets a part-time job as the janitor at my school, which means Butch and I stay after school and help him by placing all the chairs on top of the desks so he can polish the hardwood floors with a big polishing machine. After he completes a classroom, we go back and place the chairs in front of each desk.

During one afternoon the three of us were upstairs near Mrs. Sherwin's classroom, when Daddy pulls me into the nearby bathroom. It is a small space so Daddy leaves the door partially open. He begins to lift my dress when Butch comes to the door to see what we are doing. Daddy erupts in anger and yells at Butch.

"Get out of here, go to the house with your mother!"

Poor little Butch, he is only a first grader and he hasn't done anything wrong.

Years later as adults, while Butch was visiting me from Arizona he would tell me this story stating he didn't know what was going on but it felt sexual to him. I was shocked he remembered it and that his impression was correct.

It is the Fall of 1953, we enter the fourth grade in Mrs. Sherwin's class. Sharon has promised to play with me after school. I didn't see her in the school yard when we were dismissed so I start walking down the sidewalk toward home.

The sidewalk is full of kids on their way home, then up ahead in the crowd I notice Sharon walking with Celeste.

I yell out, "Hey Sharon wait up, you promised to come to my house."

Both of them look over their shoulders at me, but instead of waiting they run away from me. I chase them, yelling at them, "But you promised to play with me." They begin running faster. My temper explodes.

I yell at both of them, "You are sons of bitches! God damn you guys! I hate you! Damn sons of bitches!"

I'm running trying to catch up to them, I almost catch up but then they disappear behind the Keil Lock and hide from me. So Sharon and I do not play together as planned. My anger boils over, another broken promise and betrayal situation.

The very next day Sharon says she is sorry.

She says, "I forgot we were supposed to play together. Then Celeste said let's run and I followed her."

I don't necessarily forgive her. I do continue playing with her, but I remain angry and do not forgive Celeste.

As adults Sharon likes to tease me, "I stayed friends with you because I didn't dare not be your friend."

Whenever a person that I should be able to trust fails me, an internal spark erupts and I'm instantly filled with rage. I think it first occurred that day long ago when Daddy broke his promise to buy me two new pretty dresses after tricking me into believing we were going on a picnic.

No actually, the first betrayal was the initial woodshed abuse incident. Children depend on their parents for love and nurturing. Failure to provide these basic needs is the ultimate betrayal.

Our family is happy and thriving as we settle in at the Hoyt Mansion. Daddy is doing okay at his job in Claremont and Mommy loves working but she needs me to help her with supper. When I arrive home from school I peel potatoes and put them in cold water. This helps Mommy prepare the remainder of the meal in time for five o'clock.

As time goes on, I do more and more to help her. I also set the table and help her with dishes after supper. I become a "Mother's Little Helper." I am assuming a parent role.

Butch and I love living at the Hoyt Mansion. We see television for the first time. The Green's are a family of eight who live behind us in the former servant quarters. They invite us over on Saturday nights to watch wrestling in black and white on a small box.

The picture is fuzzy and the TV makes crackling sounds. Mr. Green gets off the couch often to rearrange the tin foil on the rabbit ears antenna in an attempt to make the picture clearer. There are twelve of us crowded into their living room and all of us are thrilled to be watching this new thing called television.

Everett and Irene are sweet, loving and giving people. With an already full house they open their home to our family so we can enjoy television. At other times Irene passes fresh homemade raised sugar donuts out the screen door to Butch and me. Our kitchen doors both open onto a shared back porch and we can always smell the delicious aroma when Irene fries her special donuts.

I continue to spend lots of time with Sharon. We have meals and sleep-overs at each other's homes. We are like sisters and are together almost every day. We watch the soaps on TV after school to include "Love of Life," "The Edge of Night" and "As the World Turns."

Sharon's sister Sally is eight years younger than we are so it is difficult to include her in our playtime. We disappoint Sally, often causing her to be extremely upset.

It is just before Christmas when Daddy and Mommy tell Butch and me that we are going to have a baby brother or sister in the summer. After seeing Sally's behavior, I'm not sure how I feel about a new baby. Mommy continues to work until the end of the school year.

During the afternoon of July 20, 1954, Mommy goes into labor. We all go to the hospital with her. I am ten-and-a-half years old and Butch has recently turned eight years old. Butch and I stay in the car in the hospital parking lot while Daddy admits Mommy to the hospital.

After a couple of hours Daddy joins us in the car to wait for the new baby to be born. Butch is sitting in the back seat and I am in the front with Daddy. He turns the radio on to listen to the news.

Then he grabs my hand while motioning for me to slide over closer to him. He puts his hand into to my panties and plays with my genitals. I am so uncomfortable. Butch is in the back seat and I am fearful he will know what is happening. I am embarrassed and I try to pull away but he will not remove his hand. After what seems an eternity he leaves the car and returns to the hospital.

Eventually he comes back to the car and announces we have a new baby brother, and then we go home for supper. Mommy will stay in the hospital for three days. That evening at bedtime Daddy makes me get in his and Mommy's bed with him.

I am getting too old for this, I know about menstruation and I know how one gets pregnant. I haven't yet started my menses but I am aware of a high school girl who recently dropped out of school because she got pregnant, which I find mortifying.

Once in bed with me Daddy pulls up my nightie, straddles me and starts to penetrate me. I feel the initial partial entry of his penis and it is instant "fight or flight" for me. I am scared to death and instantly pull away from him, jump out of bed and RUN!

Our bedrooms are joined by a small dressing room. I run into my bedroom and close both doors, crawl under the covers. I am shaking, I am so scared. I don't want to get pregnant... I must not get pregnant. I lie in bed with the covers up around my neck positive he is going to come for me. But much to my surprise he doesn't come.

The next day I am full of rage and it is spewing from me. I am slamming things around, whenever I make eye contact with him my brown eyes are black and glaring. I am angry as hell but I never say one word to him because he is the authority figure for this household and I fear him but my rage is firing on all cylinders. Every time I look his way he is fully aware of my anger and he begins to avoid making eye contact with me. HE NEVER TOUCHES ME AGAIN.

I gained my freedom on the day of my baby brother's birth, July 20, 1954. I will enter fifth grade in the fall. Mommy has no idea what has occurred and I never tell her. My anger becomes my best friend.

On day three Mommy comes home with Sidney Ovila Thibault and I am so excited when I see him, he is so cute. His crib is in Mommy and Daddy's bedroom. With my nearby bedroom it is easy for me to help Mommy with changing his diapers and giving him his bottle.

Butch and I treat him like a doll and dress him up in my baby clothes that are stored in the blue blanket chest, and then push him all over the yard in his carriage. He makes a cute little girl with curly blond hair.

One day Daddy comes home with a new car. It is a white and red trimmed 1953 Oldsmobile 98 Fiesta convertible. He tells us, "This car is very special because less than five hundred were produced."

Every weekend we go for long car rides. Sharon comes with us on several trips. Mommy usually packs a lunch and we stop along the way at scenic views. I love these drives out into the countryside with the wind blowing in my face and my hair whipping in the wind. It feels liberating.

And I like the adventurous feeling of not knowing our destination. Daddy never knows where he is taking us ahead of time. Sometimes we drive down to Connecticut to visit Daddy's sister and her family. ,

When we get to the Connecticut State line Mommy and Daddy are on alert for police cars. If there is a nearby State Police car, they make Butch and me get down on the floor of the back seat, and once they threw a blanket over us until we got to Aunt Gert's house. They remain worried about the Connecticut authorities finding me.

A few months after Sid is born I have a strange experience. I am up in my bedroom lying on my bed reading a Nancy Drew book when I put it aside for a while. I am sort of daydreaming, when in my mind's eye, I see myself as a small child repeatedly running and running between two doors terrified, screaming, "Mommy, Mommy let me in!... Mommy, Mommy let me in please!" Next I see myself helping my mother pull the nipple onto a baby bottle. But I have no other memory or know why this memory has surfaced. I go downstairs to tell Mommy about it. She is shaken by my story and has a shocked expression.

With disbelief she says, "Paula you are remembering Butch's birth at the Larrabe Farm."

She is amazed that I have been able to recall the day Butch was born. She says, "Paula you were only two-and-a-half years old on that day. Butch was born when you and I were home alone."

Mommy believes that the recent birth of Sid has somehow triggered my memory of Butch's birth. She then tells me about the entire day. Mommy begins by saying, "It was a Saturday about two in the afternoon when I began labor so I went to lie down. I had you join me in the bedroom because I was hoping to get you down for a nap."

She tells me that at the Larrabe Farm her bedroom was off the kitchen and there were two doors to go into the bedroom, one by the wood-burning cook stove and one on the opposite side down a short hallway.

Mommy says, "I tried to read you a story but you soon lost interest and wanted to get off the bed. I allowed you to return to the kitchen where you amused yourself by playing with the pots and pans in a bottom cabinet. When my hard labor began I had to close the bedroom doors. You heard me moaning and crying so you ran back and forth between the two doors and tried to open them but your hands repeatedly slipped off the white wobbly ceramic door knobs. I told you I was okay and I would open the door soon and I tried to reassure you, but a sharp pain caused me to scream. I felt so helpless, I was in the middle of childbirth and you were too young to understand, and I was terrifying you with my crying."

Mommy continues, "I can still hear you screaming Mommy... Mommy let me in, let me in," as you ran back and forth between the two doors.

Next Mommy tells me, "Daddy came home soon after Butch was born and he is the one who cut the umbilical cord. I brought Butch out to the kitchen and rinsed him off at the kitchen sink. The nearest garment was one of Daddy's flannel shirts draped over the drying rack. I swaddled Butch in it and then laid him down on the open oven door to keep him warm. Finally I was able to console you, so I gathered you up in my arms. I hugged you and wiped away your tears and sat in the rocking chair with you on my lap. After a while I told you, 'Paula, you have a new baby brother.'"

A few days later while we were home alone Mommy says, "I discovered that my right arm was too weak to put the nipple on the baby bottle. That's when I had you stand in a kitchen chair next to the table and help me with the bottle. It was a struggle but between the two of us we were able to stretch the rubber nipple onto the bottle."

After telling me about Butch's birth, Mommy decides to go through the black leather satchel for the first time since we moved to Charlestown. We are sitting together in the dining room, no one else is home. Mommy begins to talk about my father. I love hearing about my biological father and I never know what else Mommy is going to share with me. I treasure the black leather satchel.

She says, "In addition to being a big man he also has a big personality. He was the life of the party. He loved to tease and have fun and he was so proud of you. He loved you, you were his pride and joy." She tells me the Pearl Harbor Day story.

Mommy says, "We were sitting in a movie theater, when the movie was interrupted to announce the bombing of Pearl Harbor. Your Dad knew at that moment he was going to be at sea for a long time. I was so lonely when he was gone."

Then she opens the black leather satchel and takes out the wedding ring given to her by my father. She holds it for a long while, quietly reflecting on a happier time. It is a gold band with several small diamonds across the top of it.

She says, "Here Paula, I want you to have this. I think it is beautiful and I'm so proud to have it. I put it on but it is way too big for me. So I put it in my pocket."

I complete my school years at the Holden School and enter Junior High at the High School down the street from my home. It is situated halfway between Sharon's and my house. A beautiful modern, long, two story brick building on a hill with a rolling green lawn in front of it.

The first day of seventh grade is so confusing. Every forty minutes a buzzer rings and the whole class moves to another classroom for a different subject and a different teacher. But I soon adapt and enjoy my teachers and classes.

My social life also changes drastically, some I embrace and others scare the hell out of me. It is the attention from boys that I am the least capable of dealing with. I am not comfortable around them and do not know how to react to them. Part of me is flattered by their attention but mostly I remain awkward and uneasy.

Sharon, Celeste, and Pudgie behave very differently than me and seem to enjoy hanging out, flirting and dancing with the guys at the school. But for me it is as though I am in a permanent frozen state around them.

Ballroom dance lessons become available at the Town Hall and both Sharon and I go to the classes. Mommy is thrilled and shares stories with me about when she was a dancer. She relives her days of performing in shows like "Sunny Skies," when she was a pupil of a country-wide renowned ballet dancer and New York stage star, Michael Nicholoff.

Mommy buys me opulent organza dresses for each week's class and I am the only kid dressed to the nines, but for some reason I don't feel out of place. It boosts my confidence. However, I am excruciatingly self-conscious about being in contact with my male partners. I have no sense of rhythm and feel very inadequate, but I do learn the various dance steps.

I believe several situations have led to my insecurity with dancing and being around boys. I have a deep insecurity regarding music because of being shamed in front of my entire first grade class. When interacting with boys I feel sheer terror around them. Perhaps on a subconscious level I fear the return of the abuse.

Or maybe it is my history of negative experiences with my male peers like when the first grade bully hit me, or when I was in the second grade and I was shamed and ostracized by Luke and his friends. And of course there was the time when Calvin my city cousin threatened me with a switchblade knife. I only feel insecure with boys during one-on-one situations with them.

Boys seem to be attracted to me but after a while they make the assumption I am too shy to pursue. There is one male classmate, Steve, that I am okay being around because our parents know each other and we are frequently at their house for socializing. Also I seem to sense he does not have the same agenda as the other boys in my class. When he asks me to the eighth grade prom I accept. I still can't dance as well as everyone else but I get through the evening and I have a good time.

As usual my dancer Mom ensures I have a pretty prom dress and Steve brings me a corsage so my confidence is at a high. It is the only time during my adolescent years that I am fairly comfortable being alone with a male peer.

The location of the Hoyt Mansion is ideal because from my upstairs bedroom window I can spy on all my peers as they walk to and from school. I especially notice those that are going steady, holding hands with the boy carrying the girl's books, and I wonder when will I ever feel comfortable enough to have a boyfriend. I am sixteen and have yet to experience my first kiss.

Hoyt Mansion

Paula, Butch, Sid in Backyard of Hoyt Mansion

Sharon and Paula at her Uncle's Camp, Bristol, VT

Paula, Sharon and Baby Sister Sally at Camp

PAULA CZECH

Paula And Sharon, Fourth Graders At Hapgood Pond, VT

Paula in Mother Role with Sid and Butch

Chapter 10

THE ABDUCTION

After we have been in Charlestown a few years, when I am about the age of eleven, my mother decides to tell me more of my history.

On a rainy dark day, I open the door to go through the dressing room leading to my bedroom and stumble upon Mom in her bedroom, searching through papers in the black leather satchel as she leans over the blanket chest at the foot of the bed.

"Hi Mom, what are you doing?"

"Oh Paula," she said, speaking softly, "Come join me. I have something important to tell you."

Mom stands up, closes the cover of the long blue chest as we both go sit on her bed leaning against the dark oak headboard. Her bedroom is large with a marble pedestal sink near a window that overlooks a lush backyard covered with shrubs, fruit trees and flowers, although today due to rain the view is misty. There is also a white marble fireplace on the same wall as the sink.

As she begins her story, I hear the rain splatter and ping against the window, yet I feel cozy snuggled next to Mom with the purple throw across our laps.

"Paula, you were just a little baby about a year-and-a-half old when we left Connecticut. Joe and I had been in court a few days earlier and I was in a panic. The judge had awarded custody of you to your father and I knew I could never allow that to happen. I also feared the consequences, if we stayed. It was very important that we leave the legal jurisdiction of Connecticut."

"But why Mom?" I interrupt.

Mom stopped speaking for a long time and then responded, "It is too complicated to explain right now. I will tell you when you are older."

She continued, "A week later we closed out our bank accounts and packed a few of my most treasured items: a long light blue wooden blanket chest. Inside the chest are my white lace christening dress, small white socks and baby shoes, all my baby clothes, documents, photos, multiple ration booklets, old dance costumes and flapper style dresses, fur stoles along with a beautiful sterling silver cocktail shaker and colored crystal stemware."

"In the Spring of 1945, on a Friday evening and under the cover of a night sky, we crowded into Joe's blue pickup truck, overloaded and tied down with huge tarps."

Mom continues, "I was distraught. My parents were not speaking to me, I was leaving my siblings, close friends and putting all my trust in Joe that we would have a good life in Vermont. He drove quickly to the Massachusetts border being cognizant that we must not be stopped for speeding. We could not have any interaction with the Connecticut police. Once out of Connecticut I burst into tears with relief, sadness and fear. I was so confused and worried whether I was making the best decision for both our futures."

As if reliving that day, Mom becomes teary, but after wiping her eyes and blowing her nose she regains her composure.

I snuggle up closer to her. I love my Mom.

"Joe had convinced me to move to Vermont because his family would be nearby for support and we would live near the Canadian border, so if necessary we could escape to Canada. This option would ensure no one could ever take you away from me."

She says, "It was a long, difficult drive to Vermont because we were trying to avoid the main routes. Finally several hours later we arrived in the blackness of the night on the Vermont/Canadian border in the small village of Richford.

"As Joe negotiated the truck through the narrow curvy Main Street, I strained to see the landscape of my new community. But due to the darkness all I could visualize were blocks of shadowy brick buildings.

"After a while I began to relax, seeing the buildings in the soft glow of the tall street lamps flanking an iron bridge with curved railings. We drove over the bridge to the business district of Richford. There were small markets, gas stations and the Sweat-Cummings Furniture Company where many of the residents worked.

"We soon arrived at Joe's brother Raymond and his wife's small apartment up over a red brick store front on Main Street. Exhausted and afraid we had been followed, I was a relieved to be in the apartment behind closed doors."

Years later, when I met my biological father he told me he had hired a detective who tracked us to Vermont. Once in Richford on the Canadian border the detective learned that I was living in a convent in Canada. I suspect the detective lost our trail in Richford, but in order to give my father some solace he made up the story about me living in a convent in Canada.

Mom says, "It was the scariest time of my life, both Joe and I believed we might need to make a run for the border at a moment's notice, but I was comforted by the knowledge that the border customs station was within a mile of the apartment.

"The following day Raymond and Joe went looking for housing. Richford was the typical small town with a rampant grapevine so we knew Joe's overstuffed truck with its out-of-state plates had the residents buzzing and wondering who were the new people in town. The overstuffed truck was too conspicuous and needed to be unpacked promptly.

"Our stay at Raymond and Donna's was brief, within a few days Joe located the Larrabe Farm out on a back road in Burton, seven miles from Canada. Joe knew of nearby old abandoned farm roads we could use as an escape route into Canada if needed.

"The Larrabe Farm would give us the necessary seclusion to keep us safe from the Connecticut authorities and prevent my father from finding me. It was located at the Watertower Road and the corner of Mineral Brook Road in Burton.

"On the Mineral Brook side, a high tree embankment blocked a view of the red cow barn and white clapboard farmhouse situated above the barn. The driveway entrance was around the corner on the Watertower Road side. A long gravel driveway led to the red barn with the farmhouse to the left up high on a hill."

Mom continues her story, telling me living at the Larrabe Farm was a harsh transition for her, its plain mostly empty rooms so different from her cozy warm little home up on the hill in Westfield. She regretted that she had no choice but to leave many precious items behind and she especially missed her plush blue living room carpet. Her challenge was learning to cook on a black wood-burning stove.

Throughout my young childhood, my mother would often gather me close to her either on her bed or in a soft cushioned living room chair. I was always eager to see what else might be in the black leather satchel and hear more about our life before Joe. But on this rainy gloomy day she chose to only share part of our story, but she did tell me more about my biological father, Joseph Francis Czech.

Then Mom tells me that she and my father initially met in High School but didn't date seriously until several years later. My father was a football player size man, tall, rugged, good looking and the life of the party. He always dreamed of traveling and seeing the world.

Directly from High School he followed his dream by hopping onto trains, hiding in the box cars and getting out to see the sights wherever the train came to a stop. He managed to go across the country and back.

Upon his return he reconnected with my mother and they were

married about two years later. A transition moment occurred on December 7, 1941, when my father joined the Merchant Marines, causing him to be away from home for six to nine months per deployment.

Once Mom and Joe moved to Vermont, the life she experienced as a young woman, wife and new mother was never again. The days of her dancing on stage and the piano playing vanished, never to return. It was as though the lights went out on Broadway.

My Father at Coney Island

Youngest Baby Photo of Paula

Paula on Ruth Aliff's Lap

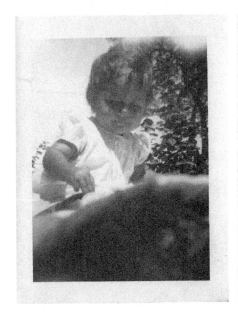

Baby photos of Paula while living in Connecticut.

Chapter 11
THE DANCER HAS NO LEGS

It is my freshman year of high school 1959, and we are moving again but this time to our own house. Dad announces he received a five thousand dollar settlement from a car accident but I wonder when was he in a car accident? I remain curious about the settlement money but I soon forget to pursue the matter. Obviously, the money came from another source because he was not in a recent car accident.

Butch and I look forward to moving to our own home. Since we left the Ben Davis Farm it feels like we are always in transition, different schools, different places to sleep, and a new brother. We yearn for a sense of stability. Perhaps our family is finally becoming part of the Charlestown community and no longer in the hiding mode.

Dad and Mom are eager to show us our new home. We drive three miles out into the countryside past a farm, a factory and an occasional house until we approach a cluster of homes. In the car Butch and I are thrilled, but we prepare ourselves to be disappointed because Dad often has big plans that never materialize.

Dad says, "We will live within walking distance to the Toll Bridge that crosses the Connecticut River into Vermont."

Dad turns left down into a settlement of homes located a short distance from the river. It is about a half mile from the last street of homes.

Midway into the small hamlet we are pleasantly surprised to see a yellow two story home with a wraparound porch and a free standing garage. There is a beautiful flowering crab tree at the entrance of the driveway and our new home sits on three acres. We seem to have the largest lot.

Butch and I begin to believe that this is really happening. We enter the house and go upstairs to see our bedrooms. It is a three bedroom house, Butch chooses the first bedroom to the left at the top of the stairs. He will share it with Sid. I have the bedroom down a short hall that overlooks the driveway, perfect spot for checking on the comings and goings. Yes, I remain in my spy mode.

Dad and Mom have the master bedroom that takes up half the upstairs area and overlooks the street and side lawn near the driveway.

I am thrilled that there is a big yard, our lot extends from street to street with the house sitting in the middle. There are a row of evergreen trees along the back boundary line obstructing the view of other neighbors. We have a nice large private lot.

There appears to be a garden area in the middle of the lawn to the left of the driveway and visible from my bedroom, and I look forward to planting flowers and digging in the dirt. Perhaps my Polish agrarian genes have been stimulated.

The Springfield Road home is smaller than the Ben Davis or Hoyt Mansion but it certainly has enough room for our family and we all soon adjust to our new residence. There is a large area for Sid to play and he especially enjoys playing hide and seek and baseball.

He is five years old and will enter first grade in the fall, enabling Mom to return to factory work. She soon finds employment with the Sylvania Company in Hillsboro. The pay is better than average making the two hour drive worth it. She drives twelve miles to Claremont where she carpools with four other women. They each take turns driving and during the winter the mountain road presents them with many challenges.

Because it is summer and I am able to care for Sid, Mom decides to begin work soon after we move. Again I see the joy return to her, she is much happier working and making friends. Mom spends her paycheck on a new house dress for work every week, a new living room set and the remainder on us kids.

Butch and I share household chores, washing and drying dishes, cooking supper, doing the laundry, caring for Sid, sometimes I even do the grocery shopping and Butch mows the lawn.

Mom does not request that I do all these chores, I sort of take over the duties as though they are my responsibility. I remain a "Mother's Little Helper." I assume a parent role and to me it feels like the natural thing to do. However, Dad does expect Butch to mow the lawn.

One day I am struggling to hang sheets on the clothesline in the backyard. Butch is mowing the lawn. He refuses to follow my instructions about not getting too close to the clothesline because the mower is throwing grass onto the wet sheets.

He is intent on getting his job done because he fears the consequences if he disobeys his father. Therefore he ignores my request and instead gives me an attitude by dismissing me with a wave of his hand. I reach the extent of my patience, my temper explodes.

I reach out and grab his shirt and slap him aside his head a couple times and yell, "I told you the grass is flying all over the sheets."

He quickly escapes my grasp and leaves for the other side of the yard.

Later that evening Butch complains to Mom and Dad, telling them I beat him. Mom soothes him and cautions me to act like a lady but Dad does not come to Butch's defense at all.

He says, "Sounds like Cooky had a good reason to kick your ass!"

We are both adolescents with too many adult responsibilities, and coupled with the usual teenage sibling rivalry these years are tough on us both. One winter day I push him out the kitchen door onto the porch and lock the door. I leave him out there freezing for ten minutes wearing only his underwear. I continue to have a short fuse.

However, during the school day at High School, my temper never erupts. I am friendly and sociable with everyone and do not become enraged. But my social skills are nonexistent when it involves the boys. I am not hanging out or making out with any of them. They tease me and flirt with me but my response is always an awkwardness with a slight smile. The guys scare me to death so I do not interact with them. Therefore, I do not experience any of the usual teenage make-out sessions in the back of a car, petting, puppy love or sexual exploration.

I make up for not interacting with the guys by concentrating on my studies. Being on the High Honor Roll gives me some name recognition throughout the school and enough popularity to compensate for not dating.

One day during science class, Mrs. Baldwin, the English and Latin teacher, enters the room and motions to me to come out into the hall with her. Instantaneously, I fear I am in trouble for something but can't imagine what I have done wrong at school.

Mrs. Baldwin says, "Paula, why are you in general science?"

I am dumbfounded that she is questioning my class schedule so I stammer, " I don't know... other than it is on my class schedule."

Mrs. Baldwin continues, "Well, wouldn't you prefer to come across the hall and be in my Latin class?"

"Yes, I would like that much better!" I say with enthusiasm.

I am eager to swap science class for Latin class because the teacher has no control over the boys. They are frequently disrupting the class with their own version of lab experiments like making stink bombs. It is hard to concentrate and learn anything because of all the commotion in the room.

I love Latin and excel at it. I receive 102% on my midterm test because I was able to do the conjugations and translations correctly plus answer the extra credit question. I am starved for any affirmation that will increase my self-esteem, because most of the time I feel tainted and less than my classmates. Doing well in my studies gives me confidence and boosts my self-image.

At the end of the school year, in the auditorium during the awards ceremony, I receive medals for having the highest grade in social studies, English, science and one for citizenship. No one from my family is there, but when I return home I am showered with praise by Mom. I'm not sure why Mom did not attend, perhaps Sid was too young to sit through the ceremony or more likely Mom was still in her hiding mode and wanted to avoid answering any in-depth questions.

When I reach my junior year of High School, again Mrs. Baldwin intercedes on my behalf. One day after class she pulls me aside and asks, "What are you doing after graduation?"

I tell her I will probably go to secretarial school, but think to myself I have no idea where I will get the money.

She says, "Have you ever thought about being a nurse?"

I say no, then add "I don't think there is any money for me to go to college." I tell Mrs. Baldwin I do work weekends at a nursing home where the charge nurse has me help with changing the patients' dressings.

Mrs. Baldwin becomes energized and orders me, "I want you to go down to Mrs. Ring's desk. In the bottom left-hand drawer is a school catalog for the New Hampshire State Hospital School of Nursing. I am sure you remember Martha Hansom, she is at that school right now."

This is a life-altering event and a serendipity moment for sure. Mrs. Baldwin is one of my "Angels."

I recognize the name of the girl, she graduated a couple years ago. So before I go home I retrieve the school catalog from the Principal's secretary's desk. I am nervous because it is the first time I've been near the Principal's office.

Because it is a State Hospital affiliated school the students pay a minimal tuition, it is about three hundred dollars. In return for their education the students work on the units caring for the patients. I begin to plan how I can earn enough money for senior expenses, college application fees and the National League of Nursing prerequisite examination and just maybe future nursing school expenses.

A few weeks later I'm sitting in the large upstairs study hall room. I'm two desks away from the teacher's desk and I'm next to the windows. I like to sit near the front because it is quieter.

Looking up from my studies, I pause and gaze out over the front lawn watching the cars traveling up and down Route 12, thinking there has to be a way for me to go to college. It is imperative that I leave Charlestown and home. I don't know how I'm going to do it, but I am determined to make a better life for myself. I want to be independent and in charge of my life because it feels like I am imprisoned under Dad's patriarchal control.

I do not understand why Dad is so stingy with money. He always has a job and he seems to have enough money, his wallet is always bulging with bills. But he is so tight with it. Neither Butch nor I get an allowance and oftentimes I will begin asking for a quarter in advance so I can attend a basketball game with Sharon and his answer is, "I will think about it."

Even by game day he will not yet have given me a response, so I can't tell Sharon if I'm going or not. Because we do not have a phone many times, Sharon will drive the three miles out to our house before the game starts at seven p.m. hoping that I can join her. Most of time Dad still has not given me his answer about the quarter. So then I have to go out to her car and tell her I can't go. Once in a while he will give me the quarter at the last minute. Sometimes Sharon gives me the quarter so Daddy is forced to let me go to the game. This begging causes me to be extremely angry, but I do not dare to express my anger.

My thoughts continue, I have a deep seated determination to be in control of my life. I am driven to earn my own money so I'm not dependent on anyone but myself. Dad controls the finances and he is never generous with money. Sure we have plenty of food and a comfortable home, but we never have any spending money or new clothes. He can't even part with a quarter!

We often wear hand-me-downs or out-of-style clothes. However, I am fortunate because Sharon's mother will frequently give me a new skirt and say, "Here, Paula, I had some extra material so I made you a skirt along with Sharon's."

Odd, because the material has a different design than Sharon's and is in my colors. Over the years she quietly passes things to me, usually with the caveat, "This does not fit Sharon any longer or these ice skates hurt her feet," when in actuality they are brand new skates. The one and only bicycle I ever had was given to me by Louise Ball.

When on a trip to Vermont with Sharon, her Mom and Sally, we visit Sharon's Gram Perry. On the back porch is an old boy's bike in need of some repairs. Louise commandeers it, brings it home with us where Mr. Ball replaces all the spokes, and gets it road-ready for me. He comments, "No child should be without a bike".

Louise Ball is another one of my "Angels."

I enjoy living at the Springfield Road home and even have near-by classmates, the Bresse twins who live up across the main road. Throughout high school I hold pajama parties where I prepare home-made spaghetti sauce for a spaghetti supper for as many of my class-mates as can come. We girls sleep on the living room floor in sleeping bags, talk and giggle about the boys into the wee hours. I may not be dating the guys but I do manage to keep tabs on them.

The 1960's are noted for rock and roll, The Beatles, The Rolling Stones, race riots and the Vietnam War but I totally miss all of these cultural events because of the effects of sexual abuse. My focus is on caretaking, I am in the parent role, confused and consumed with rage.

A highly unusual and surprising event occurs in July. Butch and I are startled when a man dressed in a brown suit comes to the kitchen door and Mom suddenly gets up and leaves with him. As she goes out the door she says, "I will be back in two hours." I only catch a glimpse of the back of him, he is short and stocky. Mom has never done this be-fore, the only time she leaves the house is to go to work or when we all go grocery shopping. She returns in two hours. I can see she has been crying and tears are still streaming down her cheeks.

Alarmed I ask, "Mom, who was that?"

Quietly she answers, "My brother." She says it so softly I'm not sure

I hear her correctly. She goes up to her bedroom and closes the door.

She never tells us any more about this unexpected visitor and sadly I do not pursue the matter with her. But I believe this is the one and only contact she ever has with her family.

Our household secrets continue.

Butch, Sid and I return to school in the fall. I am a senior and I am thrilled that I am on my way to total independence. By this time I have my driver's license. It is sort of out of character for Dad, but he generously provides various cars for me. They are second hand junkers that usually fall apart in a few weeks, but they allow me some independence. Of course in addition to driving to school every day, I also drive to Claremont and do the grocery shopping and continue my nursing home job in Bellows Falls, VT.

I enjoy my senior year of high school from 1961-62 and I maintain good grades except for the final quarter of English class. I receive my first C ever in any subject and I am devastated. Our teacher, Miss LaFrank, is in her late twenties, she is slightly overweight, appears matronly with a plain hairstyle and wire rim glasses. And we all love her! She is an amazing teacher, she takes the time to really get to know each one of us and offers individual attention as needed.

I am struggling in English because we are studying poetry and I am trying to learn the various rhythms. Even the hint of a music connection throws me into a total panic. In addition to poetry we must give oral book reports. I love reading the books and writing the reports but to stand in front of the class and speak is terrifying. Initially, I attempt to avoid the oral presentations by doing double reading and book reports but eventually Miss LaFrank insists I stand in front of the class and do a presentation.

I fail miserably, my face is white, my mouth is dry, and it takes me several seconds before I begin speaking. Once I begin the book report the paper in my hand is shaking and I am stumbling over my words. I return to my desk as soon as possible. Even Sharon is surprised to see me in such a state.

By working weekends at the nursing home I manage to earn enough money for my class ring. It is beautiful with a mother of pearl design and more expensive than the standard ring. In addition I pay for my copy of the yearbook and my cap and gown rental fee. I am happy that my entire family does attend my high school graduation, including Philippa.

Prior to the end of school, I drive myself to Concord two and a half hours away and locate the high school where I sit for hours to take the NLN exam. My admission to nursing school depends on how I score on it. All through the exam, I'm anxiety riddled, worrying that I will never pass because I have no confidence. On a later day, again I drive myself to Concord for a Nursing School entrance interview with two of the Nursing Instructors. And eventually, I learn I have passed the NLN and I am accepted for admission to the New Hampshire State School of Nursing beginning in late August.

As I graduate High School, I am optimistic and eager to embark on my future. Mom and Philippa make it a special day with lots of friends coming for dinner.

Over the summer I work at a pocketbook factory, in Bellows Falls. I sit at a sewing machine all day with Sharon to my left and other class-mates Maria and Ida nearby. We are all sewing leather pieces needed to assemble a purse. In order to obtain the job Sharon and I convince management that we intend to make factory work our vocation and plan to be there long term. But in actuality factory work pays more than the nursing home, so we are only there to earn the maximum amount of school money.

Our immediate supervisor is wise to us and realizes we will only be working for the summer. He constantly tries to trick us into admitting we are only part-time so we have fun playing a cat and mouse game with him over the summer. We tell him outlandish stories about why we are working at the factory, and enjoy our jocularity with him. It becomes a daily challenge to stay on guard and not reveal we will be going to school in the fall.

But then in the middle of August the most devastating event oc-curs, it alters the lives of every member of our family forever. I am eighteen, Butch is sixteen, Sid is nine, Mom is forty- four and Dad is forty-five years old. We are all too young to cope with tragedy. I am totally distraught but I remain in my "Mother's Little Helper" role and rise to the challenge presented. I become an adult overnight.

One evening in August 1962, Mom comes home early from work. Her usual shift is 3-11 p.m. but she arrives home about 8 p.m. I am so surprised to see her home, then I am shocked and dismayed to see her stumbling and barely standing.

"Mom what is wrong? You haven't been drinking have you?"

"No, no Paula, I'm not feeling well, please help me up to my bed."

I grab her arm and struggle to get her up the stairs and into bed. I am so worried about her. And I'm feeling guilty for thinking even momentarily that she was drunk. She rarely takes a drink and Dad does not drink often either. Once in a while with friends he may have a beer or a high ball. I berate myself for thinking that.... I don't know what made me think such a thing, I feel so ashamed to have said that to my obviously sick mother.

The next morning we all get in the car. Mom and Dad have decided to go see Dr. Pillsbury, a Chiropractor in Claremont. We kids sit in the car waiting for them. After one hour they return to the car but Mom's gait has not improved. They tell us Mom is being referred to a neurologist.

I am due to leave for Nursing School on August 26th. Two weeks before I am to leave Mom receives the diagnoses of Multiple Sclerosis. By this time she is no longer walking and is in a hospital bed in our dining room. The dining room furniture has been moved to the opposite end of the room. I don't think any of us understand the impact or the chronicity of the disease, but we do recognize Mom is acutely ill.

I think to myself there is no way I am leaving my mother home alone with only my stepfather and my brothers to care for her. I begin hovering over her, I bring her meals, help bathe her and help her on and off the bedpan. The visiting nurse comes and decides she needs an indwelling Foley catheter.

I tell Mom I am not leaving her. I am not going to nursing school.

Mom becomes very agitated, "Oh yes, you are going to school. I will need a good nurse, so you must go!"

I am so upset, anxious and conflicted. At night in bed I can't sleep, my racing thoughts repeatedly ask, what am I going to do? How can I leave Mom? How can I leave Sid, he is only a little boy!

Mom instructs Dad to hire some caregivers, so before I leave there are two older women who take turns coming Monday through Friday. I am reluctant to leave her, but Mom is adamant that I go.

Dad buys me a blue and white 1954 Chevy Bel Air car for two-hundred twenty-five dollars at Howe's Motors in Claremont and I pay close attention to his negotiating skills. I have a car with rusted rocker panels but at least it is transportation. So with much angst I load my car with my suitcase and boxes of items the school has instructed me to bring. In addition, I take the black leather satchel. It is my way of having Mom with me. I drive myself to nursing school and tell Mom I will be home every weekend to check on her.

Before leaving town I stop by Sharon's. She has already left for UNH in Durham, but I want to say goodbye to her mother, who is a nurse. Later in the day when I arrive in Concord at the dorm, Londergan Hall, I am surprised to discover Mrs. Ball had slipped a white envelope into my coat pocket with five dollars and a good luck note.

Louise, one of my "Angels," is being supportive as usual. I greatly appreciate her generosity and it lessens some of my angst. I continue to believe that God does not have my back. It will be years before I develop a relationship with a higher power. Mom's silent strength and spirit was the heart of our family and without her courageous stewardship, we children find it difficult to simply exist. Dad acts out as usual when things get tough. The Springfield Road house is our last family home and we never all live together again. With the dancer no longer conducting the show, we all become out of sync and struggle to become part of a chorus again.

Mom in Wheelchair, New Diagnosis of Multiple Sclerosis

The Springfield Road House

NOV · 60

The 1953 Oldsmobile Fiesta Convertible

SCHOOL DAYS 1958-59

Sharon Ninth Grade

"How many
hot milk?"
B.A., Columbia College
*Civics, Economics, Contemporary Problems,
History of Civilization, Senior Advisor,
Cross-Country Coach.

MRS. MONETTA BALDWIN
"Let's try that over again."
University of Vermont, Ph. B. Educa
*Latin, English, Sponsor of Nationa
Honor Society.

*Mrs. Baldwin, English and Latin Teacher
(one of my Angels)*

Newspaper Write up of my Mom,
Eleanor McCarthy

Mom (on left) Dancing in "Sunny Skies"

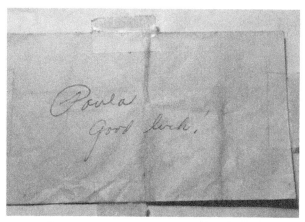

The envelope slipped into my Coat Pocket by
Louise Ball (one of my Angels)

Sharon and Paula Graduate High
School as Best Friends

Lunch Time at Margolins Pocketbook Factory

PAULA CZECH

Chapter 12

NURSING SCHOOL

September 1962, I arrive at nursing school full of trepidation, guilt, all alone but with high aspirations for a better future. I leave a mother who has sacrificed her entire life for me in bed, disabled, helpless, and two younger brothers to fend for themselves. I am eighteen years old.

Although the guilt is paramount, I allow slivers of excitement to surface in anticipation that nursing school will fulfill my dreams of becoming independent. Forefront in my heart are my sweet gentle mother, my brother Butch two-and-a-half years younger. We are no longer siblings in the throes of adolescence but allies against my stepfather. And I feel the pain of leaving my baby brother Sid, so adorable, innocent and too young, not to have a functioning mother.

Dad will not cope well with the new responsibilities of a sick wife and the raising of two young sons alone. To complicate his life, Joanne, his twenty-year-old daughter from his second marriage, is eager to come from Connecticut to meet her father. I can see from the photos she sends that she is a tall, pretty young woman with her father's stunning blue eyes.

I arrive at Londergan Hall in my '54 Chevy Bel Air on a sunny afternoon, to a beautiful four story brick and white colonial style building. It is located near several patient buildings on the campus of the New Hampshire State Hospital. A long sidewalk leads to the half circle steps accented by two white classical columns on either side. Later I discover a sundeck at the top of the building overlooking the tennis courts between the dorm and the Medical Surgical building.

On the campus reside three thousand mentally ill patients housed in seven multi-story red brick buildings. Mature trees, flowering bushes and vast lush green lawns interspersed with winding blacktop streets, complete a serene scene.

I walk up the sidewalk leading to Londergan Hall, it is both a dormitory and the School with classrooms in the basement. Upon entering I have a view of the formal living room, an elegant presentation with a fireplace, and several clusters of Queen Anne chairs for reading areas. The walls are covered with class photos of nurses dating back to the late 1800s.

I approach the house mother's desk. I am intrigued by the massive switchboard on the wall to her right. Later I learn it is the buzzer system to alert us to come to the lobby for visitors. She welcomes me and addresses me as Miss Czech, then gives me an orientation packet and my room key and directs me to the third floor via the elevator across from her desk. Riding in the elevator to the third floor, my spirits lift as I reflect on being addressed as Miss Czech, they think I am important. I navigate my way to my room through a hall full of my future classmates with their parents and siblings.

My room has a twin bed, a desk and chair near the window. The bureau is a built in three-drawer unit and mirror and I am relieved to learn that the top drawer has a lock for valuables. I look around and want to pinch myself. It is difficult to believe I am in nursing school and I'm going to be a real nurse.

A while later I hear commotion out in the hallway so I open my door to find a group of girls talking, full of excitement. I begin meeting some of them, a girl named Andrea has the room next to mine. We strike up a conversation and are both eager to begin nursing school and decide to go to supper together. There is a large dining room in the basement with white tablecloths on several tables that seat six. I appreciate dining at tables with white tablecloths and the classy presentation of our dorm appeals to my sensibilities.

Andrea tells me she lives in Hollis and has had a steady boyfriend throughout high school. Her interest in nursing stems from having a disabled brother. Over time I find her to be a moody and serious person. I have the feeling I'm not the only one entering nursing school with burdens.

The food is served cafeteria style with usually one choice, but there is always a sandwich as an alternative. Most of us enjoy the food and the servings are huge. As time goes by, one of my favorites is creamed cod served over mashed potatoes with a vegetable, rolls and always a high calorie dessert. But we seem to work off the calories on the wards.

On Monday morning, classes begin promptly with a structure and organization similar to the military. I find this irritating and I react instantly with resistance. We are a class of thirty-two and have been divided into three groups. Our instructors are dressed in white uniform dresses, white nylons and white shoes. They all wear white caps of different shapes and styles designating their individual schools of nursing.

I am enthusiastic about the subject matter and I cling to every word of the lectures, fully cognizant and thankful for the amazing opportunity I have been given. However, Nursing School is not my main focus, I am so distracted worrying about Mom and my brothers, especially little Sid. But somehow I manage to do some studying and maintain an 89% average, not as good as High School but okay under the circumstances.

I am especially drawn to psychiatric nursing and the psychology courses. I begin a self-introspection. We are taken on tours of the hospital beginning with the locked wards housing the patients who are severely mentally ill. Keys are worn on a lanyard around the waist of our pink student nurse dresses. Before entering the ward our instructor sensitizes us to our patients' feelings and emphasizes we are not to jangle the keys but keep them silent in our pockets. And to always remember to enter the ward with a smile.

These huge patient units have twenty foot ceilings, fifteen foot high windows and there are hardwood floors throughout the building. Each ward houses fifty patients. In the back of the dayroom is a dormitory, a blanket of white with rows of single beds, positioned close, all neatly made with white bedspreads. There are locked seclusion rooms stripped bare except for a rubberized twin-size mattress, a treatment room and a glass enclosed medication dispensing room the size of a walk-in closet.

In the dayroom there is a wide array of behaviors displayed, some patients remain reclusive and depressed. Along the periphery some are muttering to themselves or yelling about God, demons or electrical currents. Others pace back and forth in a strict monotonous pattern, while others are blatantly in our faces, smiling broadly with red lipstick smeared not only on their lips but onto the sides of their mouths. They are happy to see us and call out with joy, "The Pinkies are here!"

Our uniforms consist of pink dresses (therefore the nickname), with white stiffly starched bib aprons, white nylons and white oxford nurses shoes.

I am eighteen years old and have never been exposed to a mentally ill person, but I am not threatened by their bizarre behaviors and incoherent mutterings. Instead I find myself drawn to understand them. I am curious as to how they became ill and wonder what happened in their lives to contribute to their illness. I wonder why they have become so unraveled and I innately have sympathy for them.

In the beginning we are on a six-month probation period and are called Probies. We have each been assigned to a "big sister." These are students in the class above and they are meant to help us adjust to the nursing school experience. My big sister always seems too busy and I am reluctant to ask for help, so I find my own way.

I am true to my word regarding visiting my mother every weekend until the snow arrives. I don't have any snow tires so when winter arrives I am forced to leave my car parked in the school lot. We have never had a phone, so I am unable to check on Mom. But whenever

Sharon is home she makes a point to visit Mom and then gives me a report. Other times I get a ride home with a classmate who lives in Claremont.

By the end of probation period it will be determined whether we will continue in nursing or be dismissed. I feel the pressure to succeed, this is my ticket to a better life. Before the end of our probation we lose three girls who could not adjust to the demands of nursing.

In the middle of the night, about two o'clock, many of us are awakened by the elevator repeatedly going up and down. It makes a significant clang each time it stops at a floor. One of our classmates has summoned her parents to rescue her from the matriarch nursing school regimen. She feels imprisoned by the nursing school rules and believes Miss Snell will not allow her to leave.

Miss Snell and Miss Brown are extremely prim and proper registered nurses who live on the fourth floor of the dorm. Miss Brown is tall with short white hair and is the Director of the Hospital. Miss Snell is the Director of the School of Nursing, about forty-years-old and also a tall woman, with blond hair, braided and wrapped on top of her head. Her hairdo and the two inch stacked heels of her white nurses' shoes make her appear much older. Because they both live above our floor they maintain a close surveillance on us and run a tight ship.

The headlights of the student's parents' car are shining on the back of the building, and we can hear a car motor running for a quick getaway. It is a ridiculous and humorous scene but at the same time it is also pathetic. What can the parents be thinking to believe they must surreptitiously remove their daughter from nursing school?

Miss Snell, in her long flowing white nightgown and ruffled edge night cap, appears in the hall, also awakened by the elevator. She takes charge of the situation by engaging with the parents, explaining the initial few weeks can be confusing and difficult for students but to no avail, the girl is determined to leave.

There are strict rules governing our whereabouts. We all need to be in the dorm at 10:15 p.m. unless granted a late leave to 10:45 to include New Year's Eve. I find the rules a little confining and compare the nursing school experience as though we were in a convent. But some of us learn to avert the late leave and weekend passes by sneaking in and out through a side door leaving it ajar with a stick.

During the first two years of nursing school I study diligently and I especially enjoy working with the mentally ill. I am fascinated with psychology and the clinical seminars.

I follow a schizophrenic forty-year-old woman for six weeks. I learn her case history and interact with her on the ward every day. She slowly begins talking with me and we develop a quasi-therapeutic relationship. I present her case in a psychology seminar to my instructor and classmates. We are all sitting around a long conference table in Thayer Building, one of the patient residences. Near the end of my presentation, I invite the patient to the class and interview her in front of everyone. I receive a 94% for my case study.

During the next few months of our studies, we are on affiliation at Concord Hospital, a hospital less than a mile away. We are now studying Medical-Surgical Nursing. At Concord Hospital I learn to do female catheterizations, dressing changes for surgical patients, manage patients attached to Gomco suction machines, oxygen, and perfect my aseptic and sterile technique skills by working in the operating room. As part of our training we spend two nights sleeping in the call room, ready to respond to any emergency operating room surgical cases.

As anticipated one night I am awakened by the jarring of a loud bell system for the operating room at two o'clock. I quickly dress and run to the OR. I am second scrub and assist on a case involving a twenty-year-old man with a gunshot wound to his abdomen. While out on the town drinking beer and eating pizza, he gets in a bar fight and is shot in the abdomen.

Once in the OR the surgeon opens his abdomen to begin the repair, the odor of the stomach contents spilling out partially digested pizza and beer is horribly pungent and nauseating. I can barely maintain my composure but I continue to hold the retractors that keep the operating site open for the surgeon. I loved the excitement of the emergency. The operating room experience becomes one of my favorite rotations. I thoroughly enjoy it and excel.

Sharon is at UNH about one hour away and she comes to visit me often. Usually a few of my classmates are away on a weekend pass so she can sleep in their bed during her visit. She gets to know many of my friends and we have fun weekends just hanging out. She loves the meals in the school dining room and is able to dine at no charge. One weekend she helps me sew a new jumper that I am in the process of making.

While home for a weekend my thoughts drift back to my young childhood, of course all the psychology courses at school may have raised some questions in my mind. I decide to retrieve my baby clothes and some photos from the blue chest in preparation for my return to school. As I am loading my car, Dad comes out onto the porch to say goodbye. I feel compelled to get some answers. I walk up to the porch and blurt out, "I want to know why you did all those awful things to me when I was little?"

My stepfather is not expecting me to say this so it takes him a few seconds to respond and then he says, "There are things about your mother you don't understand."

I respond with rage, "No… no, don't you dare blame it on Mom!"

Feeling devastated, I storm off the porch to get in my car. I am so angry. I hate him. He is dead to me! I will have nothing more to do with him ever again! All the way to Concord, I feel a cavernous hole in the pit of my stomach and a breath-stealing pain in my chest. He feels absolutely no remorse for abusing me. I can't stop sobbing. I sob for the entire two hour trip. I am crushed and so full of anger. I vow never to speak to him ever again. By the time I arrive back at the dorm I have disowned him. He will remain dead to me. I never speak to him again except once to ask, "Where is Sid?"

In the summer of my second year of nursing, on a weekend visit home to see my Mom, I find her unusually adamant about discussing something with me. By this time Joanne has moved into the house and there is much turmoil and conflict between Butch, Joanne and Dad.

Mom grabs my hand and with difficulty due to her scanning speech, typical of a patient with multiple sclerosis she firmly instructs me, "You must try to find your real father!"

"I know Mom, I'm going to do it after I graduate."

"No, you must do it now," she says.

But with helplessness I answer, "But I don't even know where to begin."

Mom says, "Write a letter to your former babysitter, Ruth Aliff in Middletown, CT."

During the next week back at school, I follow Mom's instructions. I mail a letter simply addressed, Ruth Aliff, Middletown, CT, asking if she knows where my father lives?

Within two weeks, I receive a letter from my Aunt Julia giving me my father's Brooklyn, NY address. I am shocked and excited at the same time. I had not expected a reply so soon, thinking it was a long shot. This is the same Aunt Julia my mother would occasionally reference when I was being a stubborn teenager.

In frustration Mom would say to me, "You are being a thick-headed Polack just like your Aunt Julia!"

I write a letter to my real father but before I receive a response from him, a letter arrives from Aunt Sonya and Uncle Stan. I know that Uncle Stan is my Godfather but I haven't heard much about Aunt Sonya. But I do know they have a son who is a little younger than me.

The letter is warm and welcoming and I am thrilled to hear from them, but I am also overwhelmed by all the recent communication basically from strangers. And I am anxious because I have not yet heard from my biological father. But I continue writing to him because Aunt Julia explained he was at sea on a tour of duty.

In September 1964, as I begin my senior year of nursing school, I receive a letter from my father. I can hardly believe it. My hands are shaking as I open the envelope. It appears he had written a previous letter that included photos of me as baby that he always carried in his wallet but unfortunately it was forwarded to Charlestown. This means I will never see the letter or the photos.

My father tells me he has received some of my letters and many of them arrived on the same day because his mail is forwarded to the next port and sometimes it doesn't coincide with the ship's schedule. He has remained in the Merchant Marines all these years and is often gone for three to six months at a time.

Over the next few weeks, I also receive packages with gifts from him. My father gives me a beautiful authentic alligator leather purse. I also receive a huge smoky quartz ring in 14 carat gold for my birthday.

It is obvious he is not sure what to write to a daughter he has not seen since she was one-year-old, but his letter indicates that he is thrilled and excited about meeting me. He tells me about his routine on board ship and that he holds the rank of Quartermaster. This means his primary job is to steer the ship in and out of port.

I am excited and nervous to be communicating with my father, but what if he is disappointed once he meets me? I have difficulty maintaining my weight and often have an extra twenty pounds on my 5'4" frame, so I am self-conscious about my appearance. But we make arrangements to meet when I am on affiliation in November. I will be at the Margaret Hague Hospital in Jersey City, to study obstetrics/maternity nursing.

A few weeks before leaving for New Jersey on a Sunday afternoon, the house mother buzzes my room. I am surprised because I never have visitors, but I quickly go downstairs to learn who has come to see me.

She shows me to a small sitting room across the foyer. I enter the room to find three unfamiliar faces looking at me, a blond haired woman and two young people, a girl and a boy about my age. Almost in unison and with excitement they call out, "She looks just like Aunt Julia!"

The pretty blond woman stands up and hands me a beautiful bouquet of pink roses and white baby's breath in a round glass vase and announces, "I am your Aunt Sonya and these are your cousins Ray and Eileen."

Eileen is a tall girl for a fifteen-year-old, wears glasses and has dark brown hair and her brother Ray is tall and slender, also with dark hair and glasses. He is nineteen years old. I have Czech cousins and I am thrilled.

I am so surprised to be meeting my Czech relatives. I am not sure what to say but so happy they have come all the way from Connecticut to meet me, and I am reassured by their comment that I look like a member of the family, Aunt Julia. We make small talk for a moment and then Aunt Sonya announces that Uncle Stan is out in the car and invites me to go out to dinner with all of them.

I am pleased to see Uncle Stan has olive skin like me, he is all smiles and I feel comfortable in his presence. Other than the color of his skin I don't think we look alike. He is much shorter than what I've been told about my father. All these years I have wondered do I look like my father, although Mom did show me a photo of him when I was about ten years old. His facial features were not clear enough for me to see any resemblance.

I have always felt incomplete and wondered if I shared any physical or personality traits with my father. Now that I see the shared olive colored skin, I am encouraged. I hear their Connecticut accents, similar to Dad's sisters who live in Rockville. Uncle Stan has not seen his sister-in-law, my mother Eleanor, or me in nineteen years. He asks about her almost immediately and he is overcome by emotions when I tell him about her sickness.

Aunt Sonya is a nurse, she is a bubbly warm person and she makes it easy for all of us to become acquainted. Over dinner I exchange more information about my mother and they tell me about Aunt Julia and her family. Aunt Julia is a gardener and also has berry bushes and fruit trees behind her house. Uncle Al is a fireman.

Eileen says, "I'm so happy we have finally found you. Mommy and Daddy have always told us we had another cousin named Paula but she was lost."

When I tell them that Mom worked at the Sylvania plant in Hillsboro they react with surprise because all these years they were nearby. They had vacationed for years in the Hillsboro area.

Upon returning to the dorm I can't wait to tell Andrea, Pat and Ellen about the day. We stay up late talking about me meeting the Czech side of my family and how wonderful it will be for me to be reunited with my father. I am so eager to meet him.

JUN   63

Paula in Student Nurse Uniform

APR   65

Sharon visiting from UNH/Paula cutting out a jumper pattern.

The Czech Relatives: Uncle Stan and Aunt Sonya

Czech Cousin, Ray age 18

Czech Cousin, Eileen age 14

Paula age 19

More Czechs: Aunt Julia Czech Rasch, daughters Barbara,
Virginia and son David

Chapter 13

BITTERSWEET

On a chilly November day, fifteen of us take a bus from Concord into the Port Authority in New York City and then transfer to another bus for Jersey City. We are on our way to completing our Nursing education. We will be at the Margaret Hague for three months and then off to Boston for pediatrics. When we return to the State Hospital campus it will be time for graduation.

We arrive at Murdock Hall, Clifton Place, Jersey City, New Jersey. It is a seventeen-floor skyscraper. Upon entering the building there is marble everywhere. The lobby has high ceilings with round columns throughout the space, and a marble staircase with a glass and brass banister. There is a house mother nook on the far right to check in at to retrieve our room assignments. She directs us to a bank of elevators and to the twelfth floor. We soon learn to circumvent the house mother area on our way out because then we cannot be marked late when we return after midnight.

The next morning we access the Margaret Hague Maternity Hospital via a dank, creepy tunnel beneath the buildings that has big black bugs in puddles of water. We are repulsed and fearful of what is to come. Walking ahead of us are several groups of nurses. We later learn they are Filipino nurses and we are amused by their habit of always traveling in groups holding hands.

Before reporting to our assigned units we go for breakfast. It is served in the hospital staff cafeteria for the nurses and doctors. I am surprised to be served salsa with my scrambled eggs but I really enjoy the combination.

The Margaret Hague Maternity obstetrical curriculum is meticulously organized. In the first class we are given thick black binders with every subject/lecture fully outlined for the entire three months. This turns out be a gift due to my full social life. The next three months in the big city are a whirlwind of activities, life-altering and thankfully angel protected. At the age of twenty-one I am almost a real nurse and I experience an emotional roller coaster of life events.

A few weeks after arriving, I stand in my dorm room gazing down on all the concrete spaces and yearn for a patch of green. I miss the scenery of rural New Hampshire even though I am having fun becoming acquainted with big city life. The need to commune with nature, green grass and the woods is part of my DNA.

Andrea, Ellen and I are often out on the town. Ellen is engaged so she acts as our chaperone so we don't get into too much trouble. There is a small Greek coffee shop down one block on a corner. The three of us frequent it and soon we are being charmed by the Greek owner and one of the waiters. Vasilios (Bill) is older, and the owner, he takes a liking to me. With my olive skin, dark brown eyes and long straight brown hair, I am often mistaken for either Italian or Greek.

One night they take us to an Italian restaurant a couple of blocks east from the coffee shop. I have manicotti for the first time along with several glasses of wine. The guys are asking us to go to the movies with them after dinner, but Ellen who is not with any guy, discourages them by stating we must get back to the dorm before we are locked out.

We leave two disappointed but perfect gentlemen Greek guys and return to the dorm. We know we are past curfew so we go around the back of the building. Murdock Hall takes up a full block so it takes a while with only a few street lights to guide us to the back entrance. Fortunately, the big silver-gray metal back door is propped open. It enters directly into the stairwell. By this time Andrea is giddy with too much wine and is half laughing and half crying. She is extremely unsteady on her feet, so Ellen and I are trying to drag her up twelve flights of stairs to our rooms.

At about the fourth floor her howling is so loud it is echoing up all twelve stories of the stairwell. Ellen and I are worried that we will be detected by the night watchman so we are trying to shush her. But Andrea is too out of it to cooperate. Without any warning Ellen yells, "Andrea, you have got to shut up!" And gives her a huge slap across the face.

Andrea is shocked into soft muffled cries, so then Ellen and I run up the stairs dragging Andrea the entire way until we are safely into our rooms. We are so fortunate not to have been discovered. With the strict rules at our home school we would have been expelled without a second chance.

Soon after arriving at the Margaret Hague I receive a letter from the Visiting Nurses for Sullivan County. They have been involved in my Mom's home care for the past year. Without any previous notification, I am informed that my mother has been placed in a nursing home in Newport, NH. It located about twenty miles north of Charlestown.

I react with terror and anger. Several of my classmates hear my outburst and are alarmed. My mind is in overdrive. Did her condition worsen? What kind of place is it? I recall the questionable care the patients received at the nursing home that I worked at during high school and I'm scared to death for my mother.

I make a call to the Visiting Nurse office but do not receive any satisfactory answers. I must immediately visit my mother to see for myself how she is doing. But I have no money for bus fare and then I would only get to Claremont. Without a car, how can I travel to Newport another ten miles away?

One of my classmates who lives in Claremont hears about my distressing news and invites me to go home for the weekend with her. She is planning on going by bus, so Andrea lends me the money. It will take me several weeks to repay her because we only receive $11.54 from the school every two weeks.

Leona, a very funny girl, is our class comedian. Even though I do not hang out with her, I know her well enough to accept her invitation. We arrive at her house late Friday night. Both her parents are asleep. I wake early on Saturday morning. Before the entire family is up I am trying to get up the nerve to ask Leona's parents to drive me to Newport. But I remain reluctant to ask for help. Then I notice there is a used car lot across the street.

I develop a plan. I will go over to the car lot and pretend I'm shopping for a car. They always allow potential buyers to take the cars out for a test drive. Within twenty minutes I am at the Woodlawn Nursing Home. It is at the top of a steep hill in Newport and is a one story building with about fifty patients.

My mother has no idea that I am coming. Upon entering I ask to speak to a Supervisor, who I determine is a competent nurse and she quickly alleviates my fears around my mother's condition. She escorts me to my Mom's room that she shares with another patient.

Much to my surprise, she has a big smile and appears happy. She tells me they have her on an exercise program. I can tell she is hopeful about maybe walking again. I am so grateful to find her in good condition, in good spirits and in a nice place. My anxiety subsides for the first time in days. We have a great but short visit because I must get the car back to the used car sales lot. When I tell her how I managed to visit her, Mom reacts as always with shock at my audacity.

"Oh no, you didn't do that!"

Satisfied that my mother is in good hands, I return to Leona's house and meet her parents. They feel bad that I didn't ask them to give me a ride.

I'm in my first romantic experience with Vasilios, the Greek guy. Since I didn't date in high school all of this is foreign to me. My adolescence was confusing and scary and not like my peers'. It is as though I am experiencing puberty/adolescence and maturity simultaneously. Beneath all the emotional turmoil is a simmering rage that I do not understand. I hate the world.

I am very distracted by my heightened level of emotions so learning obstetric nursing is on the back burner. I am able to function well on the wards in both labor, delivery and in the nursery. Somehow the clinical area of nursing has always been easy for me and I am passing all my exams because of that well-organized black binder given to us on the first day. But learning obstetric nursing is not my primary day-to-day priority.

Bill (Vasilios) takes me on wonderful dates in New York City. I am thrilled by all the male attention, being in the fast paced city with beeping taxi horns, the blinking lights everywhere, and the song, "Downtown" by Petula Clark, is a No. 1 hit on Billboard and describes my life exactly. I am being wined and dined in style. We eat at several wonderful Greek restaurants, go to night clubs and to the movie, "Zorba the Greek."

Bill is about ten years older than me and remains a perfect gentlemen throughout our dates he doesn't even kiss me but is constantly saying "S' aga p" to me which he tells me means "I love you." But once after a movie he suggests we go to a hotel. It has a magnificent lobby with chandeliers and beautiful furnishings.

I am nervous and feel shamed when I notice the desk clerk looking at me with suspicion as though we do not appear to be a couple. I don't want to go to the hotel but do not have the ability to protect my boundaries because I do not know how, or realize I have the right to refuse a man. I am extremely anxious. Subconsciously, I am under the control of my stepfather.

Fortunately for me, Bill is a good person and my protective angels prevent anything but some heavy petting from occurring. I do not feel physically attracted to Bill, but enjoy being adored by him and remain confused about normal love and affection. At times the guilt I feel for not being able to return the same affection to him is overwhelming. I am not emotionally equipped to handle a healthy male/female relationship, therefore do not know how to end it. I am unable to say no to a man because I have no concept of personal boundaries, mine were broken years ago.

I have been in Jersey City for about two weeks when I receive a message from my father that he has arrived in port and wants me to come to his home in Brooklyn. This will be our first time meeting in person, although through our letters we have been getting to know one another. I am so nervous and worry about what to wear. He gives me excellent instructions on how to travel the tube from Jersey City and then catch the subway for Brooklyn. We arrange to meet at the 59th street and 5th avenue subway station in Brooklyn.

From the train window I see him and know instantly he is my father. He does not see me. On the platform is a tall man with his head down pacing back and forth. He is forty-eight years old with grayish brown hair. Like Mom's description he is a big man, three-hundred pounds and six-foot four-inches tall.

I exit the train happy but so nervous... I walk toward him and he knows immediately that I am his daughter. He says, "Hello Paula," and with tears in his eyes he gives me a big hug holding me in his arms for a long time. I'm crying too.

He is as I expected, a warm, comforting and light-hearted person. He begins telling me we only need to walk a half block to his apartment but first he is eager to present me to his friends. We walk up the stairs of the subway to 5th avenue. Within a few feet we enter a bar on the left and I am introduced to three guys. I am not comfortable but I politely say hello. I am feeling out of place because I've never been in a bar before. My Dad recognizes my discomfort so we soon leave.

Back out on the street he tells me more about Flo, who is a native Indian from Canada. They have been together for several years but are not married. At the moment her two-year-old niece is living with them because her sister cannot afford to care for own child.

He apologizes for taking me into the bar but explains it is where he was waiting for the train and his friends had requested he bring me back to meet them. I explain it is the first time I've been in a bar and that it made me nervous.

I am liking my father. He has a very relaxed manner and he has a sense of humor.

We turn the corner onto 59th street and he points down the street to the fourth brick brownstone with a five step stoop up to the door. His apartment is on the third floor, a short walk from the subway. The entryway and stairwell are neat and clean and there are not lots of people hanging out on the nearby stoops. Apparently a false impression I have of Brooklyn.

We enter the apartment into a small foyer, and to the right is a good size living room with a kitchen at one end. Down a short hallway left of the foyer are two bedrooms and a bathroom. It is nicely furnished and very neat.

Flo gives me a big hug, saying how excited both of them are to be meeting me. She has a nice smile, coal black long straight hair parted in the middle, styled behind her ears. The little girl is cute but shy, she clings to Flo's leg, peeking out at me.

Then Flo says, "You look like your father."

A serenity washes over me, after all these years I know my roots. It has always been a need of mine to know if I shared some traits or characteristics with my father. I am happy Flo sees the resemblance. Being part of a family with a different surname has always made me feel out of place even though it was my choice to keep my Czech name. I knew from an early age that I was not a Thibault and did not want that name because it was not my authentic self. I am happy Mom insisted I search for my father.

I feel guilty about a growing suspicion that my father drinks too much. It is the only negative in an otherwise wonderful reunion.... I try to push it out of my mind.

Flo brings snacks into the living room and my father grabs a beer before we sit down. Flo and the little girl go to the other end of the apartment. I am in awe at how fully my father fills the leather recliner, he is a big man. A part of me is wanting him to be infallible, I try to overlook the bottle of beer.

We seem to be quietly studying one another like we can't quite believe we are in the moment.

Out of the blue my father says, "You have a very distinctive birth-mark on your leg."

I smile and proudly respond, "I sure do."

And I pull up my slacks to reveal a gray raised crusted one inch square shaped mark on my inner thigh just above my knee. Somehow this shared knowledge is a bonding experience.

I also have a small dark brown smooth one on my mons pubis but neither one of us mentions that one, thank God!

Over the next few hours I tell him where I grew up in Vermont and that I have two brothers. He asks how old Butch is and seems somewhat disappointed when I tell him Butch is two-and-a-half years younger.

My father begins reminiscing about the last time he saw me as a baby. He takes out his wallet and shows me tattered photos of me. He has always carried them in his wallet. Tears well up and I dab them away. Then I tell him about Mom's black leather satchel.

I tell him Mom first told me about him when I was five years old and that I saw a photo of him when I was ten years old. It is a photo of him dressed in a suit sitting on a bench on the Coney Island Board-walk. I tell him how throughout the years Mom and I would sit on her bed and go through the contents of the black satchel. I tell him I've read the letters he addressed to me while at sea when I was a baby. His eyes glisten and he grabs his handkerchief to blow his nose.

After being silent for some time he begins telling me how he hired a detective to find me, but gave up after he was informed I was living in a convent in Canada. I explain that we were in Richford on the Ca-nadian border and suggest the detective probably lost the trail there so he made up the convent story.

Then with intensity he tells me he believes that if he and my moth-er had been a little older and more mature their marriage would have survived. The war years were difficult and his long tours of duty didn't help matters. I get the feeling he has remained in love with my mother. He has never remarried.

About nine p.m. my father walks me to the subway and I return to Jersey City. Over the remaining weeks at Margaret Hague, I make several of these trips out to Brooklyn and enjoy getting to know my father. I find him to be an intelligent and sensitive man. Oftentimes on the late return trip, I am on the train with only one other person, an accordion player. Although we are sitting three feet apart we do not acknowledge one another, both lost in our own thoughts with the music in the background.

On an emotional level I am flooded with a multitude of feelings. I live with underlying daily anxiety/nervousness, worrying about my mother and brothers' welfare. I have mixed feelings as I process both joy and disappointment with a new father/daughter relationship. And I can't seem to find the words to let him know how much I love him and that I am excited to be with him.

Thanksgiving arrives and very few of us can afford to go home for the holiday. While visiting my father in Brooklyn the week before, I mention that most of my classmates will not be going home for the holiday. His apartment is not large enough to have a sit down turkey dinner so he gives me two hundred dollars and tells me to take my classmates out to a nice restaurant. About five of us decide to go to dinner, Andrea, Ellen, Pat, Dottie and me. We have no idea where to dine and I don't know how to find the restaurants that Bill has been taking me to because we always go by taxi.

On Thanksgiving Day we dress up and take the Tube into Manhattan. We have become familiar with Times Square. It is a cold day and the wind is whipping between the skyscrapers almost blowing us off the street. It forces us to find a restaurant quickly. The only place we can find is Tad's Steakhouse. It is not fancy, like the restaurants I've been going to with Bill, but it is inexpensive and we have a good steak dinner but... it is not turkey. I am disappointed that I couldn't find a nicer place.

Andrea and Ellen decide they want to thank my father in person, so a few days later they come to Brooklyn with me to meet my father. It is a fun visit and my father is pleased to see who I am hanging out with and he approves.

Andrea, Ellen and I decide we want to celebrate New Year's Eve in Times Square. Oh my, what an experience it is... We are in Times Square where the huge crowd almost crushes us, making it difficult to remain on our feet. It is exciting and scary being part of the noisy crowd celebration. We have fun and we join in with our noise makers.

Toward the end of the night we are freezing cold and it is terrifying as the crowd grows larger, pushing us toward the middle. We continue to struggle to stay on our feet. It is a frightening night but for posterity's sake we can say we watched the silver ball come down in Times Square at midnight to welcome in 1965. It took us one hour just to get out of the middle of the crowd to start back to the dorm.

By February our time at Margaret Hague is nearing the end, Bill is still spending lots of money on me with dinners and beautiful gold jewelry. My father and I are having fun together. He is making plans for us to go visit Connecticut in the summer to see where he and Mom lived and to meet Aunt Julia and Uncle John. I am so excited and happy about my future.

But the week before I board the bus for Boston I get a call from Flo telling me my father has been hospitalized at the Marine Hospital on Staten Island. I am immediately concerned, but Flo reassures me he is okay. The doctors need to draw off some fluid then he will be back home in two weeks. Of course I recognize the significance of her statement and know he must have liver damage from alcoholism. I am devastated. Due to my classes and work schedule I am not able to visit my father at the hospital or see him before I leave for the pediatric hospital in Boston.

On the day of my departure for Boston, Bill sees me off at the Port Authority and gives me yet another gift. It is absolutely beautiful, 14 carat gold and pearl earrings by Krementz. I leave him heartbroken and I feel guilty that he has given me another expensive piece of jewelry. I try to give it back to him but he will not accept it. Distancing pain and compartmentalizing my feelings seems to be how I handle emotional intimacy. I do not function like a normal person when it involves a male/female situation.

The hospital in Boston is awful! The workload is heavy and fast paced with inadequate supervision. The classes are unorganized and disjointed. None of the nurse managers have time for us, instead we are simply there as free labor.

We see so many children with critical life and death illnesses. It is difficult to care for them, hemophiliacs requiring several units of blood, cleft palate babies requiring feeding with Breck feeders and the thalassemia kids going through bone marrow aspirations. We assist with all these procedures with little instruction or supervision. It is frightening. Then to make matters worse, we "the Pinkies" are given the majority of the responsibilities due to our extensive clinical experience and expertise. The university student nurses perform as if they are first year students, and so with little clinical experience they are unable to carry the patient load that we do.

We are also assigned to work the 11-7 a.m. shifts as the only nurse on the floor. The only registered nurse is the supervisor three floors down. I look down the unit and see six bags of blood hanging and wonder how am I going to be able to handle every fifteen minute vitals on all these sick children.

We live on the first floor of the dormitory and during the time we are in Boston, student nurses are raped and killed in Chicago, so as a precaution we must wait for security to escort us across the street to the hospital when we are assigned to the night shift. Having to wait for security to walk me across the street to the hospital irritates me. I do not do well with waiting.

Social life in Boston consists of walking up Washington Street and shopping in Filene's basement. I am shocked to see female customers stripped down to their slips so they can try clothes on in the aisle. They fight over dresses, sweaters and skirts on the discount tables. I am proud of myself when I snag a London Fog trench coat for eight dollars.

On one occasion a few of us go to a movie on Washington Street but once inside, the seats reek of urine so we quickly leave... horrible. Other times we walk up to the Boston Commons and wish we could afford to go on the Duck Swan Boats. In the Spring there is green grass in the Commons, the first I have seen since leaving Concord last Fall.

Throughout the three months in Boston I receive a couple of calls from Flo updating me about my father's condition. He made it home for one week but had to be re-hospitalized.

On April 30, 1965, I receive a phone call on the hall pay phone from my Uncle Stan. He tells me my father has died. I am twenty-one years old. My shrieking brings most of my classmates out of their rooms to comfort me. I only had three months with him. There must not be a God or at least not one that cares about me. I have reached my limit with stress, disappointment and abuse.

Ellen quickly takes charge of me and suggests we go for a walk. She is a good Catholic girl. We talk and walk the streets of Boston for two hours. She listens while I ramble on about my father. We end up at a Catholic Church which only brings back the memory of the time a priest pointed his finger at me.

It was during lent and I was a seventh grader. I had never been inside a church. Celeste asked me to go to church with her after school, which was next to the school. I was wearing a drab and tattered touke. Inside the beautiful Catholic Church with glistening gold, marble statues and stained glass windows, I felt unworthy to be in such a glorious place. So when we entered the pew I removed my old worn hat. As the priest came down the aisle he noticed my bare head and went into a rage. It is as though the hand of God had struck me dead. He yelled and pointed his finger at me. I was unaware of why he was screaming at me. Celeste quickly picked up my hat and whispered, "Put on your hat."

We return to the dorm and I call Flo, she fills me in on the details and tells me Aunt Julia is in charge of everything. Next I speak with Aunt Sonya who invites me to come to their house. I take a bus to Connecticut and stay with them for three days. It all seems so surreal. I recall telling Aunt Julia that my father wanted his ashes tossed into the sea but she is not receptive to that notion. I am too young and have no religious background and have yet to develop any spirituality, so I just go through the motions like a robot without any solace.

Once in the cemetery I see the CZECH family stone. I am surprised to see that my grandmother, Pauline, whom I was named for died on my seventh birthday, November 1, 1950. I was in Cooperstown with Philippa at that time. All Saints Day is November 1. All these years with serendipitous moments and interventions from those I call my Angels, Philippa, Mrs. Baldwin, and Mrs. Ball, causes me to wonder if there is a connection.

Following the funeral I return to the dorm and resume my pediatric rotation at the hospital. The remaining two weeks in Boston are nearly impossible to get through. I feel like a walking zombie. My room is at the end of the hall and I am an early riser. Each morning when I open my door to go to the bathroom, I wake my classmates by loudly screaming this rant: "I HATE THIS GODDAMN PLACE!" Not one of them complains to me about being awakened early in such a disturbing manner. They all understand and have compassion.

Another affiliation without a lot of concentration on my studies, but again our classes are not taught by seasoned educators. The lectures often feel like they are prepared on a wing and a prayer. Everything is hurried and emergent at this hospital and all these vulnerable children have life-threatening diagnoses. I am angry at the injustice of it all.

Eventually the Boston nightmare ends and we return to Concord. We are all so happy to be back at our home school and to reconnect with the other half of our class. After a couple of days it suddenly dawns on me that my nursing school years are almost completed and

I am going to be a registered nurse. I will graduate in May and be real a nurse.

Our remaining classes involve professional ethics and courses designed to prepare us for our State Nursing Board Exams. Every graduate nurse in the state must report to the state house at the same time to take the two-day-long exam. This maintains the integrity of the exam and the quality of the nurses statewide.

I do not feel like myself, can I still be grieving my father's death? It is as though I am in a fog. Events seem to occur too quickly before I am ready for them. It is hard to think and I just go through the motions to prepare for graduation. I send out the invitations and look forward to Mom, Sharon, the Czech relatives, Philippa, and Mrs. Ball attending. Butch is in the Navy and unable to get home.

Miss Brown requests we inform her if we intend to seek employment at the State Hospital, and since psychiatric nursing and surgical nursing are my favorites I decide to stay. Four of us seek employment and one of the girls, Dottie, and I decide to be roommates. I am very sad to be saying goodbye to Andrea and Ellen.

During the past three years, I have occasionally socialized with Dottie but not often, mostly because our rooms are on the opposite end of the hall. I know her to be quiet and studious, as I frequently see her sitting on her bed reading. However, I remember the day she is mischievous and ends up in trouble with Miss Snell.

Many of us have the habit of polishing our white nurses' shoes, then placing them outside our doors in the hall to dry. Dottie notices her neighbor Judy has her shoes drying out in the hall and decides to have some fun. She very artistically paints black polka dots all over the shoes with black shoe polish.

When Judy discovers her shoes, she does not think it is funny and reports the problem. The entire dorm is restricted to the campus until Dottie returns from downtown and is alerted that her artwork is causing an issue. She immediately goes downstairs to Miss Snell's office to confess to her petty crime. Dottie is totally humiliated by Miss Snell's scolding. Poor Dottie, who usually maintains a low profile and never misbehaves, is in trouble for something silly and funny.

I think she will be a fun roommate so we make arrangements to go apartment shopping before graduation. We soon find a nice first floor two-room furnished apartment on Rumford Street. I am relieved because I will have a place for out of town guests to stay during the graduation weekend.

Graduation day arrives, we are all dressed in white for the first time. We are wearing long sleeve cuffed uniforms with corsages. And most important, our caps have the wide black band that identifies us as Registered Nurses. It is a proud moment. But I am not fully participating, I am too distracted, so confused, I cannot keep up with life. We have photos taken but I barely notice. I must still be grieving my father's death. He and I had talked about him coming to my graduation. I miss him.

In attendance are Philippa who always expresses her love and pride for me, my guardian angel since age three has come to see me blossom, Louise Ball, a real nurse who noticed throughout my childhood that I did not have much. She sewed skirts for me, gave me ice skates, a bike and put five dollars in my coat pocket the day I left for nursing school, my lifelong friend Sharon, who knows all my secrets except for one, Uncle Stan who is my Godfather even though I have never received communion because I was not raised Catholic.

My mother was excommunicated from the Catholic Church which is one reason she fled Connecticut, there was no one to turn to for support. Wonderful, warm and generous Aunt Sonya, a real nurse, is here to see her niece become a real nurse. And of course my brave, loving mother is in attendance in her wheelchair and is so proud of me.

The long stairs that span the width of the Howard Recreation building make it impossible for Mom to get up to the graduation hall in her wheelchair. Uncle Stan comes to her aid and carries her up the stairs with her arms wrapped around his neck. This is the first moment they have seen each other in twenty years and it is extremely emotional for them both.

My Mom is sobbing and saying to Uncle Stan, "I am so sorry, I'm so sorry!"

Uncle Stan responds with kindness and tries to assuage Mom's guilt. Aunt Sonya carries the wheel chair to the top of the stairs.

My nursing school years come to an end. My sweet mother is safe and well cared for in a nursing home, Butch is making a life for himself in the Navy. My baby brother Sid, now age eleven, is living alone with Joe, but he may as well be homeless because his father mostly ignores him and I am worried. I have accomplished a significant goal despite many life challenges and received celebratory flowers, but I feel like the bloom is off the rose.

Paula as a Graduate Nurse

The Wallet Photo Sleeve Containing Two Baby Photos of
Paula Carried by her Father for Nineteen Years

Butch in the Navy Visiting Paula at Londergan Hall

Paula as a Registered Nurse, First Job NH Hospital
Male Admission Unit Thayer Building

Joseph Francis Czech Age Forty Three at
Home Brooklyn, NY

The Czech Monument

US Census Record,
My Grandmother Pauline Died
on my Seventh Birthday

Chapter 14
IDENTITY CRISIS

Dottie and I have been walking up and down Main Street in the pouring rain searching for a new apartment for hours. I am optimistic that we will find our perfect place but the rain is a distraction when we have so little time. The wind is blowing the rain sideways, we are getting drenched and our hair is dripping wet. We are in front of the Princess Shop, a wedding apparel store, when we encounter Marie Nelson, one of our former Nursing Instructors.

Marie says, "Hi girls, what are you doing out here in all this rain?"

I say, "We are trying to find a new apartment, we got evicted because we played our music too loud."

Dottie adds, "And we weren't even playing the stereo that loud."

Marie finds it incredulous that two of her best students have been evicted from an apartment. Typical of Marie's character and generous heart, she says, "I have a large front bedroom with two twin beds in it, you girls can stay with us until you find a new apartment."

Later that evening Dottie and I go up to School Street to see Marie and her husband Ray. He is a carpenter and is currently building a house for some friends. Ray is a big man, barrel chested, and a former city cop. He and Marie are a charismatic couple and there is always lots of laughter around them. Ray has a deep hearty laugh that makes him sound a little like Santa Claus... ho ho ho.

Marie is an excellent listener and problem solver. She is quick witted and a savvy money manager. They own a huge yellow two story home in the North end of Concord with two apartments. They live in the first floor apartment and have law students for tenants upstairs.

Marie shows us through the dining room, living room and down the front hall to a bedroom at the end of their apartment. As soon as we see it we know it will work. One side of the bedroom extends the entire width of the house. It measures about 30' x 14', and the beds are positioned at opposite ends of the room. One bed is shielded by a folding screen. Dottie and I are delighted, it is perfect.

Marie and Ray are wonderful people with a large circle of friends. They are both active in the Elks Club where they help the club raise money for school scholarships for deserving students. They are in their late thirties without any children. Marie has had five miscarriages. Over the next two years they treat us as if we are their own daughters.

It has only been about six weeks since graduation and I am enjoying being the Charge Nurse on Thayer 4, the male admission unit for the southern counties of New Hampshire, a significant responsibility for a twenty-two-year-old new registered nurse. Included in my role as Charge Nurse is holding the paddles for electric convulsant therapy, drawing blood for lab tests, administering medications and the overall management of patient care, to include giving a morning report, the status of each patient at the staff meeting attended by the psychiatrist, psychologists, charge nurses and the nursing supervisor. It is necessary that I make accurate assessments and stay alert for changes in patient symptoms and intervene appropriately.

I am thriving during work hours but when off duty, I am struggling. I feel so restless and unhappy but I can't pinpoint the reason. I seem to be full of anger. It has been five months since my father's death.

Dottie is a great roommate, very thoughtful and kind. We are good friends and are content living with Marie and Ray. She and Marie spend a lot of time in the kitchen discussing recipes and cooking. Dottie is tolerant of my angry moods and even though my reckless driving at high speeds terrorizes her, she usually maintains her quiet composure and rarely cautions me to slow down. But she does hang onto the arm rest and flinch at times when I am driving at 80-90 miles per hour. My anger and reckless driving has its genesis in my childhood abuse, but I have yet to connect those dots.

During our early months living at Marie and Ray's, our social life revolves around Marie and Ray's infamous Friday nights. Their circle of friends thrive on Marie and Ray's hospitality. The drinks and appetizers are in abundance. Marie is a good cook and always serves a variety of snacks. The small kitchen is overflowing with people, laughter, food and booze, with good clean practical jokes and fun. Their friends insist that Dottie and I participate in all the hilarity so we are often pulled out of our beds to join the kitchen group. We enjoy the attention despite not being big drinkers, so we will join them for one drink.

Eventually Dottie meets her future husband Bob who is a fireman, so she is often out with him while I am left to cope with the midnight awakenings and teasing by myself.

Several men are noticing me but like in high school the opposite sex is a challenge, and although I am flattered by the attention, I do not have a clue regarding their motivations. They flirt with me and whistle at my curvaceous figure, but I do not respond in a flirtatious manner because I am anxious. My hormones react appropriately but I am too inexperienced and do not recognize a player from a sincere guy. I am twenty-two years old, but regarding the male/ female relationship I may as well be thirteen.

The first man to approach me is Ross, the new psychologist at work from California. He is very sensual, tall, blue eyes, sandy colored hair that constantly droops down over his face. He is always tossing his head to get his hair out of his eyes. He has a sexy black convertible sports car.

One lunch time he asks me to go for a ride and I accept. Of course I find this thrilling both because of the sexy guy and the fast car. I eventually go out to dinner with him, but then he invites me back to his room. He lives on campus in one of the dorms.

I really don't want to go to his room but I don't feel like I can say no, it doesn't feel normal to refuse. I may as well be five years old and being taken to the woodshed with my stepfather. I have no frame of reference as to what is a normal dating experience.

Thankfully, Bill the Greek guy in Jersey City, was older and must have recognized my inexperience and didn't take advantage of me.

As we go up the stairs I become extremely nervous. Once again, I can't find the words to say no, I seem to be unable to verbalize my boundary lines. In his room he removes his shirt to show off his sun tanned six pack. I am definitely sexually attracted to him and think maybe we will only kiss. He begins making out with me and I actively participate. Then he strips down to total nakedness. Wow!

Now I begin thinking about the fact we work together in the same building. I can't get involved with him... it's just not right. He places a condom on the pillow of the bed where we have been making out. That does it, I push the condom off and stand up and tell him I must go. Placing the condom within my eyesight solidified his real intentions and thankfully gave me a way out without having to verbalize my answer.

It's a miracle I didn't end up getting raped after he was so aroused, but the psychologist in him recognizes something is not normal with my behavior. It appears I'm uncomfortable with any emotional intimacy but totally okay with the physical act of sex.

On the way home he encourages me to talk about anything that might be bothering me. But of course I don't because I don't trust enough to talk about my past, and I am not fully aware of what the barrier is that is interfering with my dating life.

Additionally, I am the consummate professional nurse and realize I can't be sleeping with someone from work... it just doesn't seem ethically correct and I don't trust him to be discreet because I have difficulty trusting anyone. There are many things about me even I don't understand. For example why am I so angry?

I am so confused with this male/female relationship thing. I just don't understand how it works. I become sexually aroused, but emotionally I freeze and don't know how or can't proceed to flirting or the usual banter. I think it triggers the initial trauma of when I was forced to stand in front of my stepfather.

The next guy to come into my life is a sweet licensed practical nurse also from work. He is very interested in me but I am not at all attracted to him. He is a clean cut guy but I do not have a sexual attraction to him. I hurt his feelings terribly when I don't respond to his advances which makes the work environment awkward.

Throughout my stay with Marie and Ray, I am frequently visiting my Mom at the Nursing Home to oversee her care and driving back to Charlestown to visit my baby brother Sid. I can tell Sid is lonely and my stepfather seems to be disinterested in Sid's welfare. Joe is often unshaven and disheveled looking. I know I must get Sid out of there. The need to be a caretaker experienced by sexually abused victims is surfacing, reminiscent of when I was younger and acted like a mother's helper and assumed the parent role.

It has been about one year since I graduated from Nursing School when I decide I am going to assume the responsibility of raising Sid. I also decide I want to further my nursing experience by changing jobs to pursue medical surgical nursing. Within a few weeks I obtain a position on an orthopedic floor at Mary Hitchcock Memorial Hospital in Hanover, the Medical Center for New Hampshire.

Another nursing school classmate, Pat is looking for a roommate so we decide to rent a house in West Lebanon from an elderly Greek man. Pat works at the Claremont Hospital so the location works for us both. Dottie remains with Marie and Ray for another year.

Now, I can put my plan into effect. It is a beautiful sunny summer day in July 1966, as I drive over to Charlestown to the homestead. I practice what I will say and do if I meet any resistance, but I doubt there will be an issue. I walk into the kitchen and Joe is sitting at the kitchen table with a cup of coffee.

I ask, "Where is Sid?"

He responds, "Upstairs."

I walk past him and go up to Sid's bedroom. He runs over to me and throws his arms around me and I hold him in my arms. He is a cute blond twelve-year-old boy. I sit down on his bed and ask him "Do you want to come live with me?" He is ecstatically happy and answers yes!!!

"Okay, then let's get you packed."

Within a half hour we have his suitcase packed and he has an armful of sports equipment, baseball glove, baseball bat, hockey stick and a basketball. We start down the stairs to his father.

Once in the kitchen I announce, "Sid is coming to live with me."

Joe doesn't look up at us or say a thing and out the door we go... done deal.

Over the following year we repeat the process in reverse twice. But each time I return to the driveway we both start crying and I just can't give him back to his father, so within five minutes I back the car out of the driveway and we drive two hours back to my place.

I am a twenty-three-year-old woman struggling with my own anxieties and confusion regarding male relationships and I am trying to parent a twelve-year-old. He is a good kid but I anticipate the worst behaviors so I compound the situation by suspecting him of drinking or possibly smoking pot. He is doing none of that but my constant hovering and strict rules naturally cause a strain.

In the fall I enroll Sid in the sixth grade at the West Lebanon Elementary School. He adjusts well and the four of us become a small, unusual, but happy family. Pat has her eighteen-year-old younger sister living with us and we all get along well.

On weekends Sid and I go to see Mom at the nursing home. During the summer we try to take her out for a car ride and a picnic as often as we can. I try to give Sid a normal family experience as much as possible and get him through high school as I know Mom wishes.

I'm also cognizant of teaching him the good manners Mom would have insisted on, if she were home. I take him out to dinner at the Woodstock Inn in Vermont. The table is set with a five place setting, china, crystal and a white linen tablecloth. I teach him how to fold his napkin on his lap, keep his elbows off the table and have one arm resting in his lap. He behaves like a perfect gentlemen. We have a fun time and a great meal.

I take him on a road trip to Cooperstown, and to the Baseball Hall of Fame. Dottie comes with us and I show them around town to include where I lived with Philippa during my first grade. We also visit the Farmer's Museum but the Cardiff Giant is no longer on display. At this time I am driving a white convertible with red leather seats and a black canvas top. Most of the time the top is down, we enjoy the wind whipping around us and the warmth of the sun. We stay overnight in a motel and Sid has great fun swimming in the pool. It is a nice vacation.

Another time I take him to Boston to the aquarium and out for fine dining. I'm trying to expose him to as many things as I can, knowing how important it is to Mom. In later years, I also take him to Washington, D.C.

I have been at the Mary Hitchcock about nine months when Pat and her sister decide they want to move out. Her sister is returning to Burlington and Pat is getting married. I cannot afford the rent alone so I decide to return to Concord.

Marie and Ray just happen to have an empty upstairs apartment on Tahanto Street in the house next to them. Over the years they have purchased all the homes on their side of the street for investment purposes. So I move into the upstairs apartment with Sid.

I am rehired at Thayer building but this time I am assigned to the downstairs female convalescent unit Thayer 1, a much easier assignment. However, I still interact with my former staff upstairs.

There is a tall guy with dark brown hair and brown eyes that begins to spend his coffee breaks downstairs with me. His name is Ryan. I find myself attracted to him and he is easy to talk to, for some reason he does not cause me to emotionally freeze like I usually do around guys who show an interest in me. He tells me he has a second job driving a trailer truck into Boston two nights a week. I can hold a conversation about trucks because of being around my stepfather, so the conversation flows easily between us about his second job.

A few weeks go by and I can feel myself liking him a lot. I also can tell he is attracted to me, but he isn't as blatant about it as his predecessors have been. So I am not threatened by him. One Friday after work he spontaneously asks, "Hey, how about riding into Boston with me tonight?"

Impulsively, I say "Sure, that sounds like fun."

He doesn't need to leave until seven so that gives me plenty of time to go home and give Sid supper and ask Marie to check in on him throughout the evening.

After supper I meet him at the truck terminal and climb up into the cab of the truck and we head out for Boston. It is a rough and noisy ride in the cab, but I enjoy being up so much higher than the cars. We talk a lot over the next four hours. He tells me he is building a new house and that is the reason for the second job. He is a hard worker.

When we get to the city, I love all the sounds and sights. The lights remind me of being back in New York City and I find it exciting. Once back in Concord at the terminal he kisses me goodnight and it feels different than any other kiss I've had previously. There is a spark, it surprises me.

I return home about eleven-thirty p.m. I do not see him again until Monday at work. He doesn't seem to be himself, he seems more serious than his usual demeanor. We finally find ourselves alone for a few minutes and I ask him what is wrong.

He tells me is married and has two kids. I am shocked, I am so naive when it involves men. It never occurred to me to ask that question. But because of the strong feelings I am developing for him I don't tell him to go away. Besides, I do not have a track record with being able to say no to a man.

But we do drift apart for a few weeks. I find myself thinking about him all the time and wanting to see him but I would never pursue him. I don't like asking anyone for anything.

About a month goes by without him coming downstairs for coffee breaks. I try not to run into him at work, but sometimes I see him from my office window, outside walking patients to and from the Medical Surgical building for appointments. Despite strong feelings for him, I will not act on them.

In the meantime, another guy Kyle, who is a son of one of Marie and Ray's friends, begins coming to Marie and Ray's on Friday nights and he is very flirtatious with me. He is short, not really my type, but a very good looking guy. He is my age and quite the Romeo. And of course I am flattered by his attention, but I do not flirt back because I don't know how, so instead I blush and appear uncomfortable.

We are in the same circle of friends so we are often together in a group setting. I sort of put him in the friend zone. However, one day he shows up at work at noontime in a red MG convertible sports car. He knows I like to drive fast because by now I have received several speeding tickets and the group likes to tease me about my driving.

He invites me to go for a ride and I accept. So we take a fast ride on some nearby curvy roads and I have a blast. When he returns me to the Thayer Building he walks me up the steps with his arm around my shoulder. I'm not sure what to think but again I'm flattered by the male attention.

It seems to me I attract men wherever I go. I recall walking on Elm Street, the primary street in Manchester and having men on a construction site across the street whistling and calling out, "Hey baby, let's go out." The group adulation was both flattering and threatening. My style of dress is not obscene or inappropriate, but due to my curves I have a sexy silhouette. Wherever I go, I get whistled at or hit on but because my response is such a nonresponse I do not get involved with many of them.

After two months Ryan and I resume our relationship. He is telling me he loves me and can't stand to be away from me. I am flattered but do not know what my feelings are for him other than I miss him and I want to see him. And again my conscience is nagging at me because he is married, but I accept his invitation to dinner. We drive about an hour out of town so we won't run into anyone we know. The sneaking around sort of excites me and it seems to feel familiar.

We stop out near a lake for a burger and talk in the car for a long time. It is dark when we leave the restaurant. Suddenly Ryan suggests we go to a motel. I am surprised, it is déjà vu and it brings me back when Vasilius asked to go to the New York City hotel. Except this time my feelings are saying yes, I'm not just going because I can't say no. I probably still can't say no, but I want to say yes, so I agree.

He is so loving and gentle and I love it! This is the first time I have intercourse. I am twenty-four years old. We sneak out into the countryside as often as he can get away from his wife without her being suspicious. But that guilt is back, I never seem to be able to get rid of guilt. I feel like I am falling in love with Ryan. I also realize it is all so wrong and it will never work out but I can't stop seeing him.

Wise Marie has a talk with me one Saturday afternoon. Ray has taken Sid fishing and just the two of us are at their home. We often have great life talks and Marie is so intuitive and supportive. She never pries but seems to know the right time to interject some of her wonderful wisdom.

We are in her bedroom, she is folding laundry and I'm sitting nearby talking. I am telling her about Ryan and how we need to be so discreet at work, and I am beginning to worry I will be seen as a scandalous woman. I am always the consummate Professional Nurse so this potential blemish is worrying me.

She asks me what I am doing for birth control and I tell her I am on the pill but sometimes I miss one now and then.

Then she casually says, "Oh, in that case I have a diaphragm I will give you. I don't use it anymore," and she gives me a sheepish grin indicating their sex life has declined. "You should use it as a back-up system. It has been thoroughly washed."

"Marie, I don't know anything about a diaphragm."

So dear sweet Marie tells me one of the positives is that you can put the diaphragm in hours before you have sex, but you must not remove it for a couple days after sex. Marie is another one of my "Angel" protectors.

She rummages through her dresser and comes out with a small box. This is the first time I have seen a diaphragm. She shows me how to fold it in half and then tells me how to insert it high into my vagina. I think this is probably a safe thing to do so I accept it. My angel Marie is trying to protect me from making a huge life-changing mistake.

Next I confide in her that I've been thinking I better change jobs before my relationship with Ryan is revealed and I become embarrassed at work. She wants to know where I will go and I say I am not sure. I know I can't continue with Ryan so I probably better leave town, but I'm not quite sure how to do that with Sid. He has made friends at Concord High School and he is doing very well in school.

A few days later Marie tells me that she and Ray had a talk and are willing to have Sid live with them so I can have a little break. I've been taking care of him for almost two years. I thank her and tell her I will give it some thought.

In the meantime, I have remained in contact with Uncle Stan, Aunt Sonya, Eileen and Ray. While on a weekend visit to Connecticut to see the Czech's, I decide to look for a job. Dottie is with me so we take a drive to West Haven where we stumble onto a Veterans' Hospital.

Perhaps in the back of my mind I'm thinking, if I worked in Connecticut I would have relatives nearby but still be away from Ryan.

Well within one hour I fill out an application and I am hired on the spot. The start date is in two weeks.

A goodbye party is planned for my last day at the State Hospital, but I know I will not be able to maintain my composure around Ryan, so at the last minute I don't go in for my last day at work. I say goodbye to him later that night. We are both crying but we both know I've made the best decision. There is no way he can leave his wife and two little kids.

Sid is a little sad about me leaving but he understands by staying with Marie and Ray he will remain at Concord High School and keep his friends. He is a teenager and is fully involved in being a normal teenager.

I really like my new job in West Haven VA Hospital. I am on a mental health unit and I learn the Behavior Modification Model of treatment. We have a five person team to treat a group of patients. A psychiatrist, psychologist student from Yale, RN, social worker, and mental health aide.

During my time there I witness one of the black aides being counseled several times to stop wearing hoop earrings on the unit, because it is a safety issue. An agitated patient could potentially grab the hoops and rip them out of her ears. She remains non-compliant and when the supervisor writes a reprimand for her file she complains that the supervisor is harassing her and being discriminating. Soon after this incident we hear the shouts from groups of protestors in front of the hospital calling for his resignation due to racial discrimination.

Because I witnessed the Supervisor telling her not to wear the earrings, I become involved in the aftermath. He was very professional and respectful. Later in the year, I am called down to the Chief Nurses Office. I am a nervous wreck and really don't understand what is involved in a legal deposition. I testify via phone conference about his demeanor.

I only stay six months in West Haven because I find it too much of a hassle to get on the highway on Friday nights after work to go visit Mom and Sid. Even when I leave work a few minutes early the cars are backed up several cars deep just to get on the ramp for the highway. Again waiting, or feeling like I am being restrained, is not my thing.

Upon my return to New Hampshire I rent an apartment in a rural area. Sid remains at Marie and Ray's with me continuing to pay them support money. I've been back in New Hampshire a few months when I receive a disturbing call from Marie late in the evening. She is extremely upset and angry about a missing emerald ring and is accusing Sid and his friend of stealing it.

My reaction to this news is total devastation. I am upset that I, albeit indirectly, have caused so much harm, sadness and anger to such a trusted dear friend. When I speak with Sid he adamantly denies stealing the ring and I believe him. It must have been his friend. Mom always instilled honesty and a value system incongruent with this accusation.

I am so conflicted and do not know how to resolve the issue with Marie. I offer to replace the ring but she doesn't agree to that. She does tell me Sid must move.

I am so upset and have a sinking feeling in my stomach. My anxiety is high and I feel for the first time in my life that I can't cope with this intense distress. I feel trapped with only one way out of this devastating situation.

Later during the evening I am overcome with a strong desire to push the gas pedal to the floor on my powerful Cutlass Supreme convertible and drive it into a concrete wall. My mind searches frantically to locate a concrete abutment but in my anxious and depressed mood I am unable to recall one. Because I am having such overwhelming suicidal desires, I call Dottie and her husband Bob.

Dottie says, "Stay where you are, we are on our way!"

They arrive within twenty minutes and insist I go home with them and stay overnight. My dear friend Dottie made all the difference on this terrible night. Soon thereafter Sid moves in with a teacher and his wife in Concord so he can continue in the Concord school system.

Within six months Butch is discharged from the Navy and the two of them move in together. Butch rents an apartment over a business on Main Street. They soon have it decorated like a hippie pad with beads acting as a door to the bedroom. Between the two of us we get Sid through high school.

Marie, Ray and I remain good friends despite the heart-wrenching emerald ring incident.

I am able to get a job at a local hospital on a medical surgical unit upon my return from Connecticut. But I am required to work swing shifts to include evenings and nights, sometimes within the same week. It is a stressful job compared to my experience in West Haven.

Once I am back in New Hampshire, the men return to my life, beginning with Sharon's wedding.

At Sharon's wedding I present the guest book and the best man Jay pursues me. I find him attractive, he is a sexy guy with long legs, sandy colored hair, blue eyes, and he begins flirting with me as soon as we meet at the rehearsal the night before the wedding. He reminds me of Ross. Even though he has sort of a boyish grin, he has a very seductive way of looking at me. He has a laid-back, mellow demeanor that I find very attractive. Of course I still do not feel comfortable flirting so I ignore him and even try to avoid him. He is a little too much for me.

The next day after the wedding and the reception I gather my things and leave for home in my flashy convertible. Suncook is about two hours away and I'm almost to Claremont when I notice a red Volkswagen behind me and realize it is Jay.

Oh my God, what is he doing?! I decide to pretend I don't see him and continue driving over the speed limit as usual. Within minutes after I turn into my driveway he is knocking on my door. He is very flirtatious and has a relaxed sensual attitude that is very addictive. He lives in Marblehead, MA and works for TWA, an airline. He is not a pilot but has an office job where he organizes the meals and supplies for every flight. He can fly several destinations for free... I like that idea.

He tries to kiss me but I am my usual awkward, nervous self. I hardly know him so I manage to avoid the kiss. I tell him I have to work in the morning and have laundry, etc. to prepare for the work week. We walk out to his car together and he asks to see me next weekend and I accept. But as he opens the car door, I see a six-pack of beer on the floor behind the driver's seat. A red flag goes up for me and I begin to feel negatively about him. At the hospital I have had a lot of negative experiences dealing with alcoholics, so I am immediately cautious.

While living in Suncook out in the country in an old farmhouse with a first floor apartment, my promiscuity increases significantly. I am enjoying the company of five men but I am only in love with one, Ryan, who has come back into my life, but of course he is unavailable.

Emotionally I maintain a distance from the others because it is not easy for me to show my feelings toward men. I can have sex with enthusiasm, I'm just not capable of verbally expressing feelings of intimacy. There is definitely something askew with me.

Jay and I have great sexual chemistry but because I am compartmentalizing my feelings and continue to feel the burden of caretaking my Mom and Sid, I am highly distracted. I do not really take the time or bother questioning Jay about his family or background.

On a subconscious level I am confusing sex with love and affection because I was taught that at an early age during the abuse from my stepfather. I can feel that something is missing in all these relationships. I feel shame and I am not proud that I am promiscuous, but during this time of confusion I equate sex with developing a loving relationship. So much internal conflict and confusion. Somehow I believe I must not be good enough, all my friends find serious boyfriends and eventually get married but it never works that way for me. I am becoming increasingly frustrated. And that old friend, anger, is turning more and more to rage.

At the same time an orderly at the hospital is interested in me. He is attending St. Anselm's College and has been asking me out for the past two years, but I have not given him the time of day because as a professional nurse I don't believe in dating coworkers. Don hopes to become a physician.

One day we end up in an elevator alone and I am shocked and puzzled by my reaction to him. I am nervous. He is on the way to my unit to pick up a chart. We exit the elevator and I go to the chart rack but give him the wrong chart, causing him to come all the way back from the ER. I have never been this flustered around a man and it is annoying me.

Soon after, I finally accept a date with him and find that I am attracted to his intellect and like that he treats me like a lady. He brings me roses and always takes me to upscale restaurants and Summer Theater. He is a blond, with a stocky build about six feet tall and of French/Canadian background.

I do enjoy my time with Don, he is a very kind person, although he talks nonstop and seems to be an authority on every subject. He asks me a lot of questions which I'm not totally comfortable answering, but eventually I tell him about my mother's illness and that I am helping to raise my younger brother.

He really focuses in on me, he is consumed with me even though I have informed him that there are other male friends in my life. We've only had three dates, when Marie requests that I fly out to California with her to visit her sister.

It is my first time flying and being in California. Her sister has a nice home in the suburb of Los Angeles and she takes us to visit many of the usual attractions like Disney World and Knotts Berry Farm. During my vacation I have not thought about any of the men back home.

When I return I have several messages on my phone from Don. I am a little surprised because I did tell him I was going to be away. I return his call and remind him I've been away in California. He is eager to see me so I accept a date with him.

He arrives with a bouquet of several colored roses and proceeds to tell me the significance of the various colors. First he describes the yellow one, staring into my eyes intently, he says the yellow one is for jealousy.

It is easy for me to not stay in the moment during emotional situations, so I sort of blank out and brush aside what he is trying to tell me. He is feeling jealous but I don't want to acknowledge his feelings. He continues explaining the meanings of each color, white rose is for purity and the pink is for friendship and red for love.

As usual I am very uncomfortable with intimate conversations and cannot express my feelings in these moments. But Don is beginning to get my attention so I do think about him a little more and we continue to date regularly. He has a way of summarizing what I am thinking and feeling and he often speaks for me. No one has ever been that interested or involved with me, so he is growing on me.

Meanwhile I am working long hours at the hospital. It is not uncommon to work three different shifts in one week. The evening shift is grueling. I am working on a thirty-bed medical- surgical unit that includes a two-bed coronary care unit.

On evenings there is only one RN and two orderlies. Thankfully fifteen of the patients are ambulatory and are in their convalescent phase of treatment. The remaining patients are acutely ill and bedridden. However, all thirty require medications and treatments consisting of dressing changes, breathing treatments, (IPPB) and IV's to name a few.

Then of course the two cardiac patients require constant observation and treatment. It is not uncommon to be at the end of the hall and hear the alarm sound in the CCU because a patient is having a string of PVC's (premature ventricular contractions) requiring I run the entire length of the hall to turn up the lidocaine to break the arrhythmia.

It is an unsafe environment on evenings and nearly impossible to complete all that is required. I spend most of the evening pouring medications and administering them. I never go to supper. The orderlies will bring me packages of cheese crackers and coffee from the canteen on their way back from supper which I eat on the run. I do not sit down to chart until all the care is given and I have given a report to the 11-7 nurse. Most nights I do not leave for home until two a.m. and there is no extra pay. In these days it is a nurse's "duty" to stay until all patient care is completed.

The anger that I have experienced throughout my young life is at its peak and most days my rage is evident in the workplace. I express my unhappiness with working three different shifts in one week but nothing changes.

I am so angry at the injustices that I witness and experience at the hospital. As an idealistic young nurse I am propelled to an activist state. Many of my coworkers feel the same way as me but they are not as vocal. The management, Head Nurse and Chief Nurse take notice of my disgruntled attitude.

My anger at work is escalating. One of the nurses has a connection to a state representative, Congressman Williams, and between the two of us we organize ten nurses to meet with him in his home. We are all sitting in his living room on a large curved sectional that accommodates all of us, telling him about being short staffed and about the inadequate care provided at the hospital.

Within a few days the Hospital administrator is transferred to a southern hospital but unfortunately, our Chief Nurse does not get transferred. However, some changes are made. We get a float RN to come to our floor to assist with treatments every night for a couple of hours and we are provided with one extra orderly.

My immediate supervisor suspects that I was the leader of the group that made the complaint so I am penalized. I receive only a satisfactory review which denies me a four thousand dollar raise. Of course this results in me becoming even more rebellious, so I submit a formal complaint through Human Resources. I complete reams of paperwork that is forwarded to the central office in Washington, D.C.

To this day I believe there is an FBI file with my name on it.

Because of the demands of my job I find myself not visiting my Mom or Sid as often, which results in a high level of guilt and I don't have much time for dating. Feeling guilt is a frequent emotion experienced by me.

I eventually seek counseling, my emotional health is in a free fall of rage and anxiety. I am raging constantly. Dottie witnesses me being rude to store clerks on a regular basis: "I'll tell you when I need assistance... for Christ's sake let me get in the door... before you start hounding me!"

I routinely drive my Cutlass convertible over the speed limit. Inevitably I receive three speeding tickets within a few weeks, going 80 mph in a 55 mph zone. This results in me being assigned to the automobile insurance risk pool and paying high premiums.

By the time I am in counseling Dottie and Bob are married, Butch and Sid have a hippie pad over a storefront in downtown Concord. Wonderful, generous and helpful Marie and Ray finally have their home to themselves.

Marie and Ray Taking us to Easter Sunday Services

Sid as a Boy Scout

Sid Fishing Age 12

Taking Sid to Washington DC
in Comet Convertible

Sid on Capitol Steps with Dottie
and Linda

Paula (in mother role) and Sid at Farmer's Museum

Taking Mom out of Nursing Home
for a Picnic with Sid

Paula, Midnight Awakening Asked
to Join the Party

More Partying at Marie and Ray's

Marie and Paula on California Trip, her Sister's Backyard

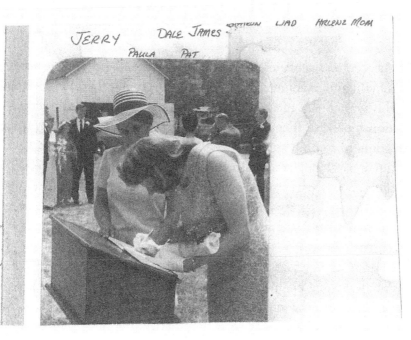

Paula Presenting the Guest Book at Sharon's Wedding

Chapter 15

LIGHT AT END OF
THE TUNNEL

At the age of twenty-eight I enter the psychologist's office for my initial visit and announce, "I don't know what... but there is something terribly wrong with me... I date plenty of men but I never develop any relationships with them. If I am not married by the time I am thirty, I'm going to commit suicide!"

Jim, a psychologist and a nice looking Greek man with a receding hairline, about five years older than me, has a stocky build and does not appear shocked by my declaration. I like him immediately, he seems to understand me and my rage. Another serendipitous moment and angel sent.

I find it strange that I have crossed paths with so many Greek men.

An awakening begins. Slowly my constant state of anger begins to make sense with the kindness and expertise of Jim. Each week, some-times twice a week I meet with him, depending on the intensity of emotional pain to be worked through. We tackle whatever issue surfaces at the time. I basically need to re-experience my adolescence in a healthy relationship within the therapeutic model and I must diffuse repressed anger and gain insight as to why I am so full of rage. It will be a long, painful journey requiring years of courage and tenacity.

I enjoy going to his office located in a home on a tree lined neighborhood street in Manchester. We meet in a comfortable room furnished with cozy upholstered chairs, plush carpeting, bookshelves and low lighting. Jim sits across from me and we begin with wherever I am at during the particular session. Mostly I am raging about my work situation, feeling monumental guilt for not visiting Mom more often at the nursing home, or dealing with the confusion around men. With his therapeutic feedback, I begin to gain insight.

Over the next few months I begin to understand that the intensity of my anger is not proportionate to my work situation. Yes, work is frustrating, but my rage is caused by something deeper.

I learn that "old business" or childhood pain is impacting my daily life and that I never fully grieved my father's death, or my mother's illness. Additionally, the issue of betrayal and lack of trust raises its ugly head, but only after Jim gains my trust.

Only with experiencing kindness, caring, love and clarity from a man in the setting of a psychologist's office does my healing begin. One day a major breakthrough moment occurs. We usually sit in comfortable soft-cushioned chairs in Jim's outer office but on this day he invites me into his inner office. He sits behind a big desk and I am across from him in a straight back cushioned chair. The session proceeds as usual until he asks a question.

"Did your stepfather ever touch you inappropriately?"

A lightning bolt of fear shoots through my chest. I attempt to speak but my throat feels like it is in a vice. I repeatedly try to answer his question. I can feel my mouth moving, opening and closing, but not a sound is coming from me. My throat feels paralyzed and I utter not a sound. I am frozen silent. Post-traumatic stress disorder has me speechless. My stepfather's repeated threat "not to tell" has penetrated my entire being.

Jim immediately takes charge. "It is okay... it is okay." He calmly says, "If you can't tell me now, over the next week, if you are able, write me a letter about what you can't tell me today and bring it with you next week."

I believe Jim expected this visceral response from me and deliberately planned the session so there was a desk between us, hoping the physical barrier would help me feel safer.

Soon after this experience I take a trip to Vermont to visit Philippa and to drive around on the back roads. I enjoy the seclusion and serenity of them, after meandering for a while I find myself near the Larrabe Farm, our first home after leaving Connecticut. I am parked and gazing at the embankment that obstructs a view of the house and barn when I experience a flashback that is very disturbing to me.

At first the repressed memory appears in fragments, some clear, others cloudy, as if I am adjusting the focus of opera glasses. Then the memories begin to unfold in bits and pieces.

We are crouched behind the sparse, scraggly underbrush along the hilltop beneath the tree canopy within view of the road below. In the distance to the left, I hear the hum of a vehicle motor as it approaches our hiding place. Instantly his hand slams across my mouth and fear rises. We hear the motor hum grow louder, soon a huge yellow road scraper comes into view in the curve of the rural gravel road. A wave of calmness washes over me as I listen to the murmuring, soft, soothing voices of the six-man work crew walking behind the scraper. I am mesmerized by the scene, as though I view it from a theater balcony.

The mammoth yellow scraper squeaks as it eases to a stop below our hiding place. With the hand firmly clamped over my mouth, fear paralyzes my throat, but I feel calmer as I look down on the men rhythmically swinging shovels, patching the potholes. I enjoy their soft murmuring voices.

But in my mind's eye, my focus is blurry. I am aware of something off to my right side and I strain to visualize. What is it? Suddenly a stream of consciousness flashes white... quickly it's gone again. But then the blurriness slowly clears and then I see it... laying atop the grass, tossed aside, is a child's white panties. I am shocked at the meaning of this flashback.

I have determined this incident took place when I was two-and-a-half years old......potholes occur in the Spring after the winter thaw and are patched at that time. I recognize the hilltop as being located on the Larrabe Farm where my brother Butch was born at home in May. We moved to the Ben Davis Farm when I was three years old, my birthday is November first, six months after the time potholes are patched.

When I was much older my mother told me I didn't speak until after I was three years old. Perhaps, this early trauma with the hand slamming across my mouth was the reason... maybe I was scared into silence. Of course I suspect it was my stepfather with me on that day.

As an adult I have analyzed this memory with an educated eye and have wondered if the stress of my brother Butch's birth could have precipitated my stepfather's behavior. After all, his outrageous behavior escalated when my second brother was born... seems like a pattern. Not that I excuse one second of it!

My mother and stepfather had only been in Vermont eighteen months when Butch was born and they were still in the hiding mode. Mom did not attempt to socialize with any of the neighbors. The visiting nurse came to the house to record Butch's home birth and prepare his birth certificate. Joe was the sole provider but was struggling to obtain jobs. With only the basic skills of farming, logging, and as a machinist it was nearly impossible for him to find a permanent job. He was twenty-seven and my mother was twenty-six.

I return to New Hampshire after my disturbing flashback and resume dating both Jay and Don. Within six months of entering therapy both of them propose marriage to me. Jay's proposal comes as a big surprise, because our connection is strictly sexual. I have lots of fun with him but because of that constant presence of a six-pack of beer in his car, I honor my instincts and turn him down.

Don checks off all the boxes, he adores me, treats me like a princess, he is intelligent and seems to have a bright future. I realize I am in love with him and accept his proposal. He is the first man with whom I can let down my walls. However, I do not notice how controlling he is... a big mistake on my part.

Soon after Don's proposal he leaves for the University of Pittsburgh to study for a Ph.D. in biochemistry. He hopes it will increase his chances of being accepted to medical school. However, after six months he drops out of the program because he misses me and wants to get married soon.

I miss him while he is away, but I am juggling so much turmoil, and distracted by all the crises in my life, that I would have been content for him to remain in school.

When I announce in my next therapy session that I am engaged, Jim is speechless. He sits with his head down for what feels like forever until he looks at me and says... keep talking.

I believe it is his way of letting me know my healing is far from over. I also question, if Don had not come into my life at that time, whether Jim and I would have started dating once I was discharged from therapy.

I am aware Jim is going through a divorce and there are moments at the end of our sessions when his comments are more personal.

A year later Don and I are married, but the ceremony is sort of a blur for me. Don and I pay for our wedding and I am responsible for the details of the plan. I make special arrangements for my Mom to stay overnight at the hotel where we hold the reception so that she can attend. One of my nurse friends volunteers to stay overnight with Mom and get her ready in the morning so my brothers can drive her back to the nursing home.

Throughout the evening reception, I am not emotionally present, I am focused on our two hundred guests, ensuring they are having a good time and of course aware of Mom's well-being. My Czech relatives, Philippa, Marie and Ray, and Dottie and Bob and Jim are in attendance. Dottie and Sharon are my bridesmaids. Butch and Sid are ushers, and wonderful, kind, loving Ray walks me down the aisle.

We have a beautiful candlelight ceremony at a Catholic Church and again I go through the motions... sort of out of it. In previous weeks I had made my first communion to please Don, not because I had a strong desire to be married in the Catholic Church.

Looking back on this day I feel really bad for Don because he is so attentive to me and I am emotionally absent. I have always been extremely responsible and duty bound so find it difficult to relinquish my caretaking role of Mom and the details of the reception.

The wedding planner is not detailed oriented and some things are not going as planned. The live band is too loud, not playing the soft background music during dinner as we had requested, making it difficult to converse. Additionally Don's sister Vivian, a beautiful soprano singer cannot be heard over the band. This makes me extremely annoyed, frustrated, and distracted.

My history has always been, when in an intense emotional situation, I block out the present and emotionally go elsewhere. So rather than live in the moment and enjoy being a joyous bride, I am concerned with the reception and not focused on my new loving husband.

Don was so thoughtful and romantic. He made reservations for our first night at a beautiful hotel with castle-like turrets, surrounded by a moat. When we drive up to it the hotel is lit up as though glowing in candlelight, an extension of the ceremony. It is so special. The next morning we travel to the Poconos for the remainder of our honeymoon.

We later move to Saratoga Springs, NY, to begin our married life. Don has a new job as a pharmaceutical representative requiring daily trips up to the Adirondacks. He soon realizes that selling and being in a car all day is not his cup of tea.

I, on the other hand, believe Don has rescued me from all my stressors, my difficult job, and all my other anxieties. In the early months I do not seek employment, subconsciously believing "the man is the supporter." Eventually I take a part-time low stress job at a local nursing home. However one day a physician says to me, "What are you doing here? Wouldn't you like a more challenging job?"

"There is a small hospital just south of here, and our head nurse's husband was just killed in an airplane crash. So there is a position open at the hospital in Ballston Spa. I think you would be perfect for the Head Nurse position."

Two weeks later I take the position at a thirty-three bed small community hospital and I find myself in management at the age of twenty-nine. I tend to always work beyond my comfort level and I remain in this role for eight years due to the high salary and because of Don's challenge to maintain jobs that satisfy his aspirations and intellect.

We have been living in Saratoga for a year, when at Christmas we receive a beautiful note from Jim wishing us Merry Christmas and hoping I am doing well. He signs it, Love, Jim.

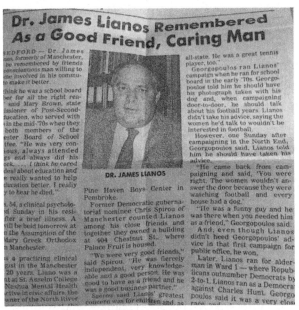

Newspaper of Jim, Paula's Psychotherapist

Philippa at my Wedding

Mom, Being Given a Perm in Preparation for Wedding

My Brothers as Ushers, Butch and Sid with Mom

Sharon, Bridesmaid Helping me get Ready

PAULA CZECH

Dottie, Maid of Honor

Ray Walking me Down the Aisle

Giving Mom my Bridal Bouquet

Chapter 16

THE DAVID

Don and I settle into married life but have difficulty agreeing on a budget. Despite this disagreement we buy a house within a year and travel to Europe during our second year of marriage.

The trip is empowering for me and provides me with a much broader world view. We visit the Louvre in Paris and see the Mona Lisa where I recall my high school English teacher, who recognized that I had poor self-esteem and wrote in my year book, "To Mona, It has been a joy to look up and see a Renaissance painting."

In Rome the Italian men do not care that I am a married woman and whistle at me and attempt to slap me on the ass, followed by a string of Italian for what sounds like "Bella donna," beautiful woman. I am intimidated by the blatant appreciation but secretly flattered. My olive skin and long straight brown hair cause me to be mistaken for an Italian. St. Peter's Cathedral is unbelievably beautiful and enormous. Needless to say, I love Italy.

But it is in Florence that I experience a significant lifelong transition, I am moved to tears. Evidence of the Medici era is throughout the city, especially in the architecture like the Duomo, Palazzo Vecchio and the Medici Chapel. The entire city is a work of art. As I walk down a long corridor, I can see a rotunda ahead with the bright sunshine shining through a skylight.

Standing in front of a seventeen-foot-tall marble nude male statue bathed in sunlight, I am overcome with emotion as I view Michelangelo's David. The marble glistens in the sunlight and I expect him to step down off the pedestal and come to life. I have never seen anything so beautiful. I am impressed with the strength and power represented by the statue's rippling muscles. Florence remains my favorite city in Europe. On our way home we buy souvenir statues of the David and the Rape of the Sabines, another symbol of power.

The experience of traveling overseas makes a huge impression on me and boosts my confidence. I remain in awe of the David and think about the power it symbolizes, wondering if I will ever feel in control of my life. I am grateful to Don for planning the trip and for escorting me through Europe.

After four years of marriage, we welcome our son Tommy and I am overjoyed. I am thirty-three years old and I give birth by an emergency Caesarean section. Partly groggy from anesthesia I ask the operating room team, "Does he have ten fingers and ten toes?" The Dr. pretends to count and then announces, "Yes, he does" and adds "He is perfect."

Don is extremely supportive during the many hours of labor before it is decided to do the surgery, remaining on a straight-back chair at my bedside the entire time. When a physician with whom I work visits, he says to Don, "You are the one that looks like you just gave birth! You look terrible, go home and get some sleep, Paula will be fine."

My maternal instinct swings into overdrive within a few hours and I become fiercely protective of our new baby boy. And my hypervigilance of our son remains throughout his younger years.

Given my history, I am unable to behave any differently. My goal is to never allow a pedophile anywhere near him. While he is at school I worry about any after school activities and when they occur I question

Tommy intently, looking for any signs of distress on his part.

We stay in the hospital eight days because of the surgery and due to the complication of mastitis. I am breast-feeding, which I am proud of because I know my immune system will benefit Tommy. There is a family history of asthma on Don's side and I hope breast-feeding will mitigate Tommy's chances of developing severe asthma. Also due to our struggle with finances, I feel the pressure to continue with breast-feeding.

Don is a great father and during the night-feeding he is the one to get out of bed, change the diaper and then bring Tommy to me to nurse. I am so grateful that he does this because I still have abdominal pain at the surgical site. It was Don's suggestion that we give Tommy my maiden name, Czech, for a middle name. He totally breaks with his family's tradition of always honoring the Godfather by using his name for the baby's middle name. I am thrilled and impressed by Don's thoughtfulness and courage or perhaps.... it is rebellion?

Tommy is four months old before I return to work. I stay home longer than the normal three months because I cannot bear to leave him in the care of a babysitter while he is so little, but this puts a strain on our finances.

I eventually find a neighbor who has her own baby boy a few months older than Tommy to babysit, so I believe it will be a perfect fit. However, about a month later I arrive at the babysitter's to pick up Tommy to find him in the care of the husband. Immediately, I am in a panic.

I ask where is Laurie, and he replies that she had to go to her craft group. I tell him we will not be returning and gather up Tommy's portable crib and belongings and we leave, never to return. I could never tolerate leaving Tommy in the care of a man.

Now I have a dilemma. I am the Head Nurse and I must be at work because it is difficult to find coverage for my position. When I call to explain the situation to the Director of Nursing, she tells me she knows someone who would be perfect.

Carol is a math teacher and mother of three daughters, but is staying home to be a full time mother. Because she comes highly recommended I go to interview her for the job. I am intense and ask her all kinds of questions like how she would handle certain emergencies and inform her she will be required to write daily notes as to Tommy's care: like what he eats, play time, nap time, new growth milestones and more. My hypervigilance status has been ramped up several notches.

She agrees to my over-protective mother demands and becomes the perfect match and even learns to handle my anxiety. One day I come to pick up Tommy and Carol begins telling me how they went to the Grand Union grocery shopping.

I am in an instant panic. How could she take him in her car, they could have had an accident! But after the initial shock wears off, I accept that this will probably happen on a regular basis. Slowly I gain trust in Carol and our arrangement works out perfectly.

The three daughters love him like a brother and have great fun playing with him and he eventually calls his new babysitters Aunt Carol and Uncle Phil. He stays with them until it is time to start kindergarten. I really don't know what I would have done without them and we remain friends to this day.

Within eighteen months of Tommy's birth, Don and I continue to struggle financially and we are arguing daily. One day I am at the gynecologist for a routine visit, and while the physician reviews my chart, he notes that I am a new mother and questions me how we are coping as new parents. I admit we are having some difficulties. He tells me this is a common occurrence and suggests we try some counseling. He gives me the name of a psychiatrist and informs me he is the best in the area and highly recommends him.

Bob is an amazing, skilled psychiatrist. He is a tall slender man, dressed in corduroy pants and a gray pullover sweater. He reminds me of "Mr. Rogers." He speaks softly and moves about the room slowly. He is very serene, peaceful and pauses for long periods before he speaks. His office is dimly lit, with soft music playing in the background. We sit across from him in a brown, soft leather couch.

Looking back on this time I am so grateful that Bob came into my life, he made all the difference. Without his wisdom and skill, I worry how my anger and at its worst my rage would have impacted the remainder of my life. Bob is one of my "Angels" and he appeared in my life when I was most in need of relief.

Initially, he leads us through financial conflict, power struggles, coping with jobs, and eventually my specific history. Bob suggests I join a women's survivors group. At the same time I continue therapy with him. Over the next two years I process anger, learn about boundary lines, and eventually I develop personal power for the first time in my life.

The women's survivor group meets in the evening twenty miles south of where we live. On the night I attend my initial meeting, I am anxious but I make myself go to the meeting. I am the third one to take a seat in the circle so I feel conspicuous and uncomfortable, but eventually there are twelve of us in the room.

My healing begins immediately, when I gaze around the circle at the women, all ages with an amazing commonality. They are all beautiful, articulate women. I am shocked at how great they all look. They do not look like the scum of the earth, or tainted in keeping with my self-image. Then as I hear their stories of abuse and share my story over the ensuing weeks, I begin to feel my esteem drastically improve. This group has the most significant impact on my self-image.

But things are not going as well at home. One day I reach my breaking point. Don and I are arguing constantly, we seem to disagree about the minutest issues. I tend to stuff my anger because I do not feel I am a good debater.

After Don leaves for work, I call in sick at the beginning of a long weekend. I am so frustrated I just want to run away. Where will I go? I am a thirty-four-year-old woman with a baby, in an unhappy marriage, without a mother or father to run home to. Marie, Ray, Dottie and Bob would welcome me but I am too proud and not willing to admit to a failed marriage. The only place calling me is the Ben Davis Farm and Philippa. But as I leave the driveway I have not decided for sure where I am going.

Tommy is almost two years old, I load the car with pillows, blankets and food in case we get stranded, there is a snow storm predicted. I am somewhat anxious because I will be totally responsible for his care and well-being during the weekend. The big question and part of the reason for this escape is to find out if I can take care of Tommy by myself. It is a trial run for a potential single mother status.

It is dark when we arrive at the Ben Davis, the driveway is not plowed but I stomp on the gas and manage to get the car out of the road. Philippa has the entire screened porch encased in plastic to keep out the cold and the door is locked. She does not hear me pounding on the door.

So I struggle through the deep snow and make my way to the living room picture window. Peering in, I can see her asleep on the pullout couch. I knock on the window for several minutes before I am able to wake her. I had not told her I was coming because initially I wasn't sure where I was going, and during the 1970s cell phones were not as common as they are now.

Philippa is shocked to see me and puzzled that Don is not with me. The only room with any heat is the living room, the pocket doors are closed and the door to the kitchen has been closed. She is heating the living room with a ceramic electric space heater but the room remains chilly.

There needs to be more heat so I go down to the cellar to stoke up the fire in the wood-burning furnace. A neighbor builds a fire daily to help Philippa. She has a bad hip so it is too difficult and unsafe for her to go up and down the stairs to keep a fire going.

I am happy to be with Philippa and despite her urging, I refuse to call Don and let him know where I am. I deliberately did not leave him a note. My anger wants him to suffer and I am in retaliation mode. We have been married only six years.

Philippa is conflicted and I can tell she does not want to be in the middle of this as she loves us both. I am enjoying my respite away from Don. Eventually after calling everyone Don can think of, to include Sharon, Dottie, Marie and Ray, he finally calls Philippa late Saturday afternoon. I refuse to speak with him, but tell Philippa to let him know I will be home on Sunday.

During the next several years we have Philippa spend the winters with us to be sure she is safe.

At our next therapy session, Bob has Don sit out in the waiting room while he speaks to me alone. Finally he asks why I left and I tell him I wanted to see if I could take care of Tommy alone.

Bob asks, "And what did you learn?"

With confidence I answer, "I can definitely take care of Tommy by myself."

Bob gives me a slight smile.

With Bob's help I am gaining personal power but have yet to fully embrace it.

I believe Don is more intelligent than me because he has a degree and that makes me feel inferior. I want to study for my Bachelor's but I am scared to death to attempt college. As a registered nurse from a three-year diploma school I realize in order to increase my salary I must have a degree, especially since I am always striving to go up the next rung of the ladder.

Within a few weeks and with Don's encouragement, I summon the courage to submit an application to the SUNY Empire State College, in Albany. As I walk up the flight of stairs to register for my classes, I am petrified and need to force myself to continue, I almost turn around and retreat down the stairs. Fear is in my chest. It is so difficult for me to take this step because of my inferiority complex. I have little confidence and because Don is so bright I feel so much less.

I begin to relax once I meet with my professors, they are not threatening after all. They are no different than the physicians with whom I work so I become comfortable discussing my lessons with them. I receive a reading assignment and a paper to write weekly and meet routinely with my professors to discuss my papers. My study time begins at three a.m., when I am awakened by the alarm so I can do my school work before leaving for the hospital. Since I am a morning person it actually works quite well.

Empire State accepts many of my Nursing credits so I only have to complete two years to receive my Bachelor's in Mental Health. A turning point comes during the summer when I sign up for a "Women in Literature" seminar.

There are ten of us women around a large conference table with the female professor. Over the summer we read several books and then discuss all the female protagonists. We read "Uncle Tom's Cabin," "Their Eyes Were Watching God," and "Jane Eyre" to name a few.

At the end of the summer I am finally a fully empowered woman. Don doesn't know how to handle me. He can no longer convince me it is my fault... I have never experienced such clarity or power. It is the beginning of the end.

During my college studies, I am given a field work assignment to complete and I am fortunate to be supervised by a psychologist and the Director of a sexual abuse treatment program for children/women.

In the beginning I shadow him in group and individual therapy as well as a court-mandated pedophile group. After a few weeks, I act as a co-therapist with the psychologist for five little girls between the ages of six and ten who are sexual abuse victims, and then as a primary therapist for a sixteen-year-old girl.

During the young girls' group, we all sit at a long table, while the children use paper and crayons to begin to tell or show their stories. I gain their trust and help them to eventually verbally tell their individual stories, by sharing my story about being thrown down the silo.

I choose not to share my sexual abuse stories because I don't feel it is appropriate self disclosure. But despite not sharing it, my silo story gives them the necessary courage to talk and therefore diffuse the power their abuse has over them, which puts them on the path to healing.

At one point I miss two sessions because of back pain. All the marital stress settles in my back and I often experience debilitating pain. One of the little girls is having a difficult time sharing her story. So the psychologist decides to use my illness as a motivator.

He asks the little girl if she would like to tell me her story privately by speaking into a recorder in a different room. She agrees and has a breakthrough moment when she is able to talk to me on the recorder about her father. I am overwhelmed with emotion knowing I helped her begin to heal.

In addition, I become the therapist for a sixteen-year-old Latino girl with a history of abuse. I am happy that she connects with me and remains in therapy with me as her counselor for the entire time of my field work. I can see I make a difference and I gain valuable counseling experience as well.

But my work with the pedophile group results in therapy for me, because part of the group goals are to hold them responsible for the crimes they have already been convicted of, and I confront them and explain how damaging it has been for me as a victim. They listen politely, but I can tell my story is falling on deaf ears.

There are five of them in the group and one of them is an attorney who arrives dressed in a suit. He has been convicted of abusing his twin eight-year-old daughters and doesn't have a clue what all the fuss is about. It is so shocking and aggravating to me.

But of course I learn that this is typical behavior for pedophiles, they never really admit responsibility and often minimize the abuse by deflecting, "It is her fault because she teased me," or like my stepfather, blame their behaviors on the mother. In my opinion pedophiles need to be locked up for life beginning with the first offense. They never change their colors.

I realize I made my stepfather stop abusing me when I was ten-and-a-half years old, but that only means he stopped abusing me. There is evidence he abused another victim after me.

I complete my field work and I am close to graduating when on my birthday, November 1, 1987, I receive an alarming phone call from Vermont. Nicole, a neighbor of Philippa's, tells me that Philippa was just taken to the local hospital and is deathly ill.

Don, Tommy and I immediately travel to the local hospital eighteen miles from the farm but we arrive too late. She has already been transferred to Fletcher Allen Medical Center in Burlington.

When we arrive at the second hospital, Philippa is already on the life support, critically ill. I am so distraught, we visit her bedside but she does not know we are there. After a while we leave for the Ben Davis to sleep. The fire in the furnace has gone out and it is freezing cold in the house. Don starts a fire, we all climb into bed fully clothed and wearing our wool hats.

By the next morning the house is still cool but getting warmer, I decide I will return to the hospital while Don stays behind to entertain ten-year-old Tommy and to cook supper.

I remain at Philippa's bedside all day... I CAN'T BE ANYWHERE ELSE. I am driven to sit at her bedside and hold her hand. The time flies by and before I realize, six hours have passed and it is time to drive one hour north to Don and Tommy.

Over the next four months we spend every weekend in Vermont with me at Philippa's bedside Friday evenings, all day Saturday and a couple of hours on Sunday before we return to New York State.

Philippa only regains consciousness once during that time, but at least I get to tell her how much I love her, and she reiterates as she has all our lives that everything she has belongs to Butch and me. But of course that is not my primary focus.

Unfortunately, I only have her financial power of attorney and not her health proxy. The physicians approach me about what I believe her wishes would be and I am positive she would not want to be on the vent. She always wanted to die in her own bed at the Ben Davis. But my hands are tied without the health power of attorney.

On March 1, 1988, while at home in New York, I have a nagging sensation in the pit of my abdomen, and with anxiousness I call the hospital to check Philippa's status. The first person to answer the phone seems to be uncomfortable and is stammering. She puts me on hold.

When she returns she tells me a nurse will call me back shortly. About one hour later a nurse calls to inform me of Philippa's death. Philippa was being coded at the exact moment I made my call.

The next week is a blur with funeral arrangements, visiting hours and the funeral. I dress Philippa in the same attire she wore to my wedding.

Typical of Philippa, everything I need to know about her affairs is in the wooden bowl on the kitchen table. She had recently sent a truck full of antiques to the auction so I will have monies to pay for her funeral. I am so sad and committed to honoring her life. I display her diplomas, photos of her on the equestrian team at Wellesley College, photos of Butch and me with her as young children, and of her beloved Elkhound, Ingrid. Ingrid has a headstone beneath a maple tree on the side lawn.

Philippa was never pretentious and none of her neighbors or towns-people have any idea of her educational background or her status in Cooperstown. I decide to honor her privacy regarding her age because nothing would ignite her temper more than when someone would ask her age. I deliberately omit her age in the obituary but lots of people think there is a mistake and insist on asking me about it. I do not re-veal her age to the public. She is eighty-years-old.

Because the ground is still frozen we do not have the burial at the time of her death. In the Spring we hold a small service at the grave site in the old country cemetery situated high on a hill in Burton, not far from the Ben Davis. Philippa always wanted to be buried with her grandparents, so I honor her wishes.

At her grave site in early summer of 1988 a profound event occurs when all the young farm kids announce, "Look, look there is a fox!" They were pointing to the edge of the woods near our small group of mourners. Of significance, it is the children whom Philippa always showered with hugs and kisses that notice the nearby fox. None of the adults see the fox.

When the service is over we walk toward our cars parked below an expansive grassy knoll. Suddenly, we are all spellbound by the sight of a beautiful strawberry blond, bushy-tailed fox running across the ridge, its tail flowing in the wind reminiscent of when Philippa would allow her long hair to air dry while she walked in the meadows.

One of the farm wives, Nicole says softly, "That's Philippa." I respond, "Yes, I know."

We both recognize the fox is Philippa and I recall that her college minor was in religion so I have no doubt the Philippa fox is letting us know she is happy and at peace.

Since that time, especially if I am sad or struggling with a problem, frequently a fox will appear within my view either along the road, in the meadows or peering from a corner of a barn.

Throughout the years, I have purposely collected fox art work and jewelry, in honor of Philippa.

It is also linked to my spirituality.

Events like the following example convince me, Philippa is always near me as my

"Guardian Angel."

During a time when I had a home job working on the computer, I had been texting with my co-worker Jamie about my frustrating day. I was most upset, and near tears. I had just ended our brief conversation with her by sending her an angry red-face emoticon, when a knock on the front door announces the arrival of the Comcast repairman.

After making his repairs to my TV he says to me, "You know, I have never seen a real fox until I was on my way over here. I saw this beautiful fox out in the meadow." He then proceeds to show me the photo of the fox on his IPhone.

Next he excitedly says to me, "Before today I had never seen a fox in the wild, then I come here and you have all these fox pictures in every room!" I reply equally as excited and explain why he has experienced this serendipitous moment.

At the time of the initial phone call notifying me of Philippa's illness I took a leave of absence from College and now it is time to return to my studies. I am so exhausted and emotionally drained from the events

of the past months that it takes every ounce of my will to resume my College education. It takes two days for me to finally rally my courage and energy. Despite it being nearly an impossible act, I have never regretted the decision and many times over the years I have counted my blessings for doing so.

Don and I continue to struggle with marital problems and we remain in therapy with Bob. I am in the beginning stages of experiencing personal power for the first time in my life. Due to school and my trip to Europe my world view has broadened and my self-esteem has had a boost. In general I am much more confident. I feel I am finally on equal footing with my peers except for my husband. Despite a college degree on the near horizon, I am locked in a power struggle with Don and I resist being controlled by him with every fiber in my body.

The Program for the Moulin Rouge in Paris

The Florence Cathedral

Arno River Florence, Italy

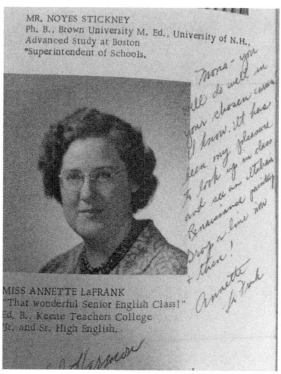

MR. NOYES STICKNEY
Ph. B., Brown University M. Ed., University of N.H.,
Advanced Study at Boston
*Superintendent of Schools.

MISS ANNETTE LaFRANK
"That wonderful Senior English Class!"
Ed. B., Keene Teachers College
Jr. and Sr. High English.

Mona — you will do well in your chosen career I know. It has been my pleasure to look up in class and see an Ithean Renaissance painting. Drop a line now + then!

*Annette LaFrank, English Teacher
(and one of my Angels)*

The Mona Lisa

Chapter 17

RAGE RESOLUTION

Shortly after Philippa's funeral I graduate from Empire State with a Bachelor's in Mental Health. The transfer of the Ben Davis goes smoothly because of Philippa's wisdom. Being the daughter of a lawyer, she had previously drawn up a joint-tenants deed between Butch and herself. This type of deed transfers the Ben Davis automatically and without the expense of probate or the need for lawyers.

At the time Philippa had wanted me to join in on this arrangement but because of my refusal to even think about her death I did not participate. However, in keeping with Philippa's desire, Butch adds my name to the property. Then Butch and I choose to also include Sid by having a lawyer prepare a trust which we name The Ben Davis Farm Trust. Don accompanies me to the lawyer's office expecting that his name will be included on the trust but the lawyer, knowing Philippa's wishes, advises against it.

Unfortunately, this angers Don, adding to our marital discord so it becomes another source of irritation to be worked through in our therapy sessions with Bob. As a result of acquiring my Bachelor's and gaining insight into my problems, I am in a good place. I am better able to deal with the power struggle between Don and myself.

Much of my anger has dissipated, but one day during a session Bob appears to take Don's side of an argument regarding our chronic issue, finances. I am confused initially and I feel a slow burn of anger growing, not understanding why Bob is supporting Don. With my brown eyes turning black I give Bob an angry glare.

Then Bob says. "I think Don has the right idea about buying a new car."

Which is totally ridiculous under our circumstances.

Instantly my betrayal button in my solar plexus explodes, as a result of my perception that Bob is betraying me. I fly out of my chair, gather up my purse and coat and storm out of the office. When I reach the door, with all my strength I slam it shut loudly... bang!

There is an elderly woman sitting on the couch in the small waiting room, and as I storm past her I see fear on her face. When I reach the second door I slam it even louder than the first door... BANG!

Bob's office is on the second floor in an office building. Outside his office there is a long landing that overlooks the lobby. Halfway along this landing and before I reach the stairs it hits me why Bob appeared to be betraying me with his outrageous statement about Don buying a car. Instantly my rage subsides and I smile... "Oh, he is so good at what he does."

By me being able to express betrayal rage at Bob, my therapeutic father figure, I have come full circle. Repressed anger (with its roots in the abuse from my stepfather) has now been diffused. By being able to direct my anger at Bob, I will be able to deal with authority figures and any future anger in a healthy manner. It is near the end of our session so I do not return to his office.

The next week when I return, Bob opens the door and I say, "Should I throw my hat in first?"

He asks, "How did you get home?" He didn't realize I had driven directly from work and was not in the same car with Don.

He was worried when I didn't return to the session so he had walked

---

down to the parking lot with Don to assess if further follow-up was necessary. Then when I wasn't there he was even more concerned. But all was well. I complete therapy within the next two sessions.

Both because I need an escape from the tension at home and because I need to begin sorting through Philippa's belongings, I begin spending almost every weekend at the Ben Davis, a three-hour drive from Ballston Spa.

In addition I see it as an opportunity to introduce Tommy to nature, especially to my childhood playground, the meadows, woods, sugar bush and the reservoir. Most times we bring his friend Steve with us and they have fun sleeping in a tent out in the woods. And later they become ambitious and build a log house type structure with tree saplings. It is my hope that Tommy will develop a love of the land, like me. I also see it as a courage building exercise being out in the woods with nearby wildlife.

These weekend retreats give me an opportunity to reconnect with Jack and Velma Dodd. Velma joins me in rocking chairs on the screened porch of the Ben Davis, where we enjoy going through Philippa's photo albums and reminiscing.

Velma grew up on the farm that she and Jack now own. She was a childhood friend of Philippa's and enjoyed many summers with her. Velma tells me about watching Philippa train her horse to stand with all four feet on the small rock out in the meadow. We both miss Philippa and love reminiscing about her. Velma is a registered nurse and assisted in getting Philippa to the hospital on the night I received the initial call about her illness.

On Friday nights when I first arrive in Vermont, I go directly to Jack's cow barn where he is usually doing chores. As I walk into the manger, I announce, "I just had to come in the barn and inhale Vermont." This always makes him laugh. Then on Sunday afternoon I stop by his house to say goodbye. It is fun reconnecting with him as an adult. He is a sweet, kind man.

The inevitable time arrives when Don and I reach the conclusion our marriage is over. The most painful thing I ever have to do is tell Tommy his parents are going to get a divorce. He is a seventh grader, the worst possible time, as he enters middle school. I feel so guilty. All these years I have remained so vigilant to protect him from a pedophile and then I ultimately cause him to be impacted by a betrayal situation anyway.

Tommy's well-being is paramount to us both, so when we tell him about the impending divorce we emphasize that only Mom and Dad are divorcing each other and not him. We will always be his parents and in his life. We co-parent amicably, attend school functions together and share custody. But of course it is an emotional and painful time for Tommy.

I deliberately inflate the value of our house so that when I buy out Don's share of our home, he has enough money to purchase a house nearby, making it easier for Tommy to move between both homes. I also do not challenge Don for a share of his teacher's pension because I do not want to delay the divorce proceedings for Tommy's sake. But my heart breaks every time I see my little son, suitcase in hand go out the door to visit his father. He shouldn't have to be living out of a suitcase. Don moves out over Labor Day weekend 1990.

The divorce is liberating for me despite the added stress from my new high-paying job. With a college degree I obtain the Infection Control Specialist position at the nearby Hospital. It is during the height of the HIV epidemic, OSHA's bloodborne pathogen standards and Universal Precautions. In my position not only do I monitor and track all nosocomial infections but teach the New York State mandated infection control course required for all licensed healthcare providers. I teach the infection control course to four-hundred nurses and sixty-two physicians.

Every day I pray repeatedly throughout my drive to the hospital just to get through the work day. I repeat the serenity prayer over and over. It is the most challenging job I have ever had and a relatively new position for nursing. But on the brighter side it is also the job I grow the most in professionally and it also complements the gains I made in therapy.

I continue to enjoy my respite weekends at the Ben Davis and I feel a monumental responsibility to honor Philippa's memory. I am overwhelmed trying to accept that we have inherited this beautiful property and all its furnishings and personal items. To me it still belongs to Philippa, I'm just the caretaker.

Knowing how much Philippa treasured the Ben Davis, I want to be a great steward of it. Because Butch and Sid live in California, I am the trustee and in charge of restoring the Ben Davis. At the time of Philippa's death the house was three different colors due to various stages of defunct paint jobs and the carriage house roof had caved in, preventing me from acquiring fire insurance on the house until I hire a demolition company to remove the carriage house. As the men destroy the structure, one of the wooden pegs rolls out from the rubble. I reach down to retrieve it for nostalgia.

So with Butch's blessings I begin to find a way to have the house painted inside and outside. In addition to the auction inventory paper in the wooden bowl there is also a claim ticket for an English Bracket clock that Philippa had taken to a clock repairman.

I decide to go find the clock but while at the clock repair shop I am informed that it is a very valuable clock. The repairmen offers to sell it for me. It is worth eight thousand dollars so I decide to sell it in order to have the house painted. It eventually sells for five thousand and we net forty-five hundred dollars, allowing the outside of the house to be restored to a beautiful rich chocolate brown. Philippa would be pleased.

Over the next ten years the Ben Davis becomes a labor of love and allows me to slowly grieve the loss of my Guardian Angel.

Jack's Farm

The Ben Davis as it Appeared at Philippa's Death

The Ben Davis Front View as Inherited

The Ben Davis After Carriage House Demolished and House Painted

Front View After House Painted

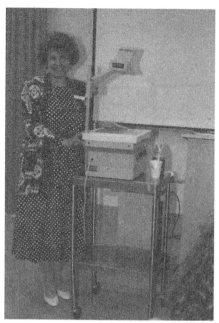

*Paula Teaching the State Mandatory Infection Control Course
to all Licensed Hospital Employees*

Photos Taken by Newspaper During a Class Break

Chapter 18
TAKING STOCK

Initially, I view my divorce as a failure. It is my first failure. All my life I have operated with the future in mind, beginning in high school, nursing, and with ensuing jobs always pushing myself toward excellence. I am never satisfied to be on the honor roll, I must be on the high honor roll, not challenged as a staff nurse, must be a nurse leader, a diploma school nursing degree is insufficient, must get a college degree and then with every job change I must have more responsibility and have a higher salary. Always reaching for the next rung of the ladder. I am a high achiever, a common trait among survivors. We see it as a way of gaining control.

In my personal life I strive to be the best mother and wife I can be, but somehow I can't reach my goal as a great wife. It is all a confusing power struggle. I am unable to accept that my husband should have the last word regarding decisions. We are basically oil and water. We share similar values but not the same goals.

I have always projected goals for at least two years in advance but that doesn't work in my marriage. However once the divorce is final, I begin implementing goals and getting long overdue projects completed.

On the day Don moves out I have a mason on the roof repairing the loose bricks on the chimney. Next Tommy and I replace the dirt path with a brick walkway leading from the side door around the house and ending at the back door. It's a fun project and makes such a difference.

Then I choose a beautiful white stockade type fence to be constructed on either side of the house to enhance the curb appeal. Little by little I catch up on house projects and at the same time I am involved with the Ben Davis projects.

Sharon comes to visit, both of us are newly divorced, both of us trim and fit and thinking about dating again but not in a hurry for it. One of my first decisions is to have a breast reduction which greatly improves my self-esteem and confidence. I am the first to venture out by joining Parents Without Partners and other singles' organizations.

But first I reconnect with a friend from my school years, initially I visit him then he follows up with visits to see me in New York. We live hundreds of miles apart, not conducive to building a relationship. However, it is a safe way to ease back into the dating world and good post-divorce damage control. We have so much fun attending the Saratoga race track. I wear my fancy hat and off to the Travers Race we go. We sit high up in the clubhouse and afterwards I take his photo with the jockeys.

Eventually I try connecting with men from the organizations and soon realize there are many valid reasons why these guys are divorced. Despite having three bouquets of red roses in the living room from three different guys, it is not at all fulfilling. Thankfully Tommy reminds me to remove two of the bouquets before my date arrives. He had sent me a dozen roses earlier in the day.

"Hey, Mom don't you think you should put the other two guys' flowers out of sight?"

Such an astute eighth grade son. We both share a good laugh about the craziness of Mom's new life.

Over the next five years, I give post-divorce dating a good chance. I am aware of safety measures and always meet these guys at public places with lots of other people nearby, from coffee shops to town squares and parks. But despite my safety measures I have some close calls.

So many disappointments; they vary from "mama's boys," sociopaths, sex addicts, gamblers, nerds, and the dysfunctional. I have difficulty screening these guys on the phone, I can't tell a player from a genuine nice guy. I did not have a normal adolescence with the usual dating experiences.

There is one guy that I do have fun with but only because he drives a red Camaro and owns a race horse. Before a date we always stop by the racetrack stable to feed the horse. I love the environment, especially being around the barns and the beautiful horses. But that is the highlight of the evening. After three dates I call it quits.

Then there is the gambler who takes me to the track and attempts to impress me with his big bets and big winnings. He gives me a winning ticket and asks me to go up to the window to cash it in for him. Imagine my shock when the teller gives me nearly two thousand dollars in cash.

He wants to celebrate by going to a hotel on our first date. I had made the mistake of riding in his car from our initial meeting spot to the nearby race track. He is so angry when I squash the hotel suggestion that he drives down Main Street of Saratoga like a maniac, screeching to a halt at my car.

Next I agree to meet a guy at the park in the parking lot. He pulls up in a pickup truck next to my car. He asks me to get in his truck so we can talk. I immediately turn down that idea and stay in my car and talk through the open window.

Within fifteen minutes he is asking me if I have ever experienced "Spanish Fly" and wants to check into a motel. I put my car in reverse and get the hell out of there!

And so it goes over the next five years. I'm often on the phone with Sharon sharing my exploits and I have her in hysterics.

To relax I continue to spend many weekends in Vermont at the Ben Davis.

The house is full of Philippa's belongings and I need to sort through everything and dispose of most of it. One bedroom has only a narrow walkway down the middle between stacks of wooden boxes stuffed with books from floor to ceiling. I order a dumpster container and have it positioned below the bedroom window.

For several weekends, I sit by the open window and review every book for first edition status, autographs or unique content before throwing it out the window into the dumpster.

It takes years to complete the process of emptying the Ben Davis farmhouse but it is also therapeutic because I'm back home where my five-year-old scribblings remain on the wallpaper near the stair landing. All those years long ago, where I had practiced writing my name and numbers on the wall. The same landing that Butch and I fell down, while I wore my new shiny shoes from Philippa.

I've been traveling to Vermont for two years when on one weekend, I learn that Velma has died. As I visit Jack I can see it is difficult for him to manage without Velma's help. He has two very arthritic knees. From the Ben Davis porch I see him slowly make his way out to the mailbox. One knee is worse than the other, so his gait is lopsided and he is bent at the waist. It is painful to watch him walk.

The local home health nursing agency provides nurses' aides to assist him with personal care, food preparation and housekeeping. At one point he hires a live-in caregiver but she is more interested in taking over his finances so he fires her. Unfortunately the proverbial line remains at the door, many others willing to take her place.

In addition, several of the Medicaid population stop by frequently requesting a few dollars, mostly for cigarettes and gas money. Jack is such a sweet, gentle soul he is unable to turn them down. He even hands out loans in the thousands of dollars, to people who will never be able to repay him. He records these loans in his twenty-fifth wedding anniversary guest book. All of this panhandling is impacting his savings.

About a year following Velma's death he says to me, "Paula, you need to move up here and take care of me."

"But Jack, I can't do that. Tommy is still in high school and besides I have this important high-paying job."

He remains tenacious and on a mission. One day near the end of Tommy's senior year and as I stop by for my usual Sunday afternoon visit, he orders, "Come in the house, I have something to talk to you about."

He leads me into his living room and has me sit right next to him on the couch. Jack asks, "Are you aware that your farm and my farm were once one big farm?"

"Yes, I remember seeing that in the old deeds that Philippa has. I think it was because they wanted to divide the big farm between their two sons."

Jack nods in agreement and then asks, "How would you like it if our farms were one big farm again?"

I am startled at what he is saying and not sure I understand. He continues "If you move in with me and take care of me it will be that way again." Jack is offering to leave me his farm in return for nursing care. I am shocked and in disbelief.

"Besides," he continues, "you have run out of excuses. Tommy will be off to college in a few months." Wow... he has given this a lot of thought.

I am a little speechless and not sure what to say, but I tell him I will think about his offer. He walks me back out to my car and I get on the road for New York.

Here I am, a fifty-two-year-old divorcee totally disillusioned with men my age, with no hope of finding a new spouse to share my remaining years. When a sweet, wonderful, highly respected much older man has just boldly propositioned me to become his live-in nurse. What am I going to do?

Tommy is accepted at Clarkson, an engineering school located in the Adirondacks and will be leaving for college at the end of August 1995, about three months away. Don and I have taken turns visiting various campuses with him. I am delighted on the day Tommy and I visit Clarkson when he announces almost as soon as we are out of the car, "Look, Mom there is grass and not concrete," with a big smile on his face. Maybe some of the Ben Davis experience has resonated with him.

I've been thinking about Jack's proposition and talking with Tommy, Sharon, Dottie, Marie and Ray about the idea, seeking their feedback and opinions. Tommy likes the idea because "Then you won't be all alone when I leave, Mom." He knows and likes Jack because of our many trips to Vermont during the past five years.

I send Sharon a copy of my pros and cons list and we discuss it thoroughly. I have determined if I accept his offer and then for whatever reason it doesn't work out, I could always move across the road to the Ben Davis house and get a job at the nearby hospital. So I have a backup plan.

Marie and Ray, always protective of me, take it one step further and ask if they can come to Vermont and meet Jack, and of course I am thrilled so we make arrangements for a weekend visit. They have been at my side for years and have seen me be impulsive, sometimes to my detriment, especially if a man is involved.

We all gather in Vermont and I am able to sleep everyone at the Ben Davis because of the five bedrooms. The decor is a little worn but it is a functional house. Having heard my childhood stories Marie and Ray are delighted to actually see the Ben Davis.

Jack's home is diagonally across the road. It is a large white two story farmhouse situated on a knoll, surrounded by magnificent maple trees with a rolling lawn sloping down to the red cow barn. Eighty acres of meadows, pasture and a sugar bush complete the property. It has a majestic, quintessential Vermont farmhouse presentation.

Despite being in his seventies and having a missing arm, Jack continues to operate a functioning farm, and he maintains the same schedule of the past fifty years. He rises early to milk his cows twice a day and he remains a good herdsmen, never missing the cycles of his cows in order to have them timely artificially inseminated. Cows must give birth to a calf every thirteen to fourteen months to maintain milk production. But in recent years it is a struggle for Jack to continue farming due to severe pain from arthritis in both knees.

But his faithful hired man, Sonny, despite having his own struggle with alcohol, shows up every day to help Jack with chores. Jack does the milking of the thirty cows and Sonny throws down the hay from the hay mow, cleans the barn by running the gutter cleaner and scraping out all the manure and takes care of the calves in the calf barn, some of the youngest require being fed by bottle. It is a lot of work even for a young man but Jack being a proud man hangs in, determined to pay off the mortgage before he retires.

Because of his courage, calm nature and his mechanical acumen especially regarding farm tractors, Jack is well known throughout the community, he is an inspiration and highly respected. I think I am drawn to Jack because of his courage and his ability to never draw attention to his obvious disability. He always finds a way to accomplish whatever challenge appears on the horizon. He is a typical stoic Vermonter.

I am not sure if Jack realizes he is being interviewed and vetted by my support group, but he passes with flying colors. They all fall in love with this seventy-four-year-old white-haired man with the twinkly blue eyes. He is soft spoken, with a dry sense of humor and has the unique ability to live in the moment. He loves to tease and can spin a yarn with everyone believing it until those twinkly blue eyes give him away.

Perhaps because of his devastating accident as a young man, he understands and appreciates the importance of each day. People are at the top of his priority list and he is always interested in their well-being. Jack always recalls the previous conversation he has with someone and consistently picks up where they ended. Everyone loves the personal touch they receive from him.

Marie and Ray are near the same age as Jack so their conversations flow easily and the three of them become instant friends. Marie likes to knit and crochet and when she notices Jack's hand without any fingers, she asks if he would wear a mitten if she custom-made one for him. He says, "Yes, that would be great." To make a pattern Marie has Jack place his hand on plain white paper and then she traces around his hand where there are no fingers and only a stub for a thumb.

I remain a little hesitant about resigning from my job because I still need to financially help Tommy get through Clarkson. I've never had any difficulty getting a job but I don't know the job market in rural Vermont. I have to do more research and come to a careful and thorough decision. I need to take my time and not be impulsive. I tell Jack I have yet to make my decision but I am giving his suggestion serious consideration.

In the meantime I continue to help Tommy plan for college and I organize a graduation party in the backyard, complemented by the new brick walkway, new steps and stockade fence. I have the party catered and Don, the Czech relatives Eileen, her husband Dennis and daughter Sonya, Marie, Ray, Dottie, "Aunt Carol and Uncle Phil" and his friends are in attendance. My gift to Tommy is a small photo album in the theme of "This is your life..." photos from birth to the present time.

So after consulting with friends and doing my research for future employment I tell Jack I will be happy to move in and take care of him. The only request I have, is that he give me a power of attorney for health care. I do not want to be in the same position I was with Philippa and watch him on life support for months. There are so many things to accomplish before I can transition to Vermont.

I decide to rent my house instead of selling it and fortunately, there is a nearby naval station with submarine trainees arriving every six months in need of housing. Because I am confident that I will have ample potential tenants I prepare the house with new carpeting and freshen the bathroom.

Finally, the worst job of all, packing up an entire house. It is a nightmare; realizing I can't take everything I reserve a large basement room and together Tommy and I build a door using folding blinds. It is a monumental job for us without the know-how or proper tools, but together we persevere and secure the room. Simultaneously, I pack the house and get Tommy ready for college. He is a great help with the packing of the house contents.

I am extremely happy to be leaving my stressful Infection Control job. At my going away party the hospital administrator attends and compliments me for my performance. Out of all the surrounding hospitals, we were the only hospital that was not fined for noncompliance with the OSHA Bloodborne Standard. The fines imposed to the other hospitals were in the thousands of dollars. Because of the AIDS epidemic, the Bloodborne standard was crucial for prevention and it had been my job to teach it and enforce it with all the hospital caregivers.

New Brick Walkway in Progress

Paula with her Vetting Group

Ray, Marie, and Dottie Getting to Know Jack

Sharon and Paula both Slim and Trim, Post Divorces

Tommy and Steve's Log Cabin During Construction in the Woods

PAULA CZECH

*Sharon and Paula at the Newly
Built Log Cabin*

Paula and Elaine (Pudgie) Friends Again as Adults

Dennis and Eileen with Daughter Sonya Visiting Paula in NY

Chapter 19
MY VERMONT

Don and I both accompany Tommy on his first day at Clarkson. It is both a joyous and sad day for me. Emotionally it is as heart-wrenching as the day I put my little kindergarten son on the bus for the first day of school. The campus is beautiful, situated on a hill with several buildings and a cluster of dorms in one area. Fortunately, Tommy will be rooming with his best friend, which is very comforting for me.

I am sobbing as I walk away from the dorm. The umbilical cord is finally cut, it will never be the same. Some parents hover over their freshman college students, calling them weekly and insisting they come home frequently. But I see this time as Tommy's moment to mature and become an independent adult, reminiscent of my own experience.

In hindsight my approach was a little harsh and I'm sorry for my actions, but I didn't know any other way. Although my check-ins with Tommy during his college years were fewer than most parents, he later told me, "Mom, I'm glad you did it the way you did, because I matured and got a good job right away, while many of my friends in their mid-twenties are still living at home."

I would often say to Don, "When Tommy turns eighteen he is going to be able to stand on his own two feet and fly right!" I had been so frustrated with adults who did not have a sense of direction despite having a college degree.

On a deeper level I also recognize my actions and expectations are a direct result of my childhood. At a very early age I learned that I could only depend on myself. On a subconscious level and for self-preservation reasons, I have always maintained some emotional distance, not sure when I will become vulnerable or betrayed. This makes me fiercely independent and with a strong will, but it is not conducive to forming male relationships because men like to be problem solvers and my approach shuts out most men. If I can't solve my problems they will go unsolved because it is extremely difficult for me to ask for help.

Moving day finally arrives, I rent the largest box truck available and a dear friend Frank, Steve's father (Tommy's childhood friend) voluntarily and unexpectedly appears and packs the truck. He manages his own Mail and More store and his expertise with packing makes all the difference. Without his help the truck would never have been packed; I had grossly under estimated the amount of work and remain indebted to him.

Around noon, I climb up on the high step of the truck and into the driver's seat of the twenty-six foot box truck to make the five-hour trip to Jack's. I am having fun, I'm on an adventure and I love the excitement of driving this big truck with no one with me. The only concern I have is to make sure when I stop for breaks that I choose a place that does not require backing out of the parking lot and I succeed.

When I reach the Davis Road, I am within one mile of Jack's, and I begin blowing the truck horn signaling to the neighborhood Paula has arrived in Vermont! The neighbors must think I am crazy.

Unknown to me, some of Jack's distant relatives, having heard through the grapevine that someone is moving in with Jack, have come to scrutinize me. So it seems both Jack and I are being vetted by our mutual parties. I think it is funny.

As I turn the huge truck into the driveway, the maple tree limbs brush along the top of the truck, I see Jack with a huge grin on his face and four strangers standing in the yard. Jack would later tell me he had not seen them in years.

I get out and give Jack a big hug and he introduces me to the relatives. I can tell they are suspicious of me by their cool response. But Jack doesn't allow them to spoil his joy. Later he tells me, "When I saw you drive in my feet were floating off the ground I was so happy!" He is such a sweet man.

Sonny takes charge and tells me to drive the truck down over the lawn then back it up to the door. He has a couple of other guys with him ready to unload the truck. The distant relatives leave.

I decide to take the upstairs front bedroom overlooking the Ben Davis farmhouse. In the morning I get up early so I can surprise Jack by baking blueberry muffins, but suddenly the door opens and a neighbor is standing in the kitchen. I feel very exposed still in my bathrobe.

He asks, "Where is Jack?"

I say, "He is still sleeping."

He quickly moves past me, walks through the dining room and living room, and into Jack's bedroom. I am in shock that someone has invaded our privacy so boldly. I'm thinking what is going on? Then I hear loud voices in the bedroom and I am alarmed.

Within a few minutes the man leaves as abruptly as he arrived. Jack comes to the kitchen and says the guy is upset over not being able to continue using the Ben Davis meadows. In recent years I have rented the meadows to Jack for the hay but apparently he has been subletting it to this guy. Probably because of his decline in health or perhaps because he couldn't say no to a bully. I find this encounter annoying and make a mental note to deal with it one day.

Later in the week one of Jack's wonderful nephews and his two kids come to meet me. I had fondly remembered the blackberry bushes with the huge berries up in the woods, so earlier in the day I had gathered a big pail of them and made an upside-down blackberry cake. During their visit I tell them my nostalgic story about going to the woods to pick blackberries and that I felt like a little kid again. I serve the cake with homemade whipped cream. The conversation between all of us flows easily with many laughs. Later Jack receives the feedback from his brother, "She is perfect for him."

One evening we drive to East Fairfield to visit Jack's youngest brother Ken and his wife Avis. They have a lovely retirement home with a gorgeous mountain view that they built on the same property as their farm.

We have only been back home a few minutes when Jack receives a call from his sister-in-law. She is calling to tell him that Ken commented after we left "She is just like us."

So apparently I am also passing with flying colors.

Over the first few weeks, I continue to unpack and blend my furniture in with Jack's. The only downside is all these various characters who continue to walk into the house without knocking at any time of the day or night. It always startles me and makes me feel uncomfortable. Mostly they want something free from Jack.

Finally, I tell Jack I can't continue living like I am in "The Burton Community Center." He understands and together we decide to start locking the door. This helps, but it doesn't stop the steady stream of cars in and out of the driveway. The panhandlers continue to ask for money for beer, cigarettes and a few more dollars to pay the rent.

Jack tells me it is okay to tell them to go away; he is not able to make it stop but is perfectly okay if I do the honors. So I assume the role of the bad guy with his full blessing.

One Saturday afternoon Dottie, Marie and Ray are visiting. We are all sitting in rocking chairs on the screened porch when an old car rattles into the driveway. A young guy jumps out of the car and runs into Jack's workshop, retrieves a large wrench, and starts back to the car with a wave toward the porch.

I jump out of my chair, step off the porch and yell, "Wait a minute, young man! What do you think you are doing?"

"I need this to change my brakes."

"Oh no you don't.... Put it back right now. Jack is not giving away any more tools or money. Please spread the word, the days of taking advantage of Jack have come to a screeching halt."

In anger he throws the wrench on the ground and squeals his tires on the way out of the driveway. I believe because he could see Jack on the porch, he realized Jack was in agreement with my declaration and he never returned. Marie and Ray are stunned to see what has been happening to Jack.

For the first few months I feel like a bouncer because there are so many people reluctant to get off the Jack gravy train.

But despite the bizarre activities, Jack and I are having so much fun living together. We are compatible, we both have quiet demeanors and are comfortable sitting and reading next to one another. Jack reads his paper every morning and his farm journals. I laugh a lot around him. Joy is in the air.

I take all his problems from his shoulders by helping him in every way possible to include his personal care. None of it feels like a burden to me, I enjoy helping him. Of course I also take over the routine household duties. The first time I vacuumed using the brand new vac Jack recently purchased was quite an experience for him. For the record, I really dislike vacuuming because the cord is always getting twisted, the vac is too heavy and I'm always running into the door jambs.

With his typical dry humor, after observing me for a while he says, "Boy, you are a little rough on rats aren't you?" I look up and see that twinkle in his eyes and burst out laughing. I promise to be more careful.

The best part of the day is right after supper when we take drives out on the back roads. I especially love the remote roads where the trees on both sides overhang and meet in the middle high above the road, making it appear as if we are driving through a tunnel. Somehow Jack is able to find a different road every night with a tree canopy. One night as dusk approaches, I am driving down a hill when I see something ahead in the middle of the road.

"Jack, what is that?"

He answers "I think it might be a bear," and sure enough as we get closer and see its identifying loping gait we know for sure. I slow down to a crawl and watch it eventually move over to the edge and then disappear into the woods. I am thrilled to have seen a black bear out in nature.

We explore rural roads bordered by brooks, streams with waterfalls and swimming holes. Sometimes we are so deep in the woods there is only a single lane with tufts of grass sprouting in the middle. Jack takes me up a mountain to visit a well-hidden covered bridge that is no longer safe to travel over by car but is open to foot traffic.

I love the serenity, the silence and beauty of this spot. Standing on the bridge, situated high above a river and peeking through broken boards, we look down and listen to the waterfall rippling over the large boulders with the river twisting through the trees, absolutely breathtaking.

Back at Jack's I continue to make a home for us both by planting lots of flowers. I add some flowers to a sap bucket and attach it to the first maple tree at the entrance of the driveway. Next I find an old wheelbarrow across the road at the Ben Davis and bring it over to plant a large display of flowers in it. I position the wheelbarrow on its side so it looks like the flowers are spilling out and place it near the mailbox. Jack is enjoying everything I am doing and I am having so much fun.

I happen to mention I would like something white strolling around the yard. Not sure if it should be a peacock, geese or ducks, but I have a romantic notion of enhancing the majestic feel of Jack's home.

"Ask, and it will be given you." One night after dark when I am finishing up the dishes, Sonny knocks on the door. I go to open it and there he is with a big white goose in his arms and he walks right into the kitchen with it.

"Oh my goodness, you can't bring that in here! What are you doing?"

He gives me his signature one tooth big grin. "I got you your goose."

"Where did you get it so quickly?"

"I got her from a woman who I do yard work for, she asked me to find Molly a new home. So I put her on the seat next to me and came right over."

I am flabbergasted but excited that I will have something white strolling up and down the driveway to complement my flowers. Sonny is always so willing to please and be helpful. He is very loyal and good to Jack. Of course he is also "three sheets to the wind," I can smell the booze. I thank him very much and tell him to put the goose in the barn for the night.

The next day I decide we also need a gander to complement the goose, so within a few days good ole Sonny arrives with another goose. To be funny, I paint a sign and place it beneath the sap bucket. In big letters the sign reads: THE GOOSE IS ON THE LOOSE AND THE GANDER IS MEANDERING.

Never did I expect the response I receive from visitors, everyone is stopping at the entrance of the driveway and not getting out of their cars. Being country folk they are aware of the mean reputations of geese who can attack people by hitting them with their flapping wings and pinch with their bills.

So everyone sees my sign as a warning and not as a joke. Fortunately, my geese seem to be easygoing and do not attack anyone. I find the entire thing humorous and it adds to the fun I am having living with Jack. In some ways I am reliving my childhood but under healthy circumstances.

I also enjoy helping Jack in the barn. He has three horses with one of the mares expecting a foal any day now. We are both so excited. One day as we walk down across the lawn toward the barn Jack says to me, "It is too bad we didn't get together when we were both much younger. We would have had a great farm!"

It is Jack's way of telling me he is so happy and appreciative of my help. His wife did not work alongside him in the barn and I obviously love being in the barn.

One day while I am brushing the burdock out of Sam's tail, one of

Jack's horses, Jack says in awe, "You are not afraid."

I'm at risk of being kicked if I pull too hard, and I say no, I want her tail to be pretty again. All those childhood years long ago spent being around the cows, horses and pigs are part of my soul.

The next morning when we go to the barn, Taffy has given birth and she is very protective. I am eager to pet the new foal but Taffy curls her lip and snarls at me, I back away immediately. She is a good Mama. Standing next to Taffy is a beautiful copper-colored baby. Jack and I are thrilled and decide to name her Penny.

I've been with Jack for about three months when he suddenly begins asking me for milk of magnesia and seems to be belching frequently. Because this is a change in his health status and because I recognize it as a red flag, being a change in his bowel habits, I write a note for him to take to his physician. (I already have a part-time job with a local Home Health Agency and I'm unavailable to go to the appointment with him.)

When I get home from work that afternoon Jack reports he has been scheduled for a colonoscopy and that the doctor told him "that was the kind of note he appreciated receiving."

Over the next two weeks Jack has several more tests and is found to have a lemon sized rectal polyp that eventually tests positive for cancer. He is scheduled for surgery and is told he will have a colostomy. Needless to say Jack is discouraged. I remain optimistic and assure him I will be able to take care of the colostomy for him.

I am on my way to visit him at the hospital one evening when an incredible moment occurs. There is not much traffic on the road but there is a large pickup truck behind me and it is near dusk. We both have our headlights lit.

Suddenly I hit black ice. At first I am able to control my car but as I enter a curve I lose it and my car does a rapid spin around. My car is now in the same lane but facing in the direction of the oncoming pickup truck.

Immediately a sense of extreme calm washes over me, everything is in slow motion, the pickup truck is heading directly for me. His headlights are within two feet of my car bumper when I think to myself, "I wonder if he can turn away from me." In that instant, the truck turns to the right, leaves the road, bounces down over a slight embankment onto a lawn and finally comes to a stop inches from a garage in someone's driveway.

I immediately move my car to right side of the road and park it out of the way of traffic. I jump out of my car and run to see how the driver of the truck is doing. He has the same impulse to come check on me and we both meet in the middle of the road.

We confirm that we are both okay. I say to him, "I can't believe you were able to turn away at the last minute," and he says "Me neither."

Again I view this as another of my serendipitous and divine moments, it confirms my belief that I have a "car angel." There is no other explanation, there is no doubt that a head-on crash should have occurred.

Jack remains in the hospital for three days. Once home I take over his post-operative care and his surgeon assures him he should be able to reverse the colostomy in three months so he won't need to wear the bag forever. Jack is very relieved.

I am enjoying my part-time job which requires me to drive out to the surrounding towns and provide nursing care to patients in their homes. The Director of Nursing soon asks me to be a consultant regarding Infection Control because the agency is applying for JCAHO accreditation. (Joint Commission Accreditation Hospital Organization.)

I assist in developing infection control policies and procedures and teach infection control to two hundred registered nurses and nurses' aides. Setting up these procedures in a patient's home is a little more difficult than in the hospital environment but I enjoy the challenge. I receive a wonderful note of gratitude from the Director of Nursing when they successfully receive their accreditation.

On a beautiful sunny spring day both Jack and I are excited because Tommy is coming home for a visit. His legal address is Vermont and it is time to have his 1987 Honda Prelude inspected. I doubt it would ever pass in New York State but with Jack's savvy Vermont ingenuity he makes it happen. Tommy and Jack patch the rusted areas with some bondo, and once the areas are dry they spray paint over the patches. Then off they go to the garage to get a new inspection sticker.

Later that night after supper Jack asks Tommy to open his safe for him. It is impossible for Jack to kneel down to put in the safe combination. I overhear their conversation as Jack reads the combination aloud. Tommy sits on the floor in front of the safe. "Okay Tommy, it is 84 right, 56 left and then 42 right," but Tommy interrupts, "Are you sure? It is usually three times to the left."

With Jack's usual dry delivery he says, "So Tommy... you do this often?"

Tommy bursts into laughter and is rolling around the floor in hysterics.

I love seeing the two of them connecting so well. Every time Tommy visits, Jack questions him about a girlfriend and encourages him to date. They have a neat relationship. Of course Jack has a history of mentoring young men because of all those years he and Velma took in the troubled high school boys.

Another funny moment occurs the next morning when Tommy comes downstairs for breakfast.

"JACK WHAT WAS THAT AWFUL NOISE, IT WENT ON AND ON?"... Then as if on cue... the rooster crows, and Tommy yells... "THERE IT IS AGAIN!!!!"

Poor Jack is laughing so hard he almost falls off his chair. It has been a wonderful visit.

Jack and I have several frequent visitors to the farm. My family and friends consider it a real treat and drive long distances to spend a weekend. And of course we love having company, it is always a lively visit with lots of laughter. And being around my laugh is not for the faint of heart. I have a very loud laugh that reverberates off the walls. Poor Tommy cringes when my laugh erupts when we are in a public place.

Oftentimes Jack and I are in the middle of a project and because the work never stops on the farm, we have no choice but to involve our visitors. At future visits, they love to tease us about providing free labor.

My cousin Eileen likes to tease me about the time I had her husband Dennis cut a huge limb with a chain saw that was in danger of falling across the main electric wire to the house. After he cut the limb into chunks suitable to fit in the old furnace, Eileen carried them down to the low ceiling basement of the Ben Davis. It was a labor intensive job, carrying heavy wood and hunched over in order to duck beneath the header of the door. I think this is when Eileen finally reached her limit with cousin Paula's chores.

Jack and I never claimed to be equal opportunity hosts, so one never knows what project will be on the weekend agenda. But despite it everyone keeps coming back for more punishment and fun. The farm experience is so different than their city lives and jobs. To me, life on the farm is always an adventure and I love every minute of it.

I had been living with Jack for one year, when he says to me, "You know when my sister and brothers retired they all built new homes on their farm properties."

"Would you like to build a new house?"

"Well, it's out of the question because I have promised you this farm."

"Jack, I already have a farm. I don't need two farms." He smiles.

So over the next few months we continue to discuss building a new house and selling his farm. But we hit an early stumbling block during the survey. We both chose the same potential house lot on Jack's property but for different reasons. Jack prefers it because of his memories of bringing the cows to the barn over this parcel of land. I chose the right-of-way section of the same parcel because of fond memories of riding on the horse-drawn sled to the Ben Davis sugar bush.

The surveyor asks, "Jack, did you sell some land in this area?"

"No, but I did sell thirty acres to a neighbor, but it is way up in the back."

The surveyor says to me, "I'm not going to continue with the survey today, I need to do some follow up and I suggest you guys consult a lawyer."

I am instantly alarmed, what is wrong? I can also see the worry on Jack's face. Back at the house he shares the story of selling thirty acres to a neighbor, but the parcel is located far away from where we plan to build. And Jack assures me he had explained to the neighbor that all three of us would be sharing the right of way.

After due diligence, we discover that the neighbor, also a surveyor, had deeded himself a one-hundred-foot wide right-of-way directly over the current tractor path right-of-way, basically the width of an interstate highway. He totally usurped the shared right-of-way that was meant to be "for as long as grass grows and water flows," in other words forever. Because of the width it impacts the site of our future house lot.

Jack is devastated and explains he totally trusted the neighbor and therefore did not attend the closing because it was chore time and he had to be in the barn.

I am protective of Jack and determined to have a legal resolution. We begin with a local attorney in the area, but he is stonewalling instead of proceeding with Jack's case. It is a small community and he doesn't want to take on such a controversial situation. My anger is rising because Jack has been betrayed. I tell Jack we have no choice but to seek legal counsel in Burlington. I am not going to allow anyone to take advantage of Jack.

We make an appointment with the most prestigious law firm in the city and they agree to take on the case, partly because Jack does not have a dishonest bone in his body, and they can see his authenticity.

Over the next three years I act as a quasi-paralegal by researching the old deeds written in calligraphy at the Burton Town Office for the law firm. Burlington is one hour away so it saves the law firm time and us money. Eventually the case is presented in Superior Court before a jury of Jack's peers. They all fall in love with Jack and believe his clear, truthful accounting of the deal between him and his neighbor, and totally reject the neighbor's incongruent story.

During the three years it takes for Jack to win his case, I draw up house and barn plans for Jack's new retirement home. It takes many drafts as Jack and I describe our wish list. I come up with the idea of having the gutter cleaner located around the perimeter of the barn to make it easier for Jack to muck out the horse stalls. By the time the lawsuit is resolved I know every inch of our new place and we present it to a contractor. But first we must sell Jack's farm.

I design a sales brochure with photos and distribute them around town and place them in the bed and breakfast homes. Additionally I advertise in the newspapers. We had determined the sale price by consulting with a realtor earlier, but to save the commission, I tell Jack I believe I can sell it.

Within two weeks we receive an offer from a new physician moving to the area from Connecticut who sees the brochure at a Bed and Breakfast. The stars are aligned. The only issue is they want to move in before the closing. I agree but I make them give us a twenty-percent down payment on the day they move. Of course our new home is not yet built so Jack and I move across the road into the Ben Davis. We pack up Jack's house and store the contents in a tractor trailer and park it at the Ben Davis.

The construction of the new home is so exciting and fun. While I am at work Jack oversees the project and then I do a daily walk through after work. If I notice any issues I call the contractor and get them resolved. At one point the contractor wants to move the slider six inches to the left and I tell him no because then my china hutch will not fit in the space. I have planned every inch of this house to include the location of all the furniture.

On the day we move in, the contractor thinks he is going to challenge my earlier decision regarding the china hutch and is very impressed when he realizes I was absolutely correct.

Our new custom-built oversize ranch is stunning. With Jack's handicap in mind I had the contractor install door latches that open with Jack pushing down on them instead of trying to turn door knobs, instead of steps we have a ramp inside the garage to access the kitchen, there is a short flight of steps leading to his workshop in the basement, there are handrails in his bathroom and an oversize shower with a seat.

I had designed the kitchen and screened porch as an exact replica of his farmhouse. As a very special surprise I found two photos of Jack on his tractors, with one that includes his beloved dog, Jenny, and brought them to an artist. He reproduced the photos as stained glass panels and then I had the contractor install them without Jack's knowledge in the cupboard doors over the sink. We also added lights so the stained glass was backlit for a beautiful effect. Jack was so surprised and pleased when we revealed them at the last moment.

We move in during the Spring of 1999, four years after my arrival in Vermont. Extremely busy years, but well worth the legal battle to retrieve Jack's land. Jack's case appears in a Vermont law journal with the title: Farmer Sues Surveyor And Wins. As a result of Jack's case it becomes illegal for only one attorney to represent both parties in a real estate transaction.

Jack and I settle into our new home, all bright and shiny new. It is immaculate and it is so easy to maintain. However, for the record I still dislike vacuuming. Every morning when I walk through the house to the kitchen I say to myself, "I love our new house!"

Jack gave me an amazing gift by giving me an opportunity to return to Vermont, enabling me to rewrite my history in the comfort of nature, my spiritual connection. The years I spend with Jack are the happiest of my entire life, other than the birth and constant joy of my wonderful son, Tommy.

Sexual abuse has had a lifelong impact on me and has shaped my destiny, but because of those intuitive, loving advocates (my Angels), I had the strength to pursue a better life and fight to overcome the "damaged goods" syndrome.

Unlike many with my same story I did not become a runaway, a prostitute, or become drug/alcohol addicted. But I did not escape unscathed. Probably the most damaging is my struggle with emotional intimacy. It is my instinct to be self-protective, so by being unable to be vulnerable and totally trusting, I have not been successful with male relationships. And perhaps the most annoying, because it is noticeable by others, is a heightened startle reflex, causing me to jump/flinch at the slightest unexpected noise.

And lastly, I have great difficulty maintaining a healthy weight. Years ago I learned that sexual abuse victims use weight gain as a defense against future perpetrators. I don't know if that is true, but I do know I am constantly dieting just to stop my weight from spiraling upward.

But despite the early onset of sexual abuse, at the age of three, I am grateful that I have a wonderful family, a large group of close friends, and that I was able to become a registered nurse, marry and give birth to a wonderful son.

During my adult Vermont years, I am treasured, appreciated and loved by a sweet man twenty-seven years older, but he is young at heart and I am an old soul so it works. We have a platonic relationship, but we are soul mates in many ways as we share similar histories. We have both overcome severe trauma, have faced challenges that have taken us to our knees, but with our strong wills and courage we have persevered. As Jack would say, we have "grit."

We love the simple things, nature, horses, farm animals, the sweet freshly mowed hay and most of all people. We both laugh easily and often, the deep scars of yesterday are in the past.

It is my hope that my story inspires an army of angels to observe all children in their communities and to shower love upon any child showing signs of distress. A little love and praise makes all the difference.

In June both Jack and I attend Tommy's graduation from Clarkson. He graduates with a double degree, BS Computer Science and BS minor Mathematics. On Monday he will begin his new job as an engineer and we are both so proud of him. I plan to add my manuscript to the Black Leather Satchel and pass it on to Tommy.

Paula About to Depart for Vermont, Driving the Moving Truck

The Creamery Covered Bridge Tucked Away in the Woods

The BLACK LEATHER SATCHEL

Jack Reading the Sunday Paper

Jack Driving Sam on the Buggy (note the location of the reins)

PAULA CZECH

Taffy with her new Foal, Penny

Molly and Sam Strolling

Silly Sharon on the Manure Pile

Sharon, Paula and Dottie "Picking Eggs"

PAULA CZECH

Cousin Dennis with Chain Saw

Cousin Eileen working hard at Paula's weekend chores.

The BLACK LEATHER SATCHEL

Thanksgiving, Dennis in Full Deer Hunting Gear

Aunt Julia, Uncle Al and Cousin Virginia Visiting New House

PAULA CZECH

Dottie Feeding Carrots to Horses, Sugar, Ginger and Penny

The New Farm, Springhill Farm

Ecstatically Happy Jack and Paula

TOPICS FOR FURTHER DISCUSSION

Sexual abuse is defined as any sexual act imposed upon a child who lacks emotional, maturational and cognitive development. When an adult with dominance and power abuses this power by engaging in sexual acts with a subordinate child, it is the ultimate betrayal. It is also an abuse of power if an older adolescent sexually abuses a younger child. A child naturally relies on an adult for basic needs: nurturing, safety, food and shelter, and when these needs are denied the child loses trust. (1) The imbalance of power allows the perpetrator to coerce the child into sexual compliance using broken promises, bribery and threats. The adult who has experienced ultimate betrayal as a child, has issues with trust and anger and therefore has difficulty forming healthy relationships. Not only do perpetrators steal childhood innocence, but they severely impact adult happiness. I believe sexual abuse results in the murder of the soul.

There are several signs of childhood sexual abuse, but for my purpose I will describe the symptoms experienced by me. Childhood sexual abuse is unlike any of the other forms of abuse because depending on the age of the child he/she may have no memories of the abuse because he/she lacks the cognitive ability to understand what has occurred. Many times the first recollection is revealed through a flashback memory as an adult.

In my situation I do recall my earliest memories of the abuse perpetrated during my young years, but I didn't realize there was a connection between the abuse and my emotional suffering until my mid-twenties when I entered therapy for clarification of my tumultuous life.

Despite being aware of my intense anger and an inferiority complex experienced as a young woman, I didn't understand the source of it. I was abused between the ages of three and eleven by my stepfather, but I have lived a lifetime with the aftermath. Fortunately, because I received exceptional mental health treatment from a psychologist and a psychiatrist, I have experienced a higher quality of life than most with similar childhoods, but I did lose most of my youth due to the abuse trauma.

THE BEHAVIORAL AND EMOTIONAL SYMPTOMS EXHIBITED BY ME AND EXAMPLES FROM MY MEMOIR WERE:
See chapters for specifics.

1. **Damaged Goods Syndrome:** a belief by a child that there has been physical injury done even if there was no pain experienced. I believed "there was something broken down there" so I did not engage in the usual teenage make-out sessions or in self-exploration until I was in therapy as an adult. Many victims have a fear that they have internal damage and will never be able to have children. See Chapters 3, 6.

2. **Guilt/shame:** occurs because the child is taught to keep the abuse a secret and because she doesn't make it stop, feels responsible for it. Of course as a child and under the control of an all-powerful adult she is helpless. If a victim does reveal the secret, she may be burdened with the responsibility that her revelations may disrupt the family dynamics. The child experiences debilitating shame as she becomes aware of societal norms. See Chapters 6, 8.

3. **Fear:** child fears further incidences, physical damage, and future disability and may experience fear from sleep disturbances to include terrifying nightmares. In my situation my nightmares occurred while I was in therapy. I would see my stepfather hanging by a rope while I repeatedly stabbed him with a knife. I only share this to exemplify the intensity of my anger. As an adult I experience fear of emotional intimacy and lack the social skills to engage in flirting. Instead, I emotionally freeze. During my adolescence when I would have been dating and learning to connect with my male peers, I was at home cooking for the family, care-taking my brothers, and doing housework. It is nearly impossible for me to develop a romantic relationship; however, sexual performance is not a problem. See Chapters 3, 6.

4. **Depression:** as a result the victim may become withdrawn, sad, act

out with self-mutilation or have suicidal ideation. See Chapter 15.

5. **Low self-esteem:** victims will often express feeling tainted, like scum, or have distorted self-images, feeling obese when in actuality they are slender. May act out sexually due to inadequate social skills. See Chapters 6, 17.

6. **Repressed anger:** on the surface may appear passive and compliant but inwardly seething with hostility and anger at the perpetrator. The victim is unable to express her anger because of the perpetrator's abuse of power and authority. The repressed anger and rage is often displayed toward innocent bystanders, friends, siblings, and others in the community. Frequently a feeling of **betrayal** triggers an eruption of rage by the victim. I expressed my anger toward store clerks, those in authority, playmates, and many others, as well as using my car as a potential weapon by consistently speeding. See Chapters 4, 7, 8, 9.

7. **Blurred boundaries and role confusion:** the premature and inappropriate sexual activity with an adult causes a great deal of confusion for the child and is magnified if the perpetrator is a family member. The child is confused by the relationship with the perpetrator, therefore the blurred boundaries between the child and adult cause the child to have role confusion. For an adult who is in a position of power and authority to have a sexual relationship with a child is criminal. See Chapter 9.

8. **Care-taking or parentification:** as a result of role confusion, the victim assumes more adult responsibilities like meal preparation, child care and general housework. Because the victim is involved in more adult responsibilities he/she is alienated from the usual social activities of peers. Therefore, the victim may not experience the usual kissing, petting or emotional intimacy of the teenager years. See Chapters 9, 11.

9. **Fire setting:** young children may use fire setting as a result of curiosity or as a cry for help due to the stress in their lives. See Chapter 3.

10. **Post-traumatic stress disorder:** is manifested by several symptoms as a result of emotional or physical trauma like:

Heightened startle reflex: as a reaction to sudden and unexpected sound.

Hypervigilance: scanning one's surroundings with extreme watchfulness and anxiety.

Flashbacks: very early memories previously not recalled to include nightmares.

Dissociation: spacing out/blocking out or escaping mentally during the abuse.

I continue to experience the heightened startle reflex.
See Chapters 2, 3, 9, 15

11. **Promiscuity:** victim attempting to seek love and affection by using sex due to poor social skills, and because it was a learned experience as a victim of sexual abuse. See Chapter 14.

12. **Suicidal Ideation:** as a result of overwhelming depression, feelings of unworthiness, and having no hope. See Chapter 14.

References used for above:
American Psychological Association
(1) Handbook of Clinical Intervention in Child Sexual Abuse, Suzanne M. Sgroi, M.D.

Fortunately for me, I was able to heal over the course of three years by being open and willing to do the work of therapy. I no longer suffer from these symptoms except for fear of emotional intimacy and the startle reflex. However, most of my youthful years were sacrificed because of sexual abuse.

It is my opinion that all perpetrators must be stopped with the initial arrest. They never stop abusing... they never change their behaviors. The laws should allow that they are immediately incarcerated for life. They destroy the lives of children/adults whether it is a one-time incident or a long slow process. We must be more observant and intercede on behalf of all children exhibiting the trauma behaviors from sexual abuse.

It is my goal that adults will become vigilant when in the presence of children and will learn to recognize damaged children. I hope they increase their observation skills and take action when they see a child with poor self-esteem, no self-confidence, withdrawal or isolating behaviors, children who steal or lie, set fires, or have an age-inappropriate interest in sexuality, and especially aggressive and hostile children. These behaviors are cries for help. Be an "Angel," any positive interaction on your part will mitigate the abuse. And remember a child rarely reveals the abuse unless asked the question, "Is someone touching your private areas?"

If you suspect a child is being sexually abused as a result of your observations, you have an obligation to report your suspicions to the sexual abuse hotline in your community. Anonymity is an option.

CPSIA information can be obtained at www.ICGtesting.com
Printed in the USA
BVOW06s0234270916

463403BV00013B/62/P